OUTLINES OF INDIAN HISTORY

OUTLINES OF INDIAN HISTORY

ALBERT WILLIAM HUGHES

GYAN

Published by

GYAN

Gyan Publishing House
5, Ansari Road
Daryaganj, New Delhi-110002
Phone: 011-47034999, 9811692060
E-mail: books@gyanbooks.com

Distribution Network
gyanbooks.com
India, USA, Canada, UK, Australia

ISBN: 978-93-7169-141-3 (PB)

First Published, 1871

2nd Impression 2025

Printed at: Gyan Press, Delhi.

OUTLINES OF INDIAN HISTORY
Author: ALBERT WILLIAM HUGHES

OUTLINES OF INDIAN HISTORY.

OUTLINES OF
INDIAN HISTORY

COMPRISING THE HINDŪ, MAHOMEDAN
AND CHRISTIAN PERIODS

FROM THE EARLIEST DATE TO THE RESIGNATION OF
THE VICEROYALTY OF BRITISH INDIA BY
SIR JOHN (NOW LORD) LAWRENCE

WITH MAPS, AND APPENDICES CONTAINING DETAILS (WITH AREA
AND POPULATION) OF THE DIFFERENT PRESIDENCIES
AND PROVINCES COMPOSING BRITISH INDIA
AND NUMEROUS EXAMINATION
QUESTIONS

BY A. W. HUGHES
BOM. UNCOV. CIVIL SERVICE
AND GRAY'S INN

1871

PREFACE.

THESE "Outlines," arranged on the plan adopted by Messrs. Ince and Gilbert in their excellent little work, "Outlines of English History," have been divided into three parts, the Hindū, Mahomedan, and Christian periods, such as are now generally recognized as correct divisions of Indian history,—the first extending from the earliest periods of Hindū history up to the date of the invasion of India by Sūltān Mahmūd of Ghuzni (A.D. 1001). This portion, which is very indistinct and unsatisfactory in character, abounds in fabulous narratives and puerile legends, and though there is much thàt is interesting in the study of the two great Hindū epic poems, the Māhābhārat and the Rāmāyāna, the subjects are essentially mythical, and there is such an utter absence of all reliable dates, as to make them altogether useless as guideposts to authentic history.

The second portion extends from the reign of Sūltān Mahmūd, the Ghuznivide, to A.D. 1761, the year which witnessed the disastrous battle of Paniput, and the consequent annihilation of the great Maratta power, while at the same time it saw the Mogul Emperor of Delhi a fugitive, and the English already sufficiently powerful to take an important political part in India. This portion of its history is one of great interest, as describing the gradual acquisition of nearly all India by the Mahomedans, and particularly so when treating of the Mogul emperors of the house of Teimūr, whose extensive conquests, as well as splendour and magnificence, have been made known not only by the native historians of those times, but by European travellers also, who were eye-witnesses of the great displays of grandeur at one or other of the imperial courts.

The third, and by far the most important portion of Indian history, is the period of Christian rule, commencing from the year 1761, when the Mogul empire was to all intents and purposes politically extinguished, and the foundation of British supremacy in Hindūsthān securely laid, and extending to the present time, which in this compilation ends with the resignation of the Vice-royalty of British India by Sir John (now Lord) Lawrence and its assumption by Lord Mayo. In this portion, which necessarily occupies the largest space, there is to be found matter of the very highest interest, as showing the wonderful progress of a body of foreigners, who, permitted at first merely to trade with the subjects of a great ruling power, found themselves under circumstances over which they had evidently no control, gradually attaining an ascendancy, which led in the end to their becoming the masters of that immense territory now recognised as British India. At no stage of this world's history is there anything to compare with the rise and progress of that great trading corporation known as the "EAST INDIA COMPANY." Consisting, in 1599, of a small capital and a few ships, its members cautiously ventured to obtain a share of that commerce in the East which the Portuguese and Dutch had enjoyed before them. By a strong and steady perseverance, and assisted at times by fortuitous circumstances, they laid the foundation of an extensive trade, and by taking part in the dissensions of the different races with whom they were brought into contact, soon obtained a political ascendancy which enabled them to become the arbiters of the rise and fall of great Asiatic princes. At length, district after district, province after province, and ultimately whole kingdoms, fell in succession under their sway, and the result has been the extension of British rule from the Punjāb to Cape Komorin. Never before had a simple trading company attained to such political power as this, and it was the more remarkable, since its directors had ever set their faces against territorial aggrandisement, and had specially desired this rule to be observed by their great officers, the Governors-General of India. How little this was heeded, and how impossible in fact it was found to attend to such an injunction, a careful perusal of the administrations of Warren Hastings, of the Marquesses Cornwallis, Wellesley, Hastings, and Dalhousie, will fully show.

The great Sepoy mutiny of 1857 shook for a time the British power in India to its foundation, and ended in the extinction of the "mighty Company," but it had the effect of removing, in a great measure, an immense native army, in itself a source of danger, more especially in Bengal, where its members consisted mostly of one caste and creed. From that time to the present, India has enjoyed, with the exception of a few petty wars, the blessings of a long peace, her trade and commerce have flourished, and her revenues have increased beyond all precedent; education has advanced among the people with mighty strides, and, to use the language of the Court of Directors of the East India Company at their last meeting in 1858, it is hoped "the millions placed under the Queen's direct, as well as sovereign dominion, may reward Her Majesty's cares in their behalf, by their faithful and firm attachment to Her Majesty's person and government."

A few remarks seem called for as to the plan here adopted for expressing Oriental words in English letters, especially as there exists much diversity of opinion on this head. Many names of places, hitherto written in maps and books with an initial and medial "c" have in this compilation, where considered necessary and without losing their proper sound, had the "c" changed into "k," thus:—Canara, Cutch, Cuttack, and Cashmir, have been spelt—Kanara, Kutch, Kuttak, and Kashmir.

Words containing a double "o," have had this changed to ū, as, Hindū instead of Hindoo; a long "a" is expressed by ā, as in Afghān, and a double "e" by i, as in Kurrachi and Mir. In this expression of letters, the plan adopted by Mountstuart Elphinstone and Eastwick has to some extent been followed, but a correct and standard system for properly expressing Hindū names in English characters, is a want greatly felt at the present time.

Two maps have been added to this compilation, one representing approximatively the kingdoms of "Bharutkund," or ancient India, with the names and position of the principal cities then existing; the other showing the extent of the Mogul empire in the time of Akbar. A map of British India has not been supplied, as large and elaborate atlases are at the present time so readily accessible to the student of history for purposes of reference. The appendices to this compilation consist of details of districts, with area and population, making up the different Presidencies and Provinces of British India, and among the numerous questions given on the history of India, are those which have from time to time been put to candidates at the examinations for appointments in the Indian Civil Service.

Among the works consulted for this compilation have been, Orme's "History of India," the Journals of the Royal Asiatic Society, Mill's "History of India," Ward's "Hindūs," Hardy's "Eastern Monachism," Mountstuart Elphinstone's "History of India," Anderson's "Western India," Taylor's and Capper's Histories of India, Chambers' "Sepoy Revolt" and "Encyclopædia," Marshman's "History of India," (Vols. I. II. and III.) and Prichard's "Administration of India," (Vols. I. and II.) besides references made to numerous government publications of recent date. To Mountstuart Elphinstone's and Marshman's histories the compiler is mainly indebted for the materials used in preparing these "Outlines."

OUTLINES OF INDIAN HISTORY.

THE HINDŪ PERIOD FROM THE EARLIEST TIMES TO A.D. 1001.

Boundaries and Divisions.

THE extensive country known as INDIA is bounded by the Himalāya mountains, the river Indus and the sea. In length from Cape Komorin to Kashmir, it is 1,900 miles, and in breadth from Kurrachi to Assam about 1,500 miles. Its superficial area, according to a late statistical report (1867), is 1,552,028 square miles, and the population 192,573,814, of which British India comprises 955,238 square miles with 144,674,615 inhabitants. The Vindya mountains divide India into two immense portions, that to the north being called Hindūsthān, and the country to the south the Dekhun. In the former there are the basins of the two large rivers, the Ganges and Indus, together with a great sandy desert on the west, and a tract now called Central India, having an altitude of from 1,500 to 2,000 feet above the sea. The latter possesses a table-land of triangular form with ranges of mountains, known as the Western and Eastern Ghauts, stretching to the south and terminating at Cape Komorin, and having between them and the sea, a narrow belt of land running round the whole peninsula.

Earliest Inhabitants of India.

The present race of Hindūs were not the earliest inhabitants of India. The original settlers are identified with the Bhils, Kolis, Gōnds, Minas, and Chūars living in the forests of the Soane, Nurbudda, and the Māhānuddi rivers, and in the hills of Surgūja and Chota Nāgpūr. Their religion differs from that of the Hindū, and their languages have no affinity with the Sungskrut. They are supposed to have formed the Sūdra or "servile" caste of the Hindū system of society, and the Sūdra kings, referred to in the Institutes of Menu, apply evidently to those aboriginal chieftains, who maintained their independence after the Hindū invasion.

Early history of the Hindūs.

The Hindūs are presumed to have come originally from the north-west, to have crossed the Indus and settled in a small tract of country called Brahmaverta, 100 miles north-west of Delhi. The India of the Vedas and of Menu applied to a region north of the Nurbudda. It was in the north that the Solar and Lunar races took their rise, the former ruling in Ayodha (the present Oudh) and the latter at Pratishtāna or Vitora. But the early history of the Hindūs is so mixed up with legends and fables, and the people are so perfectly destitute of historical records, that nothing satisfactory can be gleaned. The absurd system of Hindū chronology, which lays claim to a space of upwards of 3,900,000 years already passed and gone, has much to do with this. This space is divided into four grand periods called Yugs, the first (*Sutya*) comprising 1,728,000 years; the second (*Trita*), 1,296,000 years; the third (*Dwāpa*), 814,000 years; and the fourth (*Kāli*), which is to extend to 432,000 years, and of which 4,963 have already expired. Ikswāku is described in the Hindū annals as the progenitor of the Solar race, and Būdh of the Lunar. Between Ikswāku and Rāma, the

Hindū Chronology.

great hero and ornament of the Solar race, there occurs a long interval. This latter king so celebrated in the Rāmāyāna, a heroic poem composed by Valmiki, is supposed to have lived about 1200 years before the Christian era (though the Hindūs affirm that he reigned at the end of the Trita Yug) and is renowned for his invasion of the Dekhun and conquest of Ceylon, brought about by the abduction of his wife Sita by Ravāna King of Lunka (Ceylon). After his death he was deified by the Hindūs and is an object of general adoration among them.

Rāma.

In another poem containing not less than 100,000 verses called the Māhā-Bharat, a portion of which is said to be the composition of Vyāsa, is a description of the great war between the Pāndū and Kūrū races for the territory of Hastinapūra, ending in the success of the former. It is here that Khrishna, the favourite deity of the Hindū women, is mentioned as an ally of the Pāndūs. He is in fact the hero of the poem. Soon after his return to his capital Dwāka in Guzerat, he was killed by the arrow of a hunter who shot at him in mistake. Deified after death he became, from his adventures and flirtations, one of the most popular of gods among the Hindūs.

Māhā Bharat.

Khrishna.

From the period of this great war, probably about the fourteenth century A.C., up to the first expedition of Darius to India (sixth century A.C.) the annals of India are involved in some obscurity. The Takshūk, or serpent race, supposed to have been a tribe of Scythians professing the Būdhist creed, invaded the country about the sixth century A.C. and flourished for ten generations.

The Takshūk race.

In 518 A.C. Darius ascended the throne of Persia, and soon after he crossed the Indus and annexed a large portion of northern India to his empire. About this time appeared Gotāma (born at Kapilawastu on the borders of Nipāl, 624 A.C.) who gave a fixed character to Būdhism, a religion professed at the present time by no less than 370 millions of the human race.

Expedition of Darius.

Gotāma.

Considered generally as an offshoot of Brahminism, it will be necessary before entering into any description of it to give a brief account of this latter religion, as contained—1st, in the Vedas; 2nd, in the Institutes of Menu; and 3rd, in the Purānas. The Vedas, four in number, and the production of various authors, are supposed to have been produced in their present form in the fourteenth century A.C., one of them the Yajur Veda being a compilation by Vyāsa. They proclaimed the unity of God as a primary doctrine, the manifestations of the deity being represented by Brahma, Vishnū and Siva. No images were formerly worshipped, and the religion as primarily taught seems to have been a pure *monotheism*. Each Veda is divided into two or three parts, such as hymns and prayers (*Mantra*), and religious duties and theological arguments (*Brahmana*). The Institutes of Menu, the most celebrated of all the compendia of Hindū law, comprise a code of rules and precepts, religious and secular, supposed to have been produced in the ninth century A.C. It is in these that the Hindūs are found divided into four great classes or "*castes*," viz.:—1. Brahmins (*sacerdotal*); 2. Kshetryias (*military*); 3. Veisyas (*industrial*); and 4. Sūdras (*servile*). The Brahmin, sprung from Brahma's mouth, was the chief of all created beings, he taught the Vedas, bestowed alms, accepted gifts, was privileged from taxation, exercised all judicial authority, and interpreted the laws. The Kshetryia, sprung from Brahma's arm, had to defend the people, to give alms, sacrifice, read the Vedas, and shun all allurements of

Vedas.

Institutes of Menu.

sensual gratification. It was the duty of the Veisya, who sprang from Brahma's thigh, to keep herds of cattle, to trade, lend money at interest, and cultivate the land. The Sūdra, sprung from Brahma's foot, was to serve the other three classes, especially the Brahmins, but not to learn the law, or mode of expiating sin, nor to be allowed to amass wealth. As regards Hindū law, the Institutes are divided into 18 portions, the first nine, and the sixteenth and seventeenth treating on civil matters, the tenth to the fifteenth and eighteenth being confined to criminal subjects. The Purānas, the scriptures of the new religion, are 18 (some state 36) in number, and are said to be the work of Vyāsa, but they were composed, it is believed, by different authors between the eighth and sixteenth centuries of the Christian era. The most ancient of the Purānas is considered to be not more than 1,000 years old, and the latest 450 years old. They contain accounts of the creation of the world, of the gods, heroes and sages, fragments of history, philosophical speculations and innumerable legends. Hindū extravagance places the number of deities at 330 millions, but the following seventeen are those that are ordinarily recognized and worshipped:—

Purānas.

1. **Brahma** (*creating principle*) with his consort,
2. **Saraswutti.**
3. **Vishnū** (*preserving principle*) with his consort,
4. **Luxhmi.**
5. **Siva** (*destroying principle*) with his consort,
6. **Parvutti** (called also Dēvi and Bhāvani or Dūrga).
7. **Indra** (god of the air and heavens).
8. **Varuna** (of waters).
9. **Pavuna** (of wind).
10. **Agni** (of fire).
11. **Y ma** (of the infernal regions).
12. **Kuvēra** (of wealth).

13. **Kartikeia** (of war).
14. **Kāma** (of love).
15. **Sūrya** (the sun).
16. **Soma** (the moon).
17. **Gunnēsha** (the remover of difficulties).

Ancient Hindū Kingdoms

Mention is also made in some of the Purānas of India having formerly been divided into the following ten kingdoms, five in Hindūsthān and five in the Dekhun:—

1. **Suruswutti** (Punjāb).
2. **Kanouj** (Delhi, Agra and Oudh).
3. **Tirhūt** (from the Kusi to the Gunduk rivers).
4. **Gour** (Bengal with part of Behar).
5. **Guzerat** (Guzerat, Khandēsh and part of Malwa).
6. **Māhārāshtra** (Maratta country on western coast).
7. **Orissa** (on eastern coast).
8. **Telingāna** (lying between the Godaveri and the Kistna rivers).
9. **Dravira** (Tamul country to Cape Komorin).
10. **Kanāta** (on the western face of the Peninsula).

The languages spoken in the first seven of these were branches of the Sungskrut, with a slight modification, but those of the remaining three belong to a distinct family.

Sungskrut language.

Sungskrut, signifying "*refined,*" in which the Vedas, Institutes of Menu, and the Purānas were written, has as a language been highly commended by Sir William Jones, who describes it as "of a wonderful structure, more perfect than the Greek, more copious than the Latin, and more exquisitely refined than either."

Būdhism.

Būdhism, a branch as is supposed of Brahminism, resembles the latter in so far as the attainment of a state of perfect apathy is concerned. Būdhas are beings appearing in the world at intervals to teach men the way to attain

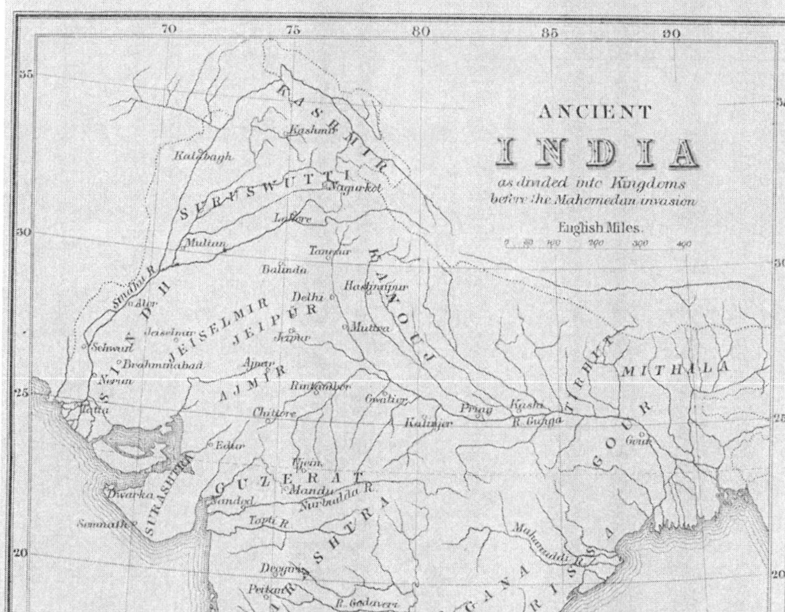

To face page 6

J. Jobbins

"*nirwana,*" or cessation of existence, the great object of the votaries of this creed. Of these, Gotāma is the chief. The Būdhist priests deny the authority of the Vedas and Purānas, live in monasteries, are bound to celibacy, receive alms, and are directed to have the greatest respect for animal life. Their principal sacred books, written in the Pāli character, are:—1. The Wināya Pitāka, or regulations for the priesthood. 2. Sūtra, or discourses. 3. Abhidharmma, or pre-eminent truths. The Būdhist religion made great strides after the death of Gotāma, and two centuries from that event it was triumphant throughout Hindūsthān. It was introduced into Ceylon about the third century A.C., and probably into Tartary and Thibet somewhat later, but into China not before 65 A.D. It does not now exist in the plains of India, but is professed in Nipāl. In the fifth century of the Christian era it had begun to decline, but it was not finally expelled from India before the tenth or twelfth century. The finest of the Būdhist cave temples in India are at Ellora and Karli, and they are justly considered to be wonderful works of art.

Jainism.

In describing Būdhism it becomes necessary to refer also to the Jaina religion, still professed to some extent in India. Like Būdhism, it is supposed to have been an offshoot of Brahminism, to have originated in the sixth or seventh century of the Christian era, reached its highest prosperity in the eleventh, and declined in the twelfth century. The Jainists deny the activity and providence of God, and consider impassive abstraction as supreme felicity; on the other hand they admit the Hindū Pantheon, maintain division of caste, and hold the Vedas as authorities in some cases. They have a belief in deified saints called Tirtankeras, of which there are 24 for the past age, 24 for the present and 24 for the future. The chief of these are Rishoba, Parusnāth and Māhāvira. They are very careful of animal life, have no monasteries, and never bathe. Their sacred language is the Magadi or Pāli, and the finest of their temples is at Mount Abū near Disa. The Jains are still numerous in Guzerat, the Rājpūt country and Kanara, where they form an opulent and mercantile class.

Invasion of Alexander the Great.

It was in the year 331 A.C. that Alexander the Great after conquering the Persian empire, arrived on the banks of the Indus with a veteran army. He crossed at Attok and received the submission of several of the principal chiefs of the country, but Porus, king of a region stretching eastwards towards Delhi, disputing his passage on the banks of the Jhilum (*Hydaspes*), was signally defeated. Thence Alexander crossed the rivers Chenāb (*Aesines*) and Ravi (*Hydraotes*), and had reached the banks of the Sutlej (*Hesudrū*), when his army became mutinous and refused to accompany him further. Returning westward he directed his admiral Nearchus to sail down the Indus, and proceed to the mouth of the Euphrates, which was accomplished, and a city and harbour built at the estuary of the former river. The great conqueror had projected a second invasion of India, when he died at Babylon from malarious fever in his thirty-second year. His able general Seleucus, who obtained the Provinces of Babylon, also invaded India in 310 A.C., but does not appear to have effected anything of importance. He was opposed by Chundragūpta (the Sandracottus of the Greeks) king of Magada. This kingdom comprised the three Kulingas, namely, the northern section of the Koromandel coast, the sea-face of Bengal from Balasore to Chittagong, and the coast of Arrakan. Its capital was Patalipūtra (the Palibothra of the Greeks). This kingdom maintained its pre-eminence under a succession of royal families from 350 A.C. to 450 A.D. The age of Vikramāditya, who

Seleucus.

reigned at Ujein, follows the supposed expulsion of the Būdhists from India. It began in the year 56 A.C. He was a powerful monarch, ruled a civilized and prosperous country, was a distinguished patron of letters, and his name is connected with the era still current through all the countries north of the Nurbudda, while that of Salivahāna (A.D. 77) is equally current in the Dekhun.

Bhoja.

The next epoch is that of King Bhoja, very renowned throughout India, but of whose exploits there is no record. From the age of Vikramāditya up to the first important invasion of India in 711 A.D. by the Mahomedans, there are to be found but barren lists of dynasties and kings, which can be turned to no account.

Dekhun.

The early history of the Dekhun is less obscure than that of Hindūsthān. The most ancient kingdoms in this part of India appear to have been those of the Pāndyas and Cholas in the extreme south, where the Tamul language prevailed. The capital of the former was at Madūra; of the latter, at Kānchi (or Konjeveram). The Pāndyas lost their consequence in the ninth century, but lingered till 1736 A.D. The Cholas maintained a feeble existence till the province was conquered in the seventeenth century by Shahji, the father of Siwuji, the founder of the Maratta empire. Of the ancient kingdoms of Kerulu (including Malabar and Kanāta), of Telingāna, Orissa, and Māhārāshtra, but little is known, their early annals being very indistinct. The same may be said of the Andra dynasty, once enjoying great power in the Gangetic provinces. A dynasty of the same name existed in the inland part of Telingāna, having their capital at Wurungol (about eighty miles north-east of the present city of Heidurabād).

The Rajpūt family of Chittore, now settled at Udipūr, rose into notice on the decay of the Andras of the Gangetic empire, about 436 A.C. They claimed a descent from Loh, the eldest son of Rāma, the hero of the Rāmayāna, and the patriarch of the Solar race, and settled at Bullabi, in Guzerat, in the middle of the second century A.D. Driven thence in 524 A.D. by a Persian army, they established a kingdom at Edur under the rule of Goha, from whom the Rajas of Udipūr are lineally descended. Eight princes succeeded Goha. Bappa, the youngest son of the last prince, proceeded to Chittore, where he was advanced to the throne after defeating an army of Mahomedans, who had invaded India under the leadership of Mahomed Kossim. It was in A.D. 664 (Hijra 44) that the Mahomedans made their first appearance in India under Mohālib; they penetrated, however, as far only as Mūltān, and no other incursion was made on the north of India during the continuance of Arab rule.

Rajpūts of Chittore.

The religion of these invaders owes its rise to Mahomed, born at Mekka in A.D. 569, by whom, and his immediate successors, province after province, and kingdom after kingdom, were conquered, and his religion established *by the agency of the sword.* The next incursion of any note by the Mahomedans into India was in A.D .711 (H. 92), when Sindh was invaded by Mahomed Kossim, and the seaport town of Dewal (supposed to have been near Kurrachi), the cities of Alor, the capital (near the present town of Rohri), and Brahminabād, and the towns of Nerūn (Heidurabād) and Sehwun were reduced, and the entire country ultimately occupied by his victorious army. Thence Mahomed proceeded to Guzerat, which he overran, and at length advanced to Chittore, where he was completely defeated by the Rajpūt army under the command of Bappa, and expelled from India. Subsequently, between the years 812 and 836 A.D., Chittore was again invaded by the Mahomedans under Mahmūn, but they

Rise of Mahomedanism.

also were signally defeated and driven out of India by the Rajpūts under Khoman, nor did they again appear until the invasion of Mahmūd of Ghūzni in A.D. 1001. For a century and a half previous to this last irruption, there is nothing deserving of notice in the history of India, and it may be useful to recollect, as far as regards Hindū chronology and history generally, that, in the words of the Honourable Mountstuart Elphinstone, "No date of any public event can be fixed before the invasion of Alexander, and no connected relation of national transactions can be attempted until after the Mahomedan conquest of the country."

MISCELLANEOUS MEMORANDA CONNECTED WITH THE HINDŪ PERIOD.

Brahmins.

A Brahmin's life was divided into four periods:—1. As a student, leading a life of abstinence and humiliation. 2nd. As a householder, living with his wife and family, teaching the Vedas, sacrificing, bestowing alms, and accepting gifts. 3rd. As an anchorite in the woods, exposed to many mortifications; and 4th. As released from all forms and outward observances, to cultivate equanimity and enjoy delight in meditating on the divinity.

Gosayens.

The name Gosayen is applied to the Hindū monastic orders in a general sense. Of the Gosayens, the followers of Vishnū are the most respectable, those of Siva the most offensive. The words "Jogi" (meaning "*abstracted meditation*") and "Bairāgi" apply to a large class of Hindū monks.

The "Avatars," or incarnations of Vishnū, are ten in number:—1. As a fish, to recover the Vedas taken by a demon in a deluge. 2. As a Boar. 3. As a Tortoise. 4. As a man with the head and paws of a lion. 5. As a Brahmin dwarf. 6. As Purshram destroying the Kshetryia, or military class. 7. As Rāmā. 8. As Balla Rāmā killing giants. 9. As Būdha, to delude the enemies of the gods. The 10th is to come, but it is expected Vishnū will appear on a white horse, with a cimetar blazing like a comet to mow down all incorrigible and impenitent offenders who shall then be on earth.

Incarnations of Vishnū.

The Hindū does not live wholly on rice; his food in Hindūsthān proper is wheat or other grains, such as joari (*holcus sorghum*) and bajri (*holcus spicatus*). In Bengal, Behar, and the country round the sea-coast of the Peninsula, it is rice; in the southern part of the Dekhun table-land it is rāgi (*cynosurus corocanus*). It is a singular fact that hedgehogs, porcupines, lizards, and tortoises, were formerly allowed as lawful food, and the flesh of *oxen* was specially permitted to Brahmins on solemn festivals.

Food.

The regular dress of the Hindū consists of two pieces of white cotton cloth, one wrapped round the middle and tucked up between the legs, while a part hangs down a good deal below the knees; the other is worn over the shoulders and occasionally stretched over the head. The dress of the women is nearly the same as that described for the men, but both pieces of cloth are larger and longer, and are of various bright colours as well as white. Both sexes have many ornaments. Children are loaded with gold ornaments, thus affording frequent temptation to child murder. At the birth of a child among the Hindūs, the religious ceremonies are numerous; and again, at the first or third year, when the shaving of the head takes place. The investiture with the sacred thread is a most important ceremonial, taking place between the ages of sixteen and twenty-four, according to the caste of the individual. It is this rite that procures for the three classes the title of

Dress.

Birth.

"twice-born" men in the code of Menu. Marriage among the Hindūs had eight forms, but seven of these are obsolete. Among these was the tying of the hands of the bride and bridegroom with a blade of sacred grass; but the most important part of the ceremony was the stepping by the bride of seven steps. When the seventh step was taken the marriage was indissoluble. Marriages are expensive, often costing laks of rupees among the rich. Where a girl was not given in marriage at the proper time, her father lost all dominion over her and she was at liberty to choose a husband for herself.

Marriage.

The ceremonies for funerals among the Hindūs are trivial and tiresome. Cremation is generally resorted to, though some classes are buried in a sitting posture cross-legged. Besides daily oblations, there are monthly obsequies to be performed to the *manes* of each Hindū's ancestors.

Funerals.

Suttis, or widows who sacrifice themselves on the funeral pile of their husbands, were common in some parts of India, but are now forbidden by law. No mention of such a rite is found in Menu's code. It was common in Hindūsthān and Bengal, but rare in Southern India.

Suttis.

In the time of Menu, the government of a kingdom was vested in an absolute monarch, subject, however, to certain divine laws, and with prescribed duties to perform. Under him were a number of councillors for the administration of the government, while a chain of civil officers, known as lords of single villages, of ten towns, of 100 towns, and of 1,000 towns, with different degrees of compensation, conducted the internal administration. The revenue was derived from taxes on all agricultural produce, on commerce, from a small annual imposition levied on petty traders and shopkeepers, and from forced service from handicraftsmen. In the administration of

Hindū Government.

criminal justice, the Hindū code was singularly inconsistent, but at the same time noted for its sanguinary punishments. Perjury was looked upon as meritorious when done to save the life of a man who had exposed himself to capital punishment, while in other parts of the Code the offence was denounced in the most awful terms. Adultery appears to have been considered the greatest of all crimes; the punishment for the woman was to be devoured by dogs, and the man to be burned to death on a highly-heated iron bed. Mutilation chiefly of the hand, was a common punishment for several offences. Trials by ordeal were also in vogue, and several are assimilated to those once prevailing among the Anglo-Saxons. Great changes have, however, taken place among the Hindūs since the time of Menu, both in caste, government, law, and religion.

Village System.

The Hindū village system is remarkable as presenting in itself a completely organized commonwealth, having nearly everything it wanted within itself, and almost independent of any foreign relations. The village system survives, notwithstanding injuries by war, famine, or disease. The kingdom might be broken up and divided, and the sovereignty changed over and over again, but the village system outlives it all. The Hindūs appear to have made settlements in Java and other Eastern islands about 75 A.C., and the histories of Java, together with the magnificent Hindū remains still existing in that island, attest the truth of this. The exports in ancient times from India to Europe by the Red Sea were cotton and silk cloths, muslins, chintzes, indigo, spices, precious stones, drugs and sugar. The imports were coarse and fine cloth, brass, tin, lead, glass, wines, principally the Italian, and a considerable quantity of specie and bullion. Roads for internal communication seem from the earliest Hindū times, to have been objects of much attention to the government.

Commerce.

Philosophical Schools.

The Hindūs recognized six ancient schools of philosophy; the chief being those of Vyāsa, Patanjali, Gotāma, and Kanāde. Logic has always been a favourite study among the Brahmins, and they have been famous from early periods for their knowledge in astronomy and mathematical science. The "Surya Siddhanta" contains an elaborate system of trigonometry. Their knowledge of geography was simply ridiculous, and in painting and sculpture their efforts were poor as regarded expression and proportion. In dramatic writings the Hindūs were more successful, the plays of Kalidāsa, one of their principal writers, presenting considerable excellence; the great strength of the Sungskrut poets lay in description. The chief dramatic authors were Kalidāsa and Bhāvabhuti.

Personal appearance and character of the Hindūs.

It is a difficult matter to give the character of so large a portion of the human race, occupying such an immense area with so many different climates. Orme says: "In Hindūsthān the common people of all sorts are a diminutive race in comparison with those of higher castes and better fortunes, and yield still more to them in all the advantages of physiognomy. There is not a handsomer race in the universe than the Banyans of Guzerat; but the Haramkores, whose business is to remove all kinds of filth, and the buriers and burners of dead bodies, are as remarkably ugly." The Rajpūts are courageous and high-spirited as a race, the Bengalees the most effeminate of all Indian people, while the Marattas are hardy and laborious but deceitful and treacherous. Taken as a whole, the most prominent vice of the Hindū is want of veracity; he is naturally well-fitted for intrigue and cunning, being patient, supple, and insinuating. He is very litigious, and will hold it meritorious to take a bribe in a good cause, but a venial offence if the cause be bad. He is deficient in manliness, dreads change, but has a contempt for death, which is remarkable, considering his timidity in small evils. He is wanting in active humanity, and though he will not kill an animal of the ox kind, there is no creature whose sufferings equal those of the labouring cattle of Hindūsthān. In comparing the Hindū character in ancient and modern times, it is generally conceded that the alteration has been for the worse; and this is thought to be owing to their religion having become debased since Menu's time, and to the restrictions of caste having been made more rigid.

Names of Note.

Rāmā, a deified hero, conqueror of Ceylon, supposed to have flourished about 14th century A. C. **Krishna**, another deified hero, king of Guzerat. **Parasara**, the first writer on astronomy (14th century A. C.). **Vyāsa**, supposed writer of a portion of the Vedas, and the Māhā Bharat, and founder of the Vedanta school of philosophy (supposed to have flourished in the 14th century A. C.). **Menu**, the celebrated Hindū law-giver (9th century A. C.). **Gotāma**, religious head of the Būdhists (middle of the 6th century A. C.). **Arya Bhatta**, writer on algebra (360 A. C.). **Kanāde**, founder of the atomic school of philosophy. **Kapila**, of the atheistical school. **Patunjali**, of the theistical school. **Vikramāditya**, king of Ujein (56 A. C.), gave his name to a Hindū era. **Salivahāna**, Hindu king (77 A. D.), gave his name to an era. **Valmiki**, author of the Rāmāyāna (2nd century A. D.). **Charaka** and **Susruta**, medical writers. **Kalidasa** (5th century A. D.) and **Bhāvabuti** (8th century A. D.), both dramatic authors. **Brahma Gūpta** (6th century A. D.) and **Bhaskur Acharya** (12th century A. D.) writers on algebra.

Table containing the names of ancient Hindū States, the mark (*) indicates that it is mentioned in the Māhā Bharat. The year generally mentioned by Ferishta is that in which they were conquered by the Mahomedans. (Mountstuart Elphinstone).

Name.	When first mentioned.	When last mentioned.	Authority.	Remarks.
Magada	*By Greeks 300 A.C.	About 5th cent. A.D.	Vishnū Purāna.	
Gour	*9th century, A.D.	A.D. 1203	Monghir Inscriptions.	
Malwa	11 generations before 56 A.C.	A.D. 1231	Ayeni Akberi.	
Gūzerat	*A.D. 144	A.D. 1297	Tod, vol. I. Mr. Wathen. Royal Asiatic Society.	
Kanouj	*A.D. 470	A.D. 1193	Tod, vol. II.	
Mithili	Rāma's time	A.D. 1325	. . . .	Mithili, the capital of father of Sita, Rāma's wife, but slightly mentioned in history.
Benares	*	A.D. 1192	. . . .	Doubtless independent at time of Māhā Bharat, afterwards subject to Magada, and later to Gour. Independent when conquered by the Mahomedans.
Delhi	*about 56 A.C.	A.D. 1192	Tod, vol. I.	After Māhā Bharat, mentioned as occupied by tribe of Rajpūts; 20 reigned in succession; dethroned in A.D. 1050, by ancestor of Pritwi Rāja, who was conquered by the Mahomedans.
Ajmir	7 generations before A.D. 695	A.D. 1192	Tod; Royal Asiatic Society's Journal, Vol. I.	The 8th prince, Manik Rai reigned in A.D. 695. His descendant Visal conquered Delhi in A.D. 1050. The two States fell together.
Mewar	A.D. 720	Still existing	Tod, vol. I.	Conquered by race of Rajpūts from Oudh, same who founded the state of Guzerat.
Jessulmir	A.D. 731	do.	Tod, vol. II.	Founded by tribe of Khrishna's family from N. West, who still hold it.
Jeipūr	A.D. 967	do.	Tod, vol. II.	Founded by a Rajpūt prince, a descendant of Rāma.
Sindh	* Independent in Alexander's time	A.D. 711.	. . . .	Mentioned in Māhā Bharat. Divided into 4 parts in Alexander's time, united in 711 A.D. when invaded by Arabs. Recovered by Rajpūt tribe of Samera, A.D. 750, finally conquered by Mahomedan house of Ghor.
Kashmir	1400 A.C.	A.D. 1015	Professor Wilson, Asiatic Researches.	According to Ferishta, after 5 dynasties conquered by Mahmūd of Ghuzni, A.D. 1015.

THE MAHOMEDAN PERIOD FROM A.D. 1001 (*THE DATE OF THE FIRST INVASION OF INDIA BY SULTAN MAHMŪD OF GHUZNI*) *UP TO* A.D. 1761.

Alptegin.

THE House of Ghuzni, which flourished about 225 years, owes its rise to Alptegin, a slave, who rose to be governor of Khorasan, but rebelling against his sovereign (Mansūr, of the house of Samāni, who ruled over Khorasan and Transoxiāna), he fled to Ghuzni in A.D. 961 (H. 350), where he became independent, and died in A.D. 975, leaving a son, Isakh, who succeeded him. He died in

Subuktegin.

A.D. 977, when Subuktegin, deputy governor of Khorasan, and formerly a slave, was acknowledged as his successor. Jeipal, Rāja of Lahore, invaded Subuktegin's territories, but returned ignominiously, after giving up fifty elephants and promising to pay a large sum of money, a promise he subsequently refused to perform. The two armies met again to the west of the Indus, when Jeipal, though assisted by the Rājas of Delhi, Ajmir, Kahuja, and Kanouj, was defeated, and all the tribes up to the Indus submitted to Subuktegin. He died in A.D. 997, and was succeeded by his son Ismāil; but he was speedily deposed (A.D. 999) by his brother, the celebrated Mahmūd, afterwards known as the "*image breaker.*"

(I.) SŪLTĀN MAHMŪD (OF GHUZNI), (A.D. 999 TO 1030).

Birth and Reign.—Was the son of Subuktegin, ruler of Khorasan and Transoxiāna, by a daughter of Alptegin. He compelled his brother Ismāil, who had succeeded Subuktegin, to relinquish the throne, which he ascended at the age of thirty, assuming the title of Sūltān (an old Arabic word for king); he reigned thirty-one years.

Issue.—Two sons, Mahomed and Musāūd.

Death.—He died at Ghuzni on the 29th April, A.D. 1030.

Character.—He possessed prudence, activity, and enterprise in the highest degree; was a patron of learned men; had the qualities of a great warrior and conqueror, and though habitually economical, displayed at times considerable liberality. He was about the middle size, athletic, and well-proportioned, but much disfigured with small-pox.

Wars.—Is chiefly known for his twelve expeditions to India. In the first (A.D. 1001) he defeated Jeipal, Rāja of Lahore, and compelled him to pay tribute. 2nd. He conquered Anungpal, Jeipal's son, for not paying his share of the tribute. 3rd (A.D. 1004). He reduced Abul Futteh Lodi, the Afghān chief of Mūltān. 4th (A.D. 1008). He attacked and defeated a Hindū confederacy of rājas, and took Nāgurkote, a fortified temple, with an immense booty. 5th (A.D. 1010). Took Mūltān. 6th. Plundered the Hindū temple of Thanēsur, near the Jumna. 7th and 8th comprised two expeditions to Kashmir. 9th (A.D. 1017). He invested and took Kanouj. 10th and 11th. Relieved the Rāja of Kanouj, and annexed Lahore and its territory to Ghuzni. 12th (A.D. 1024), was his expedition to Somnath in Guzerat, the temple at which he plundered, and carried away enormous treasures. He also conquered Persia, but tarnished his reputation by severe cruelties.

Memorable Events.—Mahmūd conquered but a small portion of India, and his authority there was limited both in degree and extent. He possessed a regular army of 54,000 horse, and had in his pay a numerous body of Hindū cavalry. He founded a university at Ghuzni, and provided a permanent sum for allowances to professors and students. He also set aside a sum equal to nearly £10,000 a year for pensions to learned men. It was at his desire that Firdusi composed his great historical poem, consisting of 60,000 couplets, on the achievements of the kings and heroes of Persia. He adorned Ghuzni with stately edifices, the chief of which was a mosque called the "Celestial Bride." The civil administration of his kingdom is believed to have been entirely conducted by Persians. Mahmūd's territories may be said, at his death, to have extended from the Persian Gulf to the Sea of Aral, and from the mountains of Kurdistan to the banks of the Sutlej. It is worthy of remark that the sandal-wood gates taken by Mahmūd from Somnath to Ghuzni were brought back to India eight centuries afterwards by an English governor-general.

Names of Note.—**Jeipal**, Rāja of Lahore; after being twice defeated by Mahmūd, he ascended the funeral pyre in regal state, and was burnt. **Unsuri** and **Firdusi**, poets; the latter, author of a celebrated historical poem. **Abul Abbas** and **Ahmed Meimendi**, viziers and administrators of the law: the former wrote all public papers in Persian, the latter, all permanent documents in Arabic.

(II.) SULTAN MASĀŪD (A.D. 1030 TO 1040).

Birth and Reign.—Was son of Mahmūd; ascended the throne five months after his father's death, having seized, blinded, and imprisoned his brother Mohamed, whom his father had selected as his successor. He reigned till A.D. 1040 (H. 433).

Issue.—Modūd.

Death.—Owing to a general mutiny of his army, he was deposed and put to death by Ahmed, son of his blind brother Mohamed.

Character.—Courageous, of a commanding temper, and energetic, he was of great personal strength and soldier-like habits.

Wars.—I. Reduced the Provinces of Mekrān, Mazanderan, and Gurgan, then in the hands of fire-worshippers. II. With the Seljūks, a horde of Tūrkis, who, under their celebrated leader Toghrul Bēg, defeated him with great slaughter, near Merv, in Persia. Masāūd then withdrew into India, where he met his death.

Memorable Events.—Notwithstanding the short reign of Masāūd, he found time to extend his patronage to learned men, and to erect magnificent buildings at Ghuzni.

(III.) SULTAN MODŪD (1040 TO 1049).

Birth and Reign.—Son of Masāūd; succeeded his father in A.D. 1040; reigned nine years.

Marriage.—With grand-daughter of Toghrul Bēg.

Death.—Died at Ghuzni in A.D. 1049.

Wars.—With the Rāja of Delhi, who had taken Nāgurkote and laid siege to Lahore, but the Hindūs were ultimately driven back by a vigorous sally of the besieged.

From the death of this prince up to A.D. 1186, when the last of the House of Ghuzni expired, there reigned a series of monarchs whose doings were, comparatively speaking, insignificant. The following table will show their names, dates of reign, &c., together with the principal events which happened.

	Began to reign.	Died.	Memorable Events.
	A.D.	A.D.	
IV. Abul Hassan	1049	1051	Murdered his infant nephew, but was himself deposed by his uncle Abul Rashid.
V. Abul Rashid.	1051	1052	Assassinated by a chief named Toghrul.
VI. Ferokhzād .	1052	1058	
VII. Ibrahim . .	1058	1089	Left 40 sons and 36 daughters.
VIII. Masāūd II. .	1089	1114	Court resided for some years at Lahore.
IX. Arslan . . .	1114	1118	Imprisoned his brothers; was defeated by the Seljūk prince Sanjar.
X. Behram . .	1118	1152	Put to death his son-in-law, Kutbudin Sūr of Ghori, and afterwards Seif-u-din, King of Ghor, on which the deceased king's brother, Ala-u-din, destroyed Ghuzni, and compelled Behram to flee into India.
XI. Khusrū . .	1152	1160	In this reign the government was permanently transferred to Lahore.
XII. Khusrū Mālik	1160	1186	Was conquered by Shahab-u-din, of Ghor, and died in exile. With this prince the race of Subuktegin expired.

At the time of the extinction of the Ghuzni dynasty, the state of that portion of Northern India under Hindu rule was one of incessant warfare. There were two parties constantly engaged in strife with each other; one comprising Guzerat (governed by the family of Bhagilas) and Kanouj (by the Rathore tribe of Rajpūts), and the other, Delhi (held by the clan of Tomāra), the Chohan of Ajmir, and the Hindū Rāja of Chittore: their wars and jealousies greatly contributed to the after-success of the Mahomedans in India, and hastened their own downfall.

HOUSE OF GHOR.

(I.) Ala-ū-din was the brother of Seif-ū-din, King of Ghor, and avenged his death by driving Behram, the Ghuzni monarch, into India, and destroying Ghuzni. He died A.D. 1156, and was succeeded by his son (II.) Seif-ū-din Ghori, who was killed by one of his own chiefs in A.D. 1157. (III.) Gheias-ū-din succeeded his cousin, and with him was associated his brother Shahab-ū-din, afterwards better known as Mahomed Ghori, whose attention was almost entirely given to India. In A.D. 1176 he entered the Punjāb, and afterwards led an expedition to Guzerat. He met with great opposition from the Rajpūts, but in A.D. 1193 defeated the King of Delhi, and took Ajmir, returning to Ghuzni with immense plunder, and leaving Kutub-ū-din, his general, to carry out his conquests, which he did with much ability, taking Delhi in the same year. In A.D. 1195 he returned and pursued his conquests as far as Bundelkund, capturing the forts of Gwalior, Kalinjer, and Kalpi. Behar and Bengal were also reduced, and as in A.D. 1202 Gheias-ū-din died, his brother at once took possession of the throne.

(IV.) MAHOMED GHORI (A.D. 1202-06).

Birth and Reign.—Was the nephew of Ala-ū-din; he ascended the throne on the death of his brother, Gheias-ū-din, and reigned from 1202 to 1206; he had no children.

Death.—Was assassinated in his tent on the banks of the Indus on 14th March 1206 by a band of Gukkars, a tribe he had subdued and compelled to embrace the Mahomedan faith.

Character.—He was an enterprising soldier, but though his conquests exceeded those of the great Mahmūd of Ghuzni, he had neither the talents nor the prudence of that eminent conqueror.

Wars.—I. With the King of Kharism (now called Khiva) on the Lake of Aral, whom he subdued, but was afterwards himself hard pressed by the Khitan Tartars with whom he effected an accommodation.

II. With his refractory dependants in India, whom he speedily reduced. He had previously during his brother's reign completely demolished the Hindū power from the banks of the Sutlej to the Bay of Bengal, and at his death the whole of Hindūsthān, excepting Malwa, was under a settled and permanent Mahomedan Government.

On the death of Mahomed Ghori, the kingdom broke up at once into separate states, of which India became independent under the rule of Kūtb-ū-din, formerly a Tūrki slave, but afterwards a successful general under the House of Ghor, and who eventually attained to the sovereignty of Mahomedan India. The Slave-King dynasty lasted 82 years, as the following tabulated statement will show :—

SLAVE KINGS (A.D. 1206 TO 1288.)

	Began to reign.	Died.	Memorable Events.
	A.D.	A.D.	
I. Kūtb-ū-din . .	1206	1210	Left at his death a permanent reputation as a just and virtuous ruler.
II. Arām	1210	1211	Son of Kūtb-ū-din; dethroned by his brother-in-law, Altamsh.
III. Altamsh . .	1211	1236	Conducted two expeditions into Sindh; the latter in 1225 was successful. In this reign the Moguls, under Zenghiz Khan, made their first irruption into India. Altamsh was occupied six years in reducing Hindūsthān, which, excepting a few insulated portions, acknowledged the government of Delhi. The Kūtb Minar, a column 242 feet high, near Delhi, was completed in this reign.
IV. Rukn-ū-din .	1236	Deposed 1236	Son of Altamsh, was deposed after a reign of seven months.
V. Rezia Begum .	1236	1239	Sister of Rukn-u-din, and distinguished for her business-like habits; she evinced all the qualities of a just and able ruler, but was deposed, and afterwards put to death.
VI. Moiz-ū-din Behrām .	1239	1241	Brother of Rezia Begum; owing to plots and seditions, was put to death.
VII. Ala-ū-din Musāūd .	1241	1244	Deposed and put to death after a licentious reign of little more than two years. Two irruptions of Moguls occurred during this reign.
VIII. Nasir-ū-din Mahmūd .	1246	1266	Grandson of Altamsh; was greatly assisted in the government by his vizier, Bulbun; reduced many of the Hindū chiefs, and repelled the attacks of the Moguls. This sūltān had but one wife, and defrayed all his personal expenses by copying books. The "Tabakāti Nāsiri," a history of Persia and India, was written at his court.
IX. Gheias-ū-din Bulbun .	1266	1286	Minister of Nasir-ū-din: his reign was disturbed by Hindū insurrections and a revolt in Bengal, all of which were suppressed. In a Mogul irruption he lost his eldest son, a prince of great promise. The poet "Amir Khusru" flourished in this reign.
X. Kei-Kobad . .	1286	1288	Grandson of Bulbun: given to pleasure and debauchery. Was dethroned and put to death by the Khiljis (mountaineers of Ghuzni and Ghōr). With this prince closed the dynasty of the slave kings.

At Kei-Kobad's death, Jelal-ū-din Khilji ascended the throne, being the first of the House of Khilji, a dynasty which extended to but 33 years, as will be seen from the following table:—

HOUSE OF KHILJI (A.D. 1288 TO 1321).

	Began to reign.	Died.	Memorable Events.
	A.D.	A.D.	
I. Jelal-ū-din . .	1288	1295	Was 70 years old at his accession: his government was remarkable for its mildness; he put down several insurrections, and defeated a Mogul invasion in 1292. His nephew, Ala-ū-din, invaded the Dekhun in 1294, obtaining immense plunder, but fearing his uncle's displeasure, he assassinated him in 1295, and took possession of the throne.
II. Ala-ū-din . .	1295	1316	Was ignorant and capricious as well as cruel, intemperate, and tyrannical. Conquered Guzerat (1297), Dekhun (1306-12), and Kanāta (1310), but failed in subjugating Telingāna. Chittore was taken in 1303, but lost in the latter part of his reign. Several Mogul invasions were so signally repelled that they ceased for many years. His general, Kafūr, formerly a slave, intrigued for the throne, and hastened Ala-ū-din's end, it is said, by administering poison to him. The land-tax was increased in this reign, and rules passed restricting persons to a certain number of cattle and servants, and fixing the prices of all commodities.
III. Mobarik Khilji	1317	1321	Third son of Ala-ū din. Reduced Guzerat, which had rebelled, restored tranquillity to the Dekhun, and conquered Malabar (1318). He was cruel, and given to debauchery and intoxication. He put to death all the survivors of Ala-ū-din's family, and lost his own life in a rebellion fomented by Ghāzi-Khān-Toghlak, Governor of the Punjāb, and with him ended the House of Khilji.

As on the death of Mobarik no member of the Khilji family remained, Toghlak was himself proclaimed king under the title of Gheias-ū-din. His dynasty reigned 91 years, ending in 1412, and is tabulated as below:—

HOUSE OF TOGHLAK (A.D. 1321 TO 1412.)

	Began to reign.	Died.	Memorable Events.
	A. D.	A. D.	
I. Gheias-ū-din Toghlak .	1321	1325	Son of a Tūrki slave; his administration was commendable. His first expedition to Telingāna failed (in 1322), but his second was successful; was killed by the fall of a pavilion erected by his eldest son during some ceremonies.

	Began to reign.	Died.	Memorable Events.
	A.D.	A.D.	
II. Mohamed Toghlak	1325	1351	Eldest son of Gheias-ū-din; was the most accomplished prince of his age, and noted for his munificence to learned men, but his judgment was perverted, and his life spent in pursuing visionary schemes. An invasion of Moguls was bought off, and an unsuccessful attempt made to conquer China with 100,000 men. The king's exactions and cruelties brought on a famine and several rebellions in Malwa, Punjāb, and Bengal in 1338-40, the two former subdued, but Bengal and the coast of Koromandel became independent. In 1344 the Hindū Kings of Kanāta and Telingāna regained their independence, the former founding a new dynasty, with Bijāyanuggur as the capital. The Mogul troops in Guzerat rebelled in 1347, but were subdued. Soon after the Dekhun revolted, and became independent under Hassan Gungū (the founder of the Bahmani dynasty). Mohamed died at Tatta in Sindh in 1351. Among the caprices of this monarch were his two attempts to remove the capital from Delhi to Deogur, called by him Dowlutabād; they failed entirely. Notwithstanding his eccentricities, the Mohamedan territory in India was at its greatest extent in this reign.
III. Firuz Toghlak	1351	1388	Nephew of Mohamed; independence of Bengal and Dekhun recognised by Firuz. Made an expedition to Sindh in 1372, where Jām Bāni, the Rajpūt prince of Tatta, submitted nominally. Firuz forbade mutilation and torture, abolished several vexatious taxes and imposts, and discouraged luxury. His public works were numerous, and comprised 50 dams across rivers for irrigation, 40 mosques, 30 colleges, 100 caravanserais, 30 reservoirs, 100 hospitals, 100 public baths, 150 bridges, besides other edifices for pleasure and ornament. He also constructed the Jumna canal for irrigational purposes. He died in 1388, at the age of 90.
IV. Gheias-ū-din II.	1388	1389	Grandson of Firuz; deposed and murdered at end of 5 months.
V. Abubukur T.	1389	1390	Another grandson of Firuz; was conquered by Nasir-ū-din, his uncle, and made prisoner.
VI. Nasir-ū-din T.	1390	1394	Son of Firuz; his reign was a scene of general disorder; Guzerat revolted, but was reduced to submission.
			Son of Nasir-ū-din; Guzerat revolted, and Malwa and Khandēsh permanently threw off the yoke, and so remained till time of Akbar. In 1398 Tamerlane (or the Amir Teimūr) invaded India, and on reaching Delhi slaughtered, it is said, 100,000 pri-

	Began to reign.	Died.	Memorable Events.
	A. D.	A. D.	
VII. Mahmūd Toghlak .	1394	1412	soners, plundered and fired the city and carried off an immense booty. He finally quitted India in March 1399. Delhi for two months after remained without a government, and almost without inhabitants. In 1400 Mahmūd Toghlak, who had previously fled to Guzerat, returned and died in 1412 after a nominal reign of 18 years, and was succeeded by Doulut Khān Lodi who in 15 months was expelled by Khizir Khān, governor of the Punjāb.

For 36 years after the expulsion of Doulut Khān Lodi there was no kingdom of India either in name or reality. The Government was administered by Khizir Khān and his family, known as the "Syuds" from their being supposed descendants of the Prophet.

SYUD DYNASTY (A.D. 1414 TO 1450).

	Began to reign.	Died.	Memorable Events.
	A.D.	A.D.	
I. Syud Khizir Khān . .	1414	1421	Styled himself the Viceroy of Teimūr; his administration was beneficial, and he added the Punjāb to the imperial dominions.
II. Syud Mubarik	1421	1435	Son of Khizir Khān; imperial territories as limited in this reign as in time of his father; was assassinated in a mosque by some Hindūs.
III. Syud Mohamed	1435	1445	Son of Mubarik. Behlol Lodi, an Afghān, made himself master of Mūltān and greater part of the Punjāb.
IV. Syud Ala-ū-din	1445	Resigned 1450	The imperial dominions much reduced in this reign, extending only twelve miles from the city of Delhi in one direction, and scarcely a mile in the other. He made over his capital to Behlol Khān Lodi, retiring on a pension to Budaon.

The family of Lodi (now known as the Lohani) owe their rise mainly to the grandfather of Behlol, an Afghān and wealthy trader, who subsequently held the Government of Mūltan and afterwards that of the Punjāb in the reign of Firuz Toghlak. The Lodi dynasty reigned for a period of 76 years, and comprised the following rulers:—

HOUSE OF LODI (A.D. 1450 TO 1526).

	Began to reign.	Died.	Memorable Events.
	A.D.	A.D.	
I. Behlōl Lodi . .	1450	1488	Attacked Jounpūr in 1452, and re-annexed it, as well as the Punjāb, to Delhi. At his death his territories extended from the Jumna to the Himālaya mountains as far east as Benares, besides a tract on the west of the Jumna extending to Bundelkund.
II. Sekundur Lodi	1488	1517	Son of Behlol Lodi; he recovered Behar. Sekundur was a poet and a great patron of letters. Died at Agra.
III. Ibrahim Lodi .	1517	1526	Son of Sekundur. Discontents and rebellions took place early in his reign. He executed one of his brothers, and imprisoned the others for life. In 1524 Bāber, king of Kabūl, invaded India at the instance of Doulut Khān Lodi, governor of the Punjāb, and defeated Ibrahim's army at Lahore, returning afterwards to Kabūl. Some time after he again engaged Ibrahim at Paniput in 1526, and utterly routed him, the Indian king and 15,000 of his army being killed. Bāber then occupied both Delhi and Agra, the latter city having lately been the royal residence. With Ibrahim ended the line of Lodi.

A period of Indian history of a most interesting nature has now been reached, but before entering upon an outline of the reigns of the kings of the **House of Teimūr,** a dynasty under which India rose to a high pitch of prosperity, it will be necessary to review briefly those States which were formed on the dissolution of the empire of Delhi, and ended about the time the House of Lodi became extinct. These are—1. The Bahmani dynasty of the Dekhun; 2. The Kings of Malwa; and 3. The Kings of Jounpūr. Some notice of the rise of the Portuguese power in India will also be given, while mention of the Kingdoms of Berar, Guzerat, Khāndēsh, and Bengal will be reserved till the close of Akbar's reign, those of Bidr and Ahmednuggur till Shah Jehān's, and those of Golkonda and Bijapūr to that of Aurungzib:—

BAHMANI KINGS OF THE DEKHUN (A.D. 1347 TO 1526).

	Began to reign.		Mem. events connected with this dynasty.
	A.D.	Hijira	
1. Hassun Gungū (or Ala-ū-din) . . .	1347	748	Hassun was an Afghān of Delhi, and the founder of this dynasty, which lasted 171 years; it took its name from a Brahmin named Gungū, a benefactor of Hassun, who, out of gratitude, assumed the name of Gungū; his capital was at Kulburga. In 1421, the kingdom of Wurungōl was conquered by the Bahmani kings. In 1477, the conquest of Rājāmundri and Masulipatam was effected, and the Kōnkan, from Bombay to Goa, was partially subdued. The Bahmani kings several times engaged in war with those of Khāndēsh and Malwa. The reign of Firuz is considered the most prosperous of this dynasty. He was a great patron of learning, established a mercantile navy, and made twenty-four campaigns. Under Mohamed II. the Bahmani kingdom reached its greatest limits, extending from the Kōnkan to Masulipatam, and from the Nurbadda to the Kistna. After his reign the kingdom gradually crumbled away, and at length resolved itself into five different states: 1. The Adil Shahi dynasty at Bijapūr; 2. The Nizam Shahi at Ahmednuggur; 3. The Imad Shahi; 4. The Kutb Shahi at Golkōnda; and 5. The Barid Shahi at Bidr.
2. Mohamed I. .	1358	759	
3. Mujahid . . .	1375	776	
4. Daūd	1378	780	
5. Mahmūd I.. .	1378	780	
6. Gheias-ū-din .	1397	799	
7. Shams-ū-din .	1397	799	
8. Firuz	1397	800	
9. Ahmed I. . .	1422	825	
10. Ala-ū-din . .	1435	838	
11. Humayūn . .	1457	862	
12. Nizam . . .	1461	865	
13. Mohamed II. .	1463	867	
14. Mahmūd II. .	1482	887	
Nominal Kings.			
15. Ahmed II. . .	1518	924	
16. Ala-ū-din II. .	1520	927	
17. Wali	1522	929	
18. Kalim . . .	1526	933	

KINGS OF MALWA (A.D. 1401 TO 1512).

	Began to reign.	
	A.D.	H.
1. Dilāwur Ghori	1401	804
2. Hoshūng Ghori	1405	808
3. Mohamed Ghori	1332	835
4. Mahmūd Khilji	1435	839
5. Gheias-ū-din Khilji	1482	887
6. Nasir-ū-din Khilji	1500	906
7. Mahmūd II. Khilji	1512	916

Memorable Events.—This dynasty was founded by Dilāwur Ghori whose ancestors were natives of Ghor. Malwa with Māndu as its capital, became independent in the reign of Sūltān Mahmūd Toghlak. It carried on frequent wars with Guzerat, Jounpūr and Khāndēsh, as well as with the Bahmani Kings in Berar. The town of Hoshūngabad derives its name from the second prince of this line, who founded it. The reign of the last king (Mahmūd II.) was more fertile in events than any that preceded it. His success was mainly owing to the support of a Rājpūt chief, Mēdni Rāi, but he was at last defeated in 1531 by Bahādūr Shah, King of Guzerat, and Malwa was permanently annexed to that kingdom.

KINGS OF JOUNPŪR (A.D. 1394 TO 1457).

	Began to reign.	
	A.D.	H.
1. Khāja Jehān	1394	796
2. Mubarik	1399	802
3. Ibrahim	1401	804
4. Mahmūd	1440	844
5. Mohamed	1457	862
6. Hossein	1457	862

Memorable Events.—Jounpūr became independent under Khāja Jehān in the reign of Mahmūd Toghlak, and stretched along the Ganges from Kanouj on the north-west to the frontier, between Bengal and South Behar on the south-east. This state carried on wars with the Kings of Delhi and Malwa. In 1476 it was subverted and restored to Delhi by Behlōl Lodi.

Rise of the Portuguese power in India.

At a time when the Bahmani kingdom of the Dekhun was fast falling to pieces, and during the reign of the first prince of the house of Lodi, another race of adventurers appeared on the western coast of India, and gave a new direction to its politics and commerce. In May 1497 the first Portuguese expedition, under the command of Vasco de Gama, after doubling the Cape of Good Hope, anchored off Kalikut, then belonging to an independent Hindū Rājā, called the Zamorin, who received them at first with cordiality, but afterwards through the influence of the Moorish traders, was induced to treat them with mistrust. A second expedition under Cabral arrived in 1500, and a third under Vasco in 1502, both of which tended to widen still further the breach already made, and resulted mainly in demonstrating the superiority of European over Asiatic troops. The Venetians who had hitherto monopolised the trade of the East induced the Sūltān of Egypt to fit out a fleet to sweep the Portuguese from the Indian seas. In conjunction with the King of Guzerat the Egyptian fleet was in 1508 at first successful, but it subsequently suffered a defeat off Diu, in Guzerat, when a peace was soon after concluded. Between the years 1507-16, the celebrated Albuquerque, the greatest of all the Portuguese commanders, placed the Portuguese power in the East on a firm basis. He secured the fine harbour of Goa on the Malabar coast, which he strongly fortified and made the capital of all the Portuguese possessions in India. Thence he sailed to the port of Malacca, took it and erected a fort there, thus opening up a new field of commercial enterprise to Siam, Java, and Sumatra. He also occupied the port of Ormuz in the Persian Gulf, which subsequently became one of the most flourishing settlements in those seas. In nine years he thus built up the power of the Portuguese in the East; and though possession of a single province on the continent of India was never obtained by them, they enjoyed for a hundred years without a rival, the command of thesea and the control of the trade throughout the Eastern archipelago. They possessed thirty factories, several of them fortified, and their authority was supreme over 12,000 miles of sea-coast.

HOUSE OF TEIMŪR.—(I.) BĀBER (A.D. 1526 TO 1530).

Birth and Reign.—Was the son of Sheik Mirza, and the sixth in descent from Teimūr; born in 1482, and was descended on his mother's side from Zenghiz Khān. He succeeded to his father's dominion of Ferghāna in 1494, but did not turn his attention seriously to India till 1524. He ascended the throne as the first Mogul emperor in 1526, and reigned from that year to 1530.

Issue.—Four sons. 1. Humayūn, who succeeded him; 2. Kāmran; 3. Hindal; and 4. Mirza Askari.

Death.—Died at Agra, 26th December, 1530, and was buried at Kabūl in a spot it is supposed he had himself selected.

Character.—Courageous and active, and more valiant as a soldier than great as a general; he never lost heart, and was as buoyant after a defeat as after a victory. He was constantly occupied with the construction of aqueducts, reservoirs, and with various improvements, and in introducing new fruits and other productions of remote countries into India. He composed many elegant Persian poems, and a history of the times in which he lived is contained in his memoirs. Among Mahomedan princes not one is held in higher estimation than Bāber.

Wars.—After defeating Ibrahim Lodi in 1526, and ascending the Indian throne, he engaged in a war with Sānga Rānā of Mēwar, whom in 1527 he routed at Sikri (twenty miles from Agra) with great loss, and occupied the province of Mēwar. In 1528, he defeated Mēdni Rāi, the Rājpūt chief of Chanderi. He then reduced South Behar, and engaged in war with the King of Bengal, who held North Behar. This prince was worsted in the field, and soon after consented to terms of peace.

(II.) HUMAYŪN (A.D. 1530 TO 1556).

Birth and Reign.—Was the son of Bāber, and born in 1517; he succeeded his father, and reigned from 1530 to 1556, including the sixteen years of his banishment from the capital.

Issue.—Akbar, who afterwards succeeded his father; Hakim, and others.

Death.—He died at Delhi, in 1556, by falling over a parapet of his palace.

Character.—Was bold and courageous in his military affairs, but wanting in enterprise; naturally he was more inclined to ease than ambition. His heart seems to have been hardened by his long misfortunes and disappointments, and he became at the end of his reign tyrannical and cruel.

Wars.—I. With Bāban and Bāyazid, Afghān chiefs of Jounpūr, who had risen in rebellion; they were defeated in 1532. II. With Bahādur Shah, King of Guzerat, in 1534, for supplying Ala-ū-din Lodi, the uncle of Sūltān Ibrahim Lodi, with men and money. Guzerat was invaded and conquered, the Moguls expelled, and the hill fort of Champaner taken in 1535-6. III. With Shir Khān Sūr of Ghor, who had, early in Humayūn's reign, obtained possession of Behar, and partly conquered Bengal. Humayūn took the fort of Chunar, near Benares, and afterwards the city of Gour; but had, in 1539, to retreat with great loss to Agra. In a second campaign he was again utterly defeated by Shir Shah, and fled at first to Lahore, and afterwards to Sindh (then in the hands of Hussein, head of the Arghūn family), the conquest of which country he attempted, but failed; thence he retired for protection to Jodhpūr, but it was refused. He made another attempt on Sindh, but again failed, and retired, in 1543, to Kandahar, then held by his younger brother, Mirza Askari. Leaving his queen and infant son Akbar there, he went to Persia, the king of which country received him and eventually furnished him with 14,000 horse, to reconquer the throne of India. With these he, in 1545, took Kandahar, and in 1547, Kabūl, but the latter fell, in 1550, into the hands of his brother Kāmran, though recaptured in 1551, when Kāmran was blinded by Humayūn's order, and afterwards permitted to go to Mekka. In 1555 he invaded the Punjāb, took Lahore, defeated Sekundur Sūr at Sirhind, captured Delhi and Agra, and once more re-mounted the throne of India.

Family of Sūr.

As during Humayūn's exile (1540-55), Shir Shah and his two successors of the family of Sūr ruled over that monarch's territories, it will be necessary here to give a brief outline of their several reigns.

(I.) SHIR SHAH (A.D. 1540-45).

This prince, after taking possession of all Humayūn's dominions, subdued a revolt in Bengal (1541), conquered Malwa in 1542, and in 1544 invaded Marwar, with 80,000 men. He afterwards reduced the Rāna of Mēwar, and in 1545, while besieging Kalinjer, he received such injuries from the explosion of a powder magazine, as to cause his death. He was a prince of consummate prudence and ability, and his measures were both benevolent and wise. He introduced many improvements in his civil government, constructed a great road, planted it with rows of trees for shade, and dug deep wells for the convenience of travellers. His right to the Indian throne was as valid as Bāber's, and his short reign is considered to be one of the most brilliant in Indian annals.

(II.) SELIM SHAH SŪR (A.D. 1545-53),

Was the second son of Shir Shah, and supplanted his elder brother, Adil Khān, the recognized heir to the throne. Soon after his accession he quelled an obstinate rebellion, and died after a peaceable reign of nine years.

(III). MOHAMED SHAH SŪR ADILI (A.D. 1553-56),

Was the brother of Selim Shah; he murdered his nephew, and then usurped the throne. He was grossly ignorant, given to debauchery, and despicable for his incapacity. By his oppressive measures he drove many of the nobles to rebellion, and Delhi and the Western Provinces were separated. The Punjāb revolted under Sekundur Sūr, Bengal under Mohamed Sūr, and Malwa also became independent. It was at this juncture that Humayūn returned to India, but he died while Hēmu, Mahomed Shah's general, was preparing to meet him. In 1556 Behram, Akbar's general, defeated Hēmu at Paniput, and Mahomed Shah, after this, lost all hope of recovering his dominions. He died soon after in battle, leaving Akbar the possessor of the Punjāb and the country round Delhi and Agra.

(II.) AKBAR (A.D. 1556 TO 1605).

Birth and Reign.—Was the eldest son of Humayūn; born at Umurkote, near Sindh, October 14th, 1542; he ascended the throne in 1556, and reigned till 1605.

Marriage.—With the daughters of the Hindū Rājas of Amber (now Jeipūr) and Marwar.

Issue.—1. Selim, who succeeded him; 2. Murād who died during his father's lifetime; 3. Daniāl, who fell a victim to intemperance in his thirtieth year, and others.

Death.—Died at Agra, October 13th, 1605. His tomb at that city is an immense structure, adorned with carving of great delicacy and beauty. The close of Akbar's life was much embittered by the misconduct of his son Selim.

Character.—Akbar was strongly built and handsome, and endowed with great personal strength and activity. Though constantly engaged in wars, he effected greater improvement in his civil government than any other king of India. He was sober and abstemious in his habits, and very fond of religious and philosophical discussions.

Wars.—Early in his reign he had to quell the rebellions of his own officers, which lasted seven years. In 1567 he engaged in war with Udi Singh, Rāna of Chittore (or Udipūr), who lost his capital, but retained his independence. In 1569, he took the strong hill forts of Rintimbor and Kalinjer. During the years 1572 and 1573 he conquered Guzerat, the pageant king Mozuffur having formally transferred his crown to the Emperor of Delhi. In 1575, Akbar subdued Bengal, which had remained under the rule of different Afghān kings; he subsequently lost the province, owing to a mutiny of his troops; but after fifteen years of disturbance, it was finally brought into subjection by his general Mān Singh, in 1592. In 1586-7, he conquered Kashmir, held by princes of the Mahomedan faith, and afterwards engaged in warfare with the North Eastern Afghāns, inhabiting a portion of the plain of Peshāwur, where his generals, Zein Khān and Rājā Birbul, were defeated, and the latter killed, and though several expeditions were sent, these tribes retained their turbulent independence to the last. In 1591, Akbar conquered Sindh by way of Umurkote; the chief of that country had in his pay Portuguese soldiers, besides 200 natives dressed as Europeans, who were probably the first sepoys in India. In 1594 he recovered

Kandahar, so that in Hindūsthān proper, the only chief that remained unsubdued was the Rāna of Udipūr. In 1595 he sent an expedition to the Dekhun, when the city of Ahmednuggur, then held by Chānd Sūltāna (or Chānd Bibi), acting as regent for her nephew, Bahādur Nizam Shah, was besieged, and subsequently taken, in 1600, but it did not lead to the submission of the kingdom. In 1601, Khāndēsh was conquered and annexed, and this last acquisition completes the long list of Akbar's wars.

Memorable Events.—At Akbar's accession the principal Rājpūt States were—1. **Mewar,** with Chittore the capital, Udipūr, not having been founded till some time before the death of Akbar by Rāna Pertab. 2. **Marwar,** under the Rahtors with its capital at Jodhpūr. Some of this tribe had about A.D. 1194 left the Ganges, and dispossessed the Jats of their country between the table-land and the Indus, while another portion at a later period (about A.D. 1459) founded 3. **Bikanir** in the desert. 4. **Jeisulmir,** under the Bhattis, who claimed to be derived from Muttra on the river Jumna; they removed their capital to Jeisulmir about A.D. 1156. 5. **Amber** (or Jeipūr) under the tribe of Kachwahā, which rose into distinction after the accession of Akbar. It was an ancient feudatory of Ajmir. 6. **Harauti,** with Būndi as its capital, under the tribe of Hāra; they settled in their present possessions in A.D. 1342 and at Akbar's accession held the strong hill-fort of Rintimbor. Besides these there were the small principalities of Parkur, under the Chouhans, and Umurkote under the Sodas, as also Sirohi and Jhalor below the Aravalli mountains and a few petty states in Bundelkund.

Rajpūt States.

Akbar's empire was divided into 15 Sūbahs (or Provinces):—1. Kabūl, beyond the Indus; 2. Lahore; 3. Mūltān; 4. Delhi; 5. Agra; 6. Oudh; 7. Allahābād;

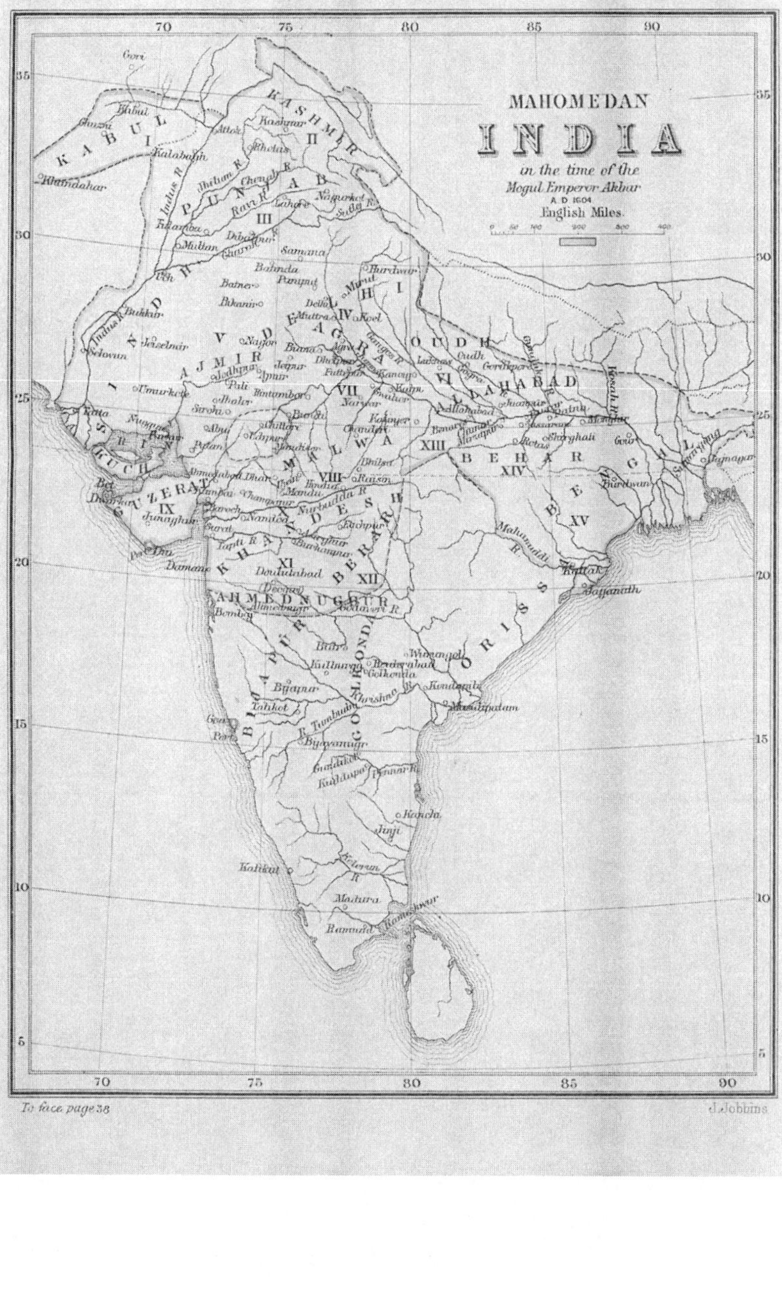

To face page 38

J. Jobbins

8. Ajmir; 9. Guzerat; 10. Malwa; 11. Behar; 12. Bengal; 13. Khāndēsh; 14. Berar; and 15. Ahmednuggur. The chief officer in each was the Viceroy (Sipah Sālar, afterwards changed to Sūbhēdar) with complete civil and military control. Under him were the Phoujdars (military commanders of districts). The police of large towns was under an officer called the "Kotwal." Justice was administered by an officer called "Mir Adel" (Lord Justice) and by a Kazi; the latter conducted the trial, and the former passed judgment. Though Akbar was nominally a Mahomedan, he had a religious system of his own, which seems to have been a pure deism. He discouraged the study of Arabic and the wearing of the beard, and changed the era of the Hijra and the Arabian months for the solar year.

Division of Akbar's Empire.

Akbar's revenue system, renowned for the benefits it conferred on India, was not an original conception, but the continuation of a plan begun by Shir Shah Sūr. The main objects were—1. To obtain a correct measurement of the land; 2. To ascertain the amount of the produce of each Bigah (nearly three-fourths of an acre) of land, and to fix the proportion of the amount each ought to pay to the Government; and 3. To settle an equivalent for the proportion so fixed in money. This settlement was made for ten years, and with the cultivators themselves, to the exclusion of all middle men. Akbar was greatly assisted in this important reform by Rājā Toda Mull, his finance minister.

Revenue System.

The army, even in its highest state of perfection, was not very well organized. There were commanders of 10,000, of 5,000, down to those of ten. Akbar paid the commanders for their soldiers by the head, a bad plan, as it led to false musters and wretched soldiery. A good horseman,

Army.

if from beyond the Indus, received 25 rupees a month, if an Indian, 20 rupees; matchlockmen had 6 rupees a month at the outside, and archers as low as 2½ rupees.

Public Works.

Akbar constructed the fort of Attok, and the walls and citadels of Agra and Allahabād. He also built and fortified the town of Futtepūr Sikri, his principal residence, and he erected the tomb of Humayūn at Delhi, a great and solid edifice, surmounted by a vast dome of white marble.

"Akbar," says Ferishta, "had never less than 5,000 elephants and 12,000 stable-horses, besides vast hunting and hawking establishments. The greatest displays of grandeur took place on the king's birthday, when he was weighed in golden scales, against silver, gold, perfumes, and other substances in succession, and these were afterwards distributed among the spectators."

The "*Ayeni Akberi*" (regulations of Akbar) by Abul Fuzl, the Prime Minister, in addition to giving long accounts of civil and military arrangements, contains also a minute description of the establishment and regulation of every department, from the Mint and Treasury to the fruit, perfumery, and flower offices, the kitchen and the kennel. Akbar encouraged schools, at which Hindū as well as Mahomedan learning was taught, and every one was educated according to his circumstances and particular views in life. To secure the loyalty of the Hindūs, he allowed them to share the highest civil offices and military commands in the state. He abolished the "*Jezzia*," or capitation tax, permitted Hindū widows to re-marry, and discouraged Suttis.

English in India.

In 1583 Fitch, an Englishman, with three other adventurers, visited India, taking with them letters of introduction from Queen Elizabeth to the Emperor Akbar. Fitch was much struck with the splendour of the court and the magnitude and wealth of the cities of Hindūsthān. It was the information gained from this visit that no doubt in a great measure opened out to English merchants the hope of a lucrative commerce with India.

Portuguese.

During the 16th century few events of consequence occurred in the history of the Portuguese in India. They formed two settlements, one at Hūghli, the other at Chittagong, ports of the Gangetic valley, and in Guzerat, Diu was taken by them and a fort built there in 1538. A great combination of Mahomedan powers was formed to extirpate them, but it ended only in the long and fruitless siege of Diu, which was gallantly defended by the Portuguese. In 1570 a combined attack of the Kings of Bijapūr, Ahmednuggur and the Zamorin of Kalikut was made on Goa with an immense army, but they were compelled to raise the siege with great loss and sue for peace. The Portuguese retained their maritime supremacy till the end of the century, when the Dutch appeared, and to them they were eventually obliged to succumb.

Names of Note.—**Behram Khān** (called also Khān Bāba) a minister of great consequence under Akbar; his arbitrary conduct disgusted all classes. Being disgraced by Akbar in 1560, he revolted, but was pardoned on his submission. He was assassinated while proceeding to Guzerat. **Raja Toda Mull,** minister of finance and author of the revenue system introduced by Akbar into India; he was also a distinguished military commander. **Bir-Bul**—A great personal favourite of Akbar, and a commander of note; he was killed in battle in 1586 while fighting against the Eusofzeis, an Afghān tribe in northern India. He was a man of very lively conversation, and many of his witty sayings are still current in India. **Chānd Sultānā** (Chānd Bibi), a princess of the house of Nizām Shah of Ahmednuggur; she defended the capital bravely against the Mogul army in 1596, and as the favourite heroine of the Dekhun is the subject of many fabulous stories; she was killed by assassins in 1600. **Feizi**, a learned Mussulman, who applied himself to a diligent study of Hindū literature and science; he translated the "Nāla and Damyanti," from the Māhā-Bhārat, and made versions of the "Bija Gunita" and the "Lilawati" of Bhaskara Achāryá. He is said to have possessed at his death a library of 4,060 books on various subjects, carefully corrected and well bound. **Abul Fuzl**, a brother of the above, and Prime Minister to Akbar; he was the compiler of the "Akbarnameh" up to the 47th year of Akbar's reign; this was continued for three years afterwards either by Enāyut Ullah or Mahomed Salliá. Abul Fuzl was murdered near Gwalior in 1602, at the instigation of Prince Selim, Akbar's eldest son. **Tansen**, a celebrated musical composer. **Abdul Khadir**, author of the "Muntakhab-ul-Tawarikh," a history of the Mahomedan kings of India. **Nizam-u-din Hevei**, author of the "Tabakāti Akbari," a history of the Mahomedan kings, down to the 37th year of Akbar. **Mirza Khān** (Khān Khānam), son of Behram Khān, and translator of Bāber's memoirs from Turkish into the Persian language.

KINGS OF BENGAL (A.D. 1338 TO 1575).

	Began to reign.	
	A.D.	H.
1. Fakhr-ū-din	1338	739
2. Ala-ū-din	1340	741
3. Hafi Elias (Shums-ū-din)	1342	743
4. Sekundur	1357	759
5. Gheias-ū-din	1367	769
6. Sūltān-ū-Salatin	1374	775
7. Shums-ū-din II.	1383	785

	Began to reign.	
	A. D.	H.
8. Rājā Kans	1386	788
9. Jitmull (Jilal-ū-din)	1392	795
10. Ahmed	1409	812
11. Nasir-ū-din	1426	830
12. Nasir	1426	830
13. Barbik	1428	832
14. Eusof	1445	849
15. Futteh	1461	866
16. Shazāda	1481	886
17. Firuz	1481	886
18. Mahmūd	1493	899
19. Mozuffur	1494	900
20. Ala-ū-din II.	1497	904
21. Nusrut	1521	927
22. Mahmūd II.	1534	940
23. Shir Shah	1537	945
24. Selim	1545	952
25. Adili	1548	955
26. Bahādur	1553	961
27. Jilal-ū-din	1560	968
28. Sulimān Kerāni	1563	971
29. Bāyazid	1573	981
30. Dāūd	1573	981

Memorable Events.—The kingdom of Bengal, after its revolt from Mohamed Toghlak, lasted upwards of 200 years, but there are no events worthy of record. This kingdom at one time seems to have included North Behar. It possessed Sūndurgong (Dakka), and Jajnuggur (Tipperah) was tributary. Assam was occasionally plundered. Kuttak and the adjoining parts of Orissa were not acquired till just before the extinction of the kingdom. At the time of Akbar's accession, Bengal was in the hands of a revolted officer of one of the successors of Shir Shah of the family of Sūr, who conquered the kingdom in 1541.

KINGS OF GUZERAT (A.D. 1396 TO 1572).

	Began to reign.	
	A. D.	H.
1. Mozuffur Shah I.	1396	799
2. Ahmed Shah I.	1412	815
3. Mohamed Shah	1443	847
4. Kūtb Shah	1451	855
5. Dāūd Shah (reigned one week)	—	—
6. Mahmūd Shah Bēgarra	1459	863
7. Mozuffur Shah II.	1511	917
8. Sekundur Shah	1526	932
9. Mahmūd Shah II.	1526	932
10. Behādur Shah	1526	932
11. Miran Mahomed Farukhi	1536	943
12. Mahmūd Shah III.	1553	961
13. Ahmed Shah II.	1561	969
14. Mozuffur Shah III.	1561	969

Memorable Events.—On the separation of Guzerat from Delhi, the extent of the kingdom consisted of but a narrow territory on the plain between the hills and the sea, the hilly and forest tracts were mostly held by mountain tribes of Bhils and Kūlis; the Rājā of Edur (a Rajpūt) being in possession of the western part of the hills. This dynasty was founded by Mozuffur, son of a Rajpūt convert. The kings had frequent wars with Malwa, Khāndēsh and the Bahmani kings of the Dekhun, and they obtained in 1429 the islands of Bombay and Salsette from the latter. Ahmed Shah I. built the towns of Ahmednuggur and Ahmedabād. Mahmūd Shah, the sixth king, was noted for his vigorous government and maritime expeditions. He co-operated with the Mamlūks of Egypt in a naval war against the Portuguese, but was defeated in 1508, near Diu in Guzerat. Bahādur Shah, the tenth king had his supremacy acknowledged by the kings of Khāndēsh, Berar, and Ahmednuggur; in 1531 he conquered Malwa and annexed it to Guzerat. He was killed in an affray which took place between him and the Portuguese off Diu. Nothing further of any note occurred till 1572, when Guzerat was conquered by Akbar and annexed to his dominions.

KINGS OF KHĀNDĒSH (A.D. 1399 TO 1596).

	Began to reign.	
	A. D.	H.
Malik Rājā	—	—
1. Nasir Khān (first king) . . .	1399	801
2. Miran Adil Khān	1437	841
3. Miran Mobarik	1441	844
4. Adil Khān I.	1457	861
5. Dāūd Khān	1503	909
6. Adil Khān II.	1510	916
7. Miran Mohamed Shah . . .	1520	926
8. Miran Mūbarik II.	1535	942
9. Miran Mohamed Khān . . .	1566	974
10. Rājā Ali Khān	1576	984
11. Bahādur Shah	1596	1005

Memorable Events. — The kingdom of Khāndēsh comprised the lower part of the valley of the Tapti; to the south it was bounded by the Dekhun table-land, and to the north by the Injadri range. The country was rich and well-watered, and seems to have enjoyed a high state of prosperity under its kings, as the numerous remains of irrigational works evidently show. The capital was Burhanpūr, near the strong hill fort of Asīrgarh. There is nothing worthy of note in the domestic history of these kings. The founder of the dynasty was Malik Ambur, a person of Arab descent. Khāndēsh was re-annexed to Delhi by Akbar in 1599.

DYNASTY OF IMĀD SHAHI IN BERAR.

	Began to reign.	
	A. D.	H.
1. Futteh Ullah	1484	890
2. Ala-ū-din	1504	910
3. Deria	1529	936
4. Burhan (doubtful)	1560	968
5. Tufal	—	—

Memorable Events.—This dynasty was founded by Futteh Ullah, who was descended from a converted Hindū. This small kingdom extended from the Injadrī hills to the Godaveri, and it bordered on Ahmednuggur and Khāndēsh on the west. On the east its limits were uncertain, but it is supposed not to have included Nagpūr. This state merged in that of Ahmednuggur in 1572.

(III.) JEHĀNGIR (A.D. 1605 TO 1627).

Birth and Reign.—Was the eldest son of Akbar; born in 1568, and on his accession assumed the title of Jehāngir (Conqueror of the World). He reigned till 1627.

Marriage.—With Nūr Jehān (Light of the World), widow of Shir Afghān Khān, a woman of remarkable grace and beauty, and of great capacity in state affairs. She survived Jehāngir, and died in 1646. She was buried in a tomb she had herself erected close to that of Jehāngir at Lahore.

Issue.—1. Khusru, who died in 1621. 2. Parviz. 3. Khurram, afterwards Shah Jehān.

Death.—Died of asthma on his way from Kashmir to Lahore, October 28th, 1627, in the 60th year of his age. Was buried at Lahore, where his tomb still exists.

Character.—This prince was wanting in neither good feelings nor good sense, but he was the slave of favourites and wine. His intelligence was of a low order, and he fully believed in magical performances, regarding them as the results of supernatural power.

Wars.—With the Rāna of Udipūr in 1607, and against Malik Ambur in the Dekhun. In 1614 the Rāna submitted on honourable terms. In the Dekhun the imperial armies were repeatedly defeated by Malik Ambur, but in 1617, he was forced to submit; the fort of Ahmednuggur was restored as well as all the territory he had re-conquered from the Moguls. In 1621 Malik Ambur renewed the war, but peace was again concluded on a further cession of territory and the payment of a sum of money by the Dekhun prince. Jehāngir's reign was also disturbed by the rebellions of his sons and subjects. The first was fomented by his eldest son Khusru in 1606, but was quelled in about a month. The second by his third son, Khurram, in 1623, owing to a mutual distrust between him and his father. He obtained possession of Bengal and Behar, but was defeated by his brother Parviz and Mohābet Khān; he then united his fortunes with Malik Ambur in the Dekhun, but being deserted by his army, submitted to the emperor in 1625. The third rebellion was that of Mohābet Khān, one of Jehāngir's generals, and the most eminent of all the emperor's subjects. Driven to rebellion by the persecutions of the empress (Nūr Jehān) in 1626, he seized Jehāngir as the latter was preparing to cross the Jhilum, but the emperor was soon after rescued, and terms were granted to Mohābet Khān provided he used his services against Shah Jehān, then once more in rebellion. Instead, however, of following up Shah Jehān he joined him, but all further hostilities were avoided by the death of Jehāngir, which occurred in 1627.

Memorable Events.—It was in 1611 that Jehāngir married Nūr Jehān. She was of Persian extraction, and her grandfather held an office of high trust under the government of that country. Her name was put on the coin together with the emperor's. Her conduct in rescuing her husband from the hands of Mohābet Khān was most spirited. After the death of Jehāngir, she was allowed a stipend of £250,000 a year; she wore no colour but white after his decease, and appeared to devote her life to the memory of her husband.

East India Company.

It was in 1599 that the first East India Company was formed, with a capital of £30,133, to open a trade with Hindūsthān. In 1600 a charter was obtained from Queen Elizabeth, and in 1601 the first venture, consisting of five ships with goods valued at 68,000 rupees (£6,800) and a quantity of bullion, under the command of Captain Lancaster, sailed for the East. No part of India was touched at, but the fleet proceeded to Sumatra, and afterwards to Bantam, where a factory was erected; it returned to England in 1603 with a satisfactory profit. In 1608 their fleets touched for the first time on the coast of India. In 1611 the Company sent two ships to Surat (Sūrut), where they defeated four Portuguese ships of war. In 1612 Captain Best settled the English factory at Surat, and in 1613 a "*firman*" was obtained from Jehāngir, allowing the establishment of factories at Surat, Ahmedabād, Kambay, and Gogo. In 1616 the title of President was first given to Thomas Kerridge, superintendent of the Surat factory, and this town became the chief seat of English commerce on the western coast of India. On the Koromandel Coast the Company's first factory was opened at Masulipatam, and removed thence in 1625 to Armegan. In 1615 Sir Thomas Roe arrived at the Court of Jehāngir as Ambassador from King James I. He describes the magnificence of the court, the great display of gold plate, jewelled vases and goblets, and the throne covered with diamonds, rubies, and pearls. The language of the court was Persian, but all classes spoke Hindūsthāni. He represents the great men as being nearly all open to corruption. He accompanied the emperor in his marches to Mandū and Guzerat, but met with many inconveniences, which he ascribes "to an ill government and an intemperate climate." He left the imperial camp at the end of 1618, having obtained some valuable privileges for the East India Company.

Names of Note.—**Nūr Jehān** (Light of the World), the Queen of Jehāngir; she died in 1646. **Mirza Gheias,** the father of Nūr Jehān; he rose to be prime minister to Jehāngir; he was wise and upright. **Mohābet Khān,** a renowned general under Jehāngir; he was a native of Kabūl, and was raised to the highest dignities and employments by the emperor before he rebelled in 1626. **Malik Ambur,** the chief of the Abyssinian nobles at Ahmednuggur, and a statesman of great genius; he introduced a revenue settlement into the Dekhun, and for twenty years upheld the fortunes of the Nizam Shāhi dynasty with great energy. He died in 1626, at the age of eighty.

(IV.) SHAH JEHAN (A.D. 1627 TO 1658).

Birth and Reign.—Was the third son of the Emperor Jehāngir; born in 1591, proclaimed at Agra, January 26th, 1628, and reigned till 1658.

Marriage and Issue.—Married Mumtaz Mehāl. He had four sons and two daughters. 1. Dara, frank and high spirited, but impetuous and imprudent. 2. Shujā, given to wine and pleasure. 3. Aurungzib cautious, artful, and designing; and 4. Murād, brave and generous, but dull in intellect. The daughters were Padshah Begum and Roushanāra.

Death.—He died in 1665, seven years after his deposition by his son Aurungzīb.

Character.—Shah Jehān's personal conduct when on the throne appears to have been blameless; he was beneficent and paternal in his administration, and though fond of magnificence and pageantry, was noted for the incomparable order and arrangement of his finances.

Wars.—In the beginning of this reign Khān Jehān Lodi, an Afghān commander, revolted, and having obtained assistance from the King of Ahmednuggur, endeavoured to make head against the imperial forces. He was defeated, and fled towards Bundelkund, but was killed by a Rajpūt, and his head sent to the emperor, in 1630. Through this rebel, war ensued with Ahmednuggur and Bijapūr, attended with varying success, when peace was concluded in 1636 with the latter state; but the kingdom of Ahmednuggur was extinguished in 1637, and a portion made over to Bijapūr. In 1655 the war in the Dekhun was renewed under the emperor's son Aurungzib, who treacherously attacked and plundered Heidurabād, the capital of the kingdom of Golkōnda, and then in 1656 provoked a war with the Bijapūr State, which ultimately fell in 1686. At the latter end of this reign disputes took place between Shah Jehān's four sons as to the succession to the throne, ending in the success of Aurungzib and the discomfiture of his three brothers, and also in the deposition of the emperor in 1658.

Memorable Events.—Shah Jehān on his accession abolished the ceremony of prostration, and restored the Mahomedan lunar year in ordinary correspondence. A famine and pestilence took place in the Dekhun, owing to a failure of the periodical rains in 1629 and 1630. Thousands of people emigrated, vast numbers died, whole districts were depopulated, and some did not recover under forty years. In 1653 a revenue survey of the Dekhun, which had occupied Shah Jehān nearly twenty years, was completed, and Todar Mull's system of assessment and collection was introduced. Shah Jehān, though deposed by his son Aurungzib in 1658, was treated with the highest respect; he lived seven years after this. The famous Delhi Canal was constructed in this reign, under the superintendence of the emperor's architect, Ali Murdan Khān. It took its course from the Feroze Canal, was carried through the Aravilli Mountains, and thence brought into Delhi. Native tradition mentions that the revenue from it maintained 12,000 cavalry. For working and protecting it, there were employed 1,000 armed Peons, 500 horsemen, and a large staff of officers, masons, and others. Shah Jehān founded a new city at Delhi on a regular plan, and enriched it with several structures of great elegance and grandeur; but his reign will always be remembered as that in which the "Taj Mahāl" (a corruption of Mumtaz Mehāl, the name of Shah Jehān's queen) was erected at Agra. It is a mausoleum of white marble decorated with mosaics, with a high cupola and four minarets. The peacock throne, valued at six and a half millions sterling, was also constructed by him. It represented a peacock, with its outspread tail formed of sapphires, emeralds, rubies, and other jewels. Notwithstanding the expense of these undertakings, Shah Jehān is said to have left at his death a treasure in coin ranging from six to twenty-four millions sterling.

Portuguese in India.

In 1632 the fortified factory of the Portuguese at Hūghli, in Bengal, was captured by the Mogul Subhēdar of that province, and the Portuguese power there irretrievably broken.

In 1634 Shah Jehān granted a "*firman*" for the establishment of a factory in Bengal. In 1636, owing to the fortuitous circumstance of Mr. Boughton, an English surgeon, successfully treating the emperor's daughter who had fallen sick, the privilege was granted of trading in Bengal free of duty, and of establishing factories in the interior; these were afterwards allowed to be formed at Balasore and Hūghli. In 1639 the Madras factory was established by Mr. Day on a plot of land granted to the East India Company by the Rājā of Chundagiri, and called Fort St. George; this was subsequently declared a presidency in 1653. In Western India, Surat still continued to be the seat of trade for the East India Company, and the principal person in the factory there was styled "Chief for the Honourable Company of English Merchants trading to the East." In 1652 Captain Jeremy Blackman was president, with a salary of £500 per annum. The Dutch were at this time formidable rivals of the English.

English.

Names of Note.—**Ali Merdān Khān**, a governor of Kashmir and Kabūl, noted for his public works, and especially for a canal at Delhi, which still bears his name. **Saād Ullah Khān**, the prime minister of Shah Jehān, considered to have been the most able and upright statesman that ever appeared in India. He died in 1655. **Sundar**, a poet; his works were written in Hindi.

DYNASTY OF BARID SHAH AT BIDR.

	Began to reign.	
	A. D.	H.
1. Kasim	1498	904
2. Amir	1504	910
3. Ali	1549	945
4. Ibrahim	1562	990
5. Kasim II.	1569	997
6. Mirza Ali	1572	1000
7. Amir II.	—	—

The Barids appeared first as the ministers and representatives of the Bahmani kings. The territories of this dynasty were small and ill-defined, and the period of its extinction uncertain.

DYNASTY OF NIZAM SHAH AT AHMEDNUGGUR (A.D. 1490 TO 1637).

	Began to reign.	
	A. D.	H.
1. Ahmed	1490	896
2. Burhān	1508	914
3. Husen	1553	961
4. Murtezza	1565	972
5. Mirān Husen	1588	996
6. Ismāil	1588	997
7. Burhān II.	1590	999
8. Ibrahim	1594	1003
9. Ahmed II.	1594	1004
10. Bahādūr	1595	1004
11. Murtezza Nizam Shah	—	—

Memorable Events.—Ahmed was the founder of this dynasty, and was declared king on the dissolution of the Bahmani government. In combination with the Adil Shāhi, Barid, and Kutb Shāhi governments, this dynasty destroyed, in 1565, at the battle of Talikote, the Hindū kingdom of Bijāyanuggur, then comprehending almost all the south of India. It engaged also in war with the other kingdoms of the Dekhun, and subverted Berar in 1572. The celebrated gun now at Bijapūr is said to have been taken from one of the kings of Ahmednuggur. At its greatest extent this kingdom comprehended all that was afterwards called the Sūbah of Aurungabād, and all to the west of that of Berar. It also possessed a portion of the sea-coast in the Kōnkun, between the tracts belonging to Guzerat and Bijapūr. The Nizam Shāhi dynasty was extinguished in 1637, by Shah Jehān, and a portion of its territory ceded to the Bijapūr State.

(V.) AURUNGZIB (OR ALUMGIR) (A.D. 1658 TO 1707).

Birth and Reign.—Was the third son of Shah Jehān; born in October, 1618, he ascended the throne in 1658, during the lifetime of his father, and reigned till 1707.

Issue.—1. Moazzim, who succeeded him; 2. Azim; 3. Kambuksh; and 4. Akbar.

Death.—At Ahmednuggur, on 22nd February, 1707, in the eighty-ninth year of his age.

Character.—Mild in temper but cold in heart; a perfect master of dissimulation, but a sincere and bigoted Mussulman. His government was a system of continual mistrust, and he cordially detested the Hindūs. In his old age he is described as being of low stature, with a long nose and a round beard. Of all the kings of India, Aurungzib is the most admired among Mahomedans.

Wars.—With his brothers, Dara, Shūja, and Murād, for the sovereignty of India. Dara, after being defeated, fled to Guzerat and Sindh, but being betrayed by the chief of Jūn, he was put to death by Aurungzib in 1659. Shūja fled to Arrakan, but his subsequent fate is uncertain. Murād was shortly after executed in his prison. In 1661, an expedition against Assam was undertaken, but it ended disastrously, and in the death of the Mogul general, Mir Jūmla. His first rupture with the Maratta freebooter, Siwuji, took place in 1662, and in 1665, the latter submitted, but the war was renewed in 1670, and it continued till Siwuji's death, in 1680. In 1673, the emperor was occupied with a war against the North-eastern Afghāns, which ended unsuccessfully in 1676. In 1677, a combination of Rājpūts was formed against Aurungzib, his own son Prince Akbar joining them; nearly all the Rājpūt States continued in open hostility till the end of this reign. In 1683, he went to the

Dekhun in person at the head of his army, and invaded Bijapūr, but failed ; he afterwards attacked the Golkonda State, which he crippled, and compelled to sue for peace. In 1685, he had the English to contend with, both in Bengal and on the western coast, but a reconciliation was effected in 1690, and the English were invited back to Bengal. In 1686, he again invaded Bijapūr, took the capital, and destroyed the monarchy. In the following year, the kingdom of Golkonda fell in the same manner, and the territories of these states were seized upon as far as Tanjore. In 1692, the war between the Moguls and Marattas was renewed with varying success, but the emperor being hard pressed, was, in 1706, compelled to fall back on Ahmednuggur, where he died in the following year.

Rise of the Marattas.

Memorable Events.—One of the most remarkable events in this reign, was the rise of the Maratta dynasty under the celebrated Siwuji, a member of the Bhonslē family. Siwuji was the son of Shahji Bhonslē, and by his mother's side had claim to Rājpūt descent, she being the daughter of Jadow Rao. He was born in 1627, and was brought up at Pūna (then a petty Jagir of his father's), by a Brahmin called Dadaji Kōndu. In 1646 he commenced his predatory career by taking the hill fort of Torna, and in 1647, the stronger forts of Purundhur and Singhur. In 1648 he openly rebelled against the Bijapūr government, and took possession of the Northern Kōnkan, but as that state had secured his father Shahji as a hostage for his son, the latter remained quiet till his father's release in 1653, when he again renewed his encroachments, and even invaded the Mogul territories, but in 1658 obtained forgiveness from Prince Aurungzib, then in command of the Dekhun army. His renewed attacks on the Bijapūr State,—the wily assassination of Afzul Khān, and the defeat of the Bijapūr army, brought the king of that state himself into the field in 1661, when most of Siwuji's conquests were at first recovered, but subsequently lost. In 1662, peace was concluded, Siwuji's territories then including 250 miles on the sea-coast (between Goa and Kalliān), while above the Ghāts they extended more than 150 miles in length from north of Pūna to south of Merich, on the Krishna, and about 100 miles from east to west. He had then an army of 50,000 foot and 7,000 horse. Between 1662 and 1665, he engaged in warfare occasionally with the Moguls and the Bijapūr State, plundered Surat (1664), and in 1665, after his father's death, assumed decisive marks of independent sovereignty, but a large Mogul army being sent against him under Rājā Jei Singh, he submitted, and joined it in a campaign against Bijapūr. He was afterwards induced to go to Delhi, but finding himself closely watched, he managed to escape, and reached his capital, Rāighur, in the Konkun, nine months after his departure for Delhi. After making peace with the emperor on favourable terms, he commenced levying tribute on both Bijapūr and Golkonda. This peace was, however, broken by Aurungzib in 1670, and the war renewed by Siwuji taking several forts, plundering Surat again, and ravaging the Mogul territories. He now levied, for the first time, "*Chout*" (one fourth of the revenues of a state), and in 1672, defeated the Moguls in the open field. During 1673-4, he got possession of the whole of the Southern Kōnkun, except the tract held by the English, Abyssinians (Hubshis), and Portuguese, and on 6th June, 1674, was formally crowned king at Raighur. In 1676, he allied himself with the king of Golkonda against the Moguls and the Bijapūr State, and in 1677 recovered all his father's Jagir in Mysore. In 1679, he engaged to assist the regent of Bijapūr, then hard pressed by a Mogul army, for a cession of territory called the Raichore Doāb, and it was owing to his troops that the Mogul general was compelled to raise the seige of

Bijapūr. Siwuji died at Rairi, in the Kōnkun, in 1680, in the fifty-third year of his age, and was succeeded by his son, Sambaji, whose time was mainly spent in idleness and debauchery. In the invasion of the Dekhun in 1683 by Aurungzib, Sambaji harassed the Mogul army by ravaging the country in the emperor's rear, but he afterwards displayed great inertness, and was, in 1689, captured by Aurungzib, and put to death with studied barbarity. Sambaji's infant son, Sahū, was proclaimed Rājā, with his uncle, Rājā Rām, as regent. In 1690, the infant Rājā was captured at Raighur, the regent fleeing to the fort of Jingi, in the Karnatik, which was invested and taken by the Moguls in 1698. In 1700, Sattara fell into their hands, but Rājā Rām had died previously at Singhur, and was succeeded by his infant son, Siwuji, under the regency of Tāra Bāi. The Marattas now began to recover their forts, and even to extend their ravages to Malwa, Berar, and Khāndēsh. They also followed up the imperial army in its retreat to Ahmednuggur, whither Aurungzib had fallen back in 1706. The Marattas were little, active men, accustomed to hard work and hard fare. Their arms were a sword and matchlock, but oftener a bamboo spear thirteen or fourteen feet long, which they used with skill. Their horses were small, strong, active, and of great endurance.

Aurungzib, in 1659, forbade the solar era as an invention of fire worshippers, and directed the lunar year to be used on all occasions. He discountenanced poets and abolished the office and salary of royal poet. He also revived the "*jezzia*," or poll tax on infidels, and this excited great discontent among the Hindūs.

Aurungzib desired in his will that his funeral expenses should be defrayed from the price (4½ rupees) of caps he had made and sold. He ordered also that 805 rupees earned by him in copying "Korans," should be given to the poor.

English in India.

In 1662 the island of Bombay, held by the Portuguese since 1530, was acquired by Charles II. as part of the dower of his wife, an Infanta of Portugal, but the Crown held it for six years only, when it was made over to the East India Company. Sir George Oxenden was the first governor of the island. Surat retained a president till 1688, when the office was abolished and an agent substituted. In 1702 the English had on the western coast factories at Surat, Swalli, Broach, Ahmedabād, Karwar, Tellicheri, Anjengo, and Kalikut. Money was first coined in Bombay in 1687. On the Koromandel Coast besides Madras, the company had factories at Chingu, Fort St. David, Kuddalūr, Porto Nuovo, Madapollam, Pettipoli and Vizagapatam. In Bengal, besides Kalkutta (Calcutta) they had Chuttanutti, Balasore, Kossimbazar, Dakka, Hūghli, Malda, Rājmahāl, and Patna. The English trade in Bengal rapidly increased from ten laks in 1666, to one hundred laks in 1682. In 1685 owing to disputes with the Bengal Viceroy, war was declared against the Mogul empire, and an expedition sent out from England, entered the Hūghli, bombarded the town, and destroyed much property. Bengal was abandoned in 1688, but a reconciliation was afterwards effected with the emperor in 1690, and Mr. Job Charnock, the English chief, and his people, were invited back to the province, where on the 24th of August of that year he laid the foundation of the city of Kalkutta, which was subsequently fortified and named Fort William in compliment to the then reigning King of England. In 1693 a rival East India Company was established, but it led to so many difficulties and mutual bickerings, that the two companies were amalgamated in 1702 under the title of the "United Company of Merchants trading to the East." The yearly salary of the President was fixed at £300, that of eight members of council at £40 each, junior merchants at £30, factors at £15, and writers at £5, but the privilege of *private* trade was permitted. This latter was so lucrative that junior servants are said to have "sat down to dinner with a band of music, and to have ridden out in a coach and four." Up to 1707, when Kalkutta was created a Presidency, the English settlements in Bengal had been under the control of Madras.

French.

In 1664 the French, under the auspices of their great minister Colbert, formed an East India Company, and soon after a French fleet sailed up the Hūghli, and established a settlement at Chandernagore near Kalkutta.

Dutch and Danes.

In 1667 the Dutch established a factory first at Hūghli, but afterwards at Chinsura, ten miles distant, and erected a fort there, and about the same time the Danes entered the river and embarked in the trade of the country.

DYNASTY OF ADIL SHAH AT BIJAPŪR (A.D. 1489 TO 1686).

	Began to reign.	
	A. D.	H.
1. Eusof Adil Shah	1489	895
2. Ismāil Adil Shah	1510	915
3. Mallu Adil Shah	1534	941
4. Ibrahim Adil Shah	1535	942
5. Ali Adil Shah	1567	965
6. Ibrahim Adil Shah II.	1579	987
7. Mahomed Adil Shah	1626	1034
8. Ali Adil Shah II.	1656	1064

Memorable Events.—This dynasty was founded by Eusof Adil Shah, a Turkish slave. His kingdom extended from the Bhima and Krishna rivers on the east, to the sea from near Goa and Bombay on the west, and from perhaps the Nira river on the north to the River Tumbūdra on the south. He is said to have entertained a large number of Marattas in his pay, who were then known under the name of Bergis, and that to this the Marattas owe their rise. Ibrahim, the fourth king introduced the Maratta language into the accounts instead of Persian. The kings of this dynasty waged constant wars with the other Mahomedan kings, especially with the Nizam Shah of Ahmednuggur. Bijapūr was twice besieged in the reign of Shah Jehān, but without success; it was eventually captured by Aurungzib in 1686. In works of utility and magnificence this dynasty had no rival in India. The tombs, mosques, and palaces of Bijapūr are still splendid even in their ruins, and the mausoleum of Mahomed Adil Shah, though entirely devoid of ornament, is, from its enormous dimensions, a grand edifice, its dome filling the eye from every point of view. The lofty walls of the city were of hewn stone and six miles in circumference. It is puzzling to conjecture how so small a state could have maintained such a large capital.

DYNASTY OF KUTB SHAH AT GOLKONDA (A.D. 1512 TO 1687).

	Began to reign.	
	A. D.	H.
1. Sūltān Kūli	1512	918
2. Jamshid	1543	940
3. Subhān Kūli	1550	957
4. Ibrahim	1550	957
5. Mohamed Kūli	1580	988
6. Abdula Kūtb Shah	—	—
7. Abul Hassan	—	—

Memorable Events.—This dynasty was founded by Sūltān Kūli Kūtb Shah, a Turkoman soldier; he was governor of Telingāna when the Bahmani kingdom broke up. This state extended from the Godaveri to beyond the Krishna, and from the sea to a line drawn west of

Heidurabād, about the 78th degree of east longitude. The greater part of Sūltān Kūli's conquests were from the remains of the Wurungol family and other chiefs of Telingāna. The kings of this dynasty took part in the various wars and alliances of the other Mahomedan monarchs. Mahomed Kūli, the fifth king, in addition to Rājamundri and the country north of the Godaveri up to Chikakōl gained by his predecessor, conquered Gundikote, Kuddapa, and the rest of the country up to the River Penaar. This king built Heidurabād and made it his capital. In 1686 Aurungzib crippled the Golkonda State, then under the rule of Abul Hassan, and in the following year took the capital and subverted the monarchy.

(VI.) BAHĀDŪR SHAH (A.D. 1707 TO 1712).

Birth and Reign.—Was the eldest son of Aurungzib, and known before his accession as Prince Moazzim; he was born in 1642, and reigned from 1707 to 1712.

Issue.—1. Jehāndar Shah, who succeeded him. 2. Azim-ū-Shan and two other children.

Death.—Died at Lahore in 1712 in the 71st lunar year of his age and the fifth of his reign.

Character.—This prince appears to have possessed vigour and activity, and his conduct generally in his wars with his brothers and the Sikhs, does not seem to have been stained with any cruelties.

Wars.—I. With his brother Prince Azim for the throne in 1707, ending with the defeat and death of the prince and his two grown-up sons. II. With his brother Kāmbuksh near Heidurabād in the Dekhun, ending also in that prince's defeat and death. III. With the Sikhs, a religious sect in Sirhind, who had ravaged the country in the neighbourhood of Lahore and Delhi. The emperor defeated them, but could only partially check their depredations, as their power was again in the ascendant at the date of Bahādūr Shah's death in 1712.

Memorable Events.—This reign is chiefly remarkable for the severities used against a religious sect called the Sikhs, founded about the end of the 15th century, by one Nanuk, a Hindū, whose peculiar tenet was universal toleration. The sect was noted for its quiet character, but the bigotry of the Mahomedans gave it no peace, and in 1606 the Sikhs revolted and became fanatical warriors. They were formed in 1675 under Govind Gurū into a religious and military commonwealth, and they engaged always to carry steel about their persons, to wear blue clothes, allow their beard and hair to grow, to reverence the Hindū gods and Brahmins, and prevent the slaughter of kine. Gurū Govind found his plan unsuccessful, he was overpowered, and at length murdered by a private enemy at Nānder in the Dekhun. Under a chief named Bandū they overran the Punjāb in the reign of Bahādūr Shah, committing terrible ravages and cruelties. The emperor drove them into the hills, but Bandū escaped capture, and at the end of this reign their power was once more on the increase.

On the death of Bahādūr Shah the usual contest for sovereignty took place between his sons, ending in the eldest, afterwards known as (VII.) **Jehāndar Shah** securing the throne through the artifices of Zulfikar Khān, formerly a general in Aurungzib's service, and who afterwards became Jehāndar Shah's vizier. He reigned but one year (1712-13) amid general discontent, putting all the princes of the blood within his reach to death; but his nephew Prince Farokhsir revolted, and with the assistance of the brothers, Syud Abdūla and Syud Hosein Ali (descendants of the Prophet), the one governor of Behar, and the other of Allahabād, he defeated the imperial army, putting Jehāndar Shah and his betrayer Zulfikar to death. (VIII.) **Farokhsir** ascended the throne in 1713 and reigned till 1719; he was the most contemptible prince of his line, utterly incapable and unworthy of his high office, and ruled as a matter of course by the brothers, the Syuds, who had helped him to the throne. Owing to their overbearing conduct the emperor intrigued for their destruction, instigating one Dāūd Khān Panni, Governor of Guzerat, and a man of reckless courage, to resist Hosein Ali, but Dāūd was defeated and killed in 1716. The Sikhs were nearly extirpated during this reign and their chief Bandū cruelly executed. In his contest with the Marattas, Hosein Ali was unsuccessful, he made peace in 1717 with Rāja Sāhū, and agreed to pay "*chout*," but Farokhsir refused to ratify it. In 1718 Hosein Ali returned to Delhi and Farokhsir was deposed and put to death in February, 1719, the Syuds setting up two young princes one after the other as nominal emperors, but both died within a few months. Roushen Akhter (or Rūstum Khān) a grandson of Aurungzib was in 1719 selected and raised to the throne by the title of **Mahomed Shah.**

(IX.) MAHOMED SHAH (A.D. 1719 TO 1747).

Birth, Reign and Death.—This prince was a grandson of Aurungzib and reigned from 1719 to 1747, he died in April, 1748.

Character.—Feeble and utterly incompetent to check the rapid decline of the Mogul dynasty, now hastening to its fall. He was indolent, given to pleasure, and ruled by favourites.

Wars.—Numerous insurrections occurred at the beginning of his reign in the provinces of Allahabād and the Punjāb, which it was found difficult to quell. Chin Kilich

Khān, the Viceroy of the Dekhun, better known as **Asof Jah** and **Nizam-ūl-Mūlk**, whose descendants are the present Nizams of the Dekhun, revolted in 1720 and defeated the imperial troops in several battles. In 1738 the celebrated **Nadir Shah**, King of Persia, the ablest warrior that country has ever produced, invaded India on the plea of no notice having been taken of his application to the Court of Delhi for the seizure of some Afghāns who had fled into India. He was met in 1739 at Kurnāl (within 100 miles of Delhi) by Mohamed Shah, whose army was utterly routed, and Nadir marched on Delhi, accompanied by the defeated monarch. An insurrection of the inhabitants stirred up by a report of Nadir's death, provoked a general massacre by the Persians, and 30,000 persons were put to the sword and the city of Delhi fired in several places. The imperial treasures and jewels and the celebrated peacock throne, together with money amounting to between eight and nine millions sterling were taken by the invaders. Many elephants, horses, and camels, as well as hundreds of skilful workmen and artizans, were led away by Nadir, who marched from Delhi after a residence there of fifty-eight days. This merciless conqueror was assassinated by the Persians in 1747. In that year Ahmed Khān Abdāli, after being crowned king at Kandahar, occupied the Punjāb, but was repulsed at Sirhind by Prince Ahmed, the heir apparent to the Delhi throne.

Memorable Events.—One of the most important events during this reign was the invasion of India by Nadir Shah, of which an account has been given under the heading, Wars. The condition of Delhi after Nadir's departure was deplorable, and the entire empire presented as lamentable an aspect of ruin and desolation as the capital. Of the two brothers, the Syuds, who had been instrumental in placing Mahomed Shah on the throne, Hosein Ali was assassinated at the emperor's instigation by Mir Heidur, a savage Kalmūk in 1720. The other, Abdūla revolted, but was defeated in the same year by the emperor in person. Chin Kilich Khān (Asof Jah), the viceroy of the Dekhun, was appointed vizier at Delhi in 1722, but becoming disgusted with matters there, resigned his office, and set out for the Dekhun in 1723; he fixed his residence at Heidurabād, declared his independence, and tried to foment dissensions among the Marattas. They invaded his territories in 1727, and forced him to make concessions. In 1731 he effected a compromise with the Peishwa, Bāji Rao, but was afterwards, in 1736, reconciled to Mahomed Shah, and assisted the latter in 1738 against the Peishwa's attacks, but was ultimately compelled to make great concessions on the emperor's part. In 1740 his second son, Nasir Jung, defeated the Marattas under Bāji Rao at Būrhanpūr. In 1741 this son headed a revolt, but it was suppressed by Asof Jah himself, who afterwards died, in 1748, at the great age of 104, leaving his territories in the Dekhun to be contended for by his sons.

Marattas.

After the death of Aurungzib the Marattas were weakened by intestine discord, owing to the rivalries of Sāhū, the son of Sambāji, the legitimate heir to the throne, and Tāra Bāi, the regent, ending in the former taking Sattara and assuming the functions of royalty in 1708. Sambaji, a son of Rām Rāja, was placed on the throne at Kolapūr, which thus became a rival to Sattara. In 1714 Ballaji Vishwanath, the Peishwa, by his energy and ability restored the fallen fortunes of his nation, and in 1717 he brought about a convention with the Moguls, by which, on paying an annual tribute of ten laks of rupees and furnishing a contingent of 15,000 troops, Sāhū was recognized as an independent sovereign, and the "*fourth*" and "*tenth*" of the revenues of the six Sūbahs of the Dekhun and the states of Tanjūr, Maisūr, and Trichinopoli, were conferred upon him. In 1720 Ballaji died, and was succeeded by his son Bāji Rao, who in talent and vigour was second only to Siwuji. In 1729 he obtained the "chout" of Guzerat, and it was during his absence there that Sambaji plundered the territory of his cousin Sāhū, but being defeated he, in 1730, acknowledged his sovereignty to the entire Maratta country, excepting a small tract round Kolapūr, to which his branch of the family were to be confined. Dabāri, the Maratta commander-in-chief, instigated by the Nizam, marched upon Sattara to release Sāhū from the tyranny of the Peishwa, but he was defeated and slain in 1731; his office was nevertheless conferred on his infant son, and the management of affairs entrusted to Pilaji Geikwar, whose ancestor was a cow-herd, and whose descendants *now* occupy the throne at Baroda.

Geikwar.

It was at this time also that the great families of **Holkar, Sindia,** and **Powar** took their rise. Mulhar Rao Holkar was a shepherd on the Nira, south of Pūna. Ranāji Sindia was a menial servant of Bāji Rao's, and Udaji Powar was a chief before his connection with the Peishwa. In 1731 a compromise was entered into between Bāji Rao and Asof Jah, when the former at once laid waste the province of Malwa, which in 1736 was ceded to him by Rājā Jei Singh the viceroy. In 1737 he appeared before Delhi, but soon after retreated to the Dekhun. It was about this time that he was engaged in wars in the Kōnkan with Angria of Kolaba,—the Abyssinians (Hubshis) of Jinjira and the Portuguese. In 1738 Asof Jah, who had previously been reconciled to the emperor, marched against Bāji Rao, but was defeated near Bhopal, and obliged to make great concessions. In 1739 Bāji Rao resumed offensive operations by attacking Asof Jah's possessions, but he was repulsed by Nasir Jung, Asof's son. Bāji Rao died soon after on the Nurbudda, in April, 1740. Of his three sons, Ballaji Rao succeeded him, though his father's enemies, Ragōji

Bhonslé and Damaji Geikwar, intrigued together, but in vain to prevent it. In 1742 Ballaji marched into Malwa, and revived his father's demands on the court of Delhi, and Mahomed Shah, to obtain his aid against Ragoji Bhonslé, who had invaded Bengal, ceded Malwa to the Peishwa. In 1743 Ragoji was defeated by the Peishwa and driven out of Bengal, but in the following year, owing to fresh combinations against himself, Ballaji bought him over by liberal cessions, and ultimately (1751) Ragoji obtained the "*chout*" of Bengal and the cession of Kuttak.

Oudh Family.

It was during Mahomed Shah's reign that Saādut Ali, a Khorasan merchant, who had raised himself by his talents to the charge of Biāna, was made Sūbhēdar of Oudh (1721), where he founded the royal dynasty which was extinguished in 1856.

Angria.

In this reign flourished Angria of Kọlaba (near Bombay); he was noted for his piracies, which he called "levying *chout* on the seas." He was frequently attacked by the English, and at one time (1719) in conjunction with the Portuguese, but they all failed. In 1724 the Dutch sent an expedition against him, but without success. In 1734 a dispute took place between two brothers of the family, in which the Peishwa interfered with some success.

Portuguese.

The Portuguese engaged in war with Bāji Rao Peishwa; it ended in 1739 in the loss of their possessions in Salsette, Bassein (Wusāi) and the neighbouring parts of the Konkun.

English & French.

During the viceroyalty of Mūrshed Kūli Khān in Bengal, the East India Company, in 1715, sent an embassy to the Emperor Farokhsir at Delhi, to seek for redress of grievances. This was successful, owing to the circumstance of the surgeon of the embassy, Mr.

Hamilton, curing the emperor of a disease. When requested to name his recompense, he begged that the concessions prayed for by the embassy might be granted. The following privileges were then accorded:—1st, That the president's pass should exempt goods from examination by native servants of government; 2nd, That money should be coined for the Company *three* times a week at Mūrshedabād; and 3rd, that the English should be at liberty to purchase the lordship of thirty-eight towns in the vicinity of Kalkutta. Up to 1720 the English possessions in India were Kalkutta and Madras, with some small estates around each, and the island of Bombay. During the viceroyalty of Sūjah-ū-din, son-in-law of Mūrshed Kūli, who died in 1725, the Ostend East India Company, established by the emperor of Germany at Banki-bazar, opposite Chandernagore, was destroyed by the viceroy through the jealousies of the English and Dutch, who paid him 320,000 rupees as a bribe. Sūjah-ū-din died in 1740. In 1736 the Karnatik, which had been included by Aurungzib in the Sūbah of the Dekhun, became a scene of contention between two parties, Chunda Sāhib and Sufdūr Ali, the former a son-in-law, and the latter the son of Dost Ali, the nabob of that country. In 1741 Chunda Sāhib was captured by the Marattas and confined in Sattara, and in 1742 Sufdūr Ali was assassinated, as was his infant son soon after. Anwar-ū-din, in whose hands the Nizam had placed the administration of the province, then took the vacant post, and thus founded the family of the Nabobs of the Karnatik. In 1744 the English engaged in war with France, and in September, 1746, the town of Madras, with a population of 250,000, but poorly fortified, was captured by the French under Labourdonnais, and held to ransom for 44 laks of rupees. Owing to dissensions between Labourdonnais and Dupleix, the Governor of Pondicherri (Puducheri), as well as to the setting in of the monsoon that year with extraordinary violence, the other English settlements in India were saved from capture.

It is worthy of notice that the first Protestant mission in Madras was established as early as 1726. The Danes were, however, the first people who sent a Protestant mission to India; this was in 1705, to their settlement at Tranquebar, on the Koromandel Coast.

After the death of Mohamed Shah in 1748, his son (X.) **Ahmed Shah**, ascended the throne, but his reign was short, lasting only six years, when he was deposed and blinded by his overbearing minister Ghāzi-ū-din. In 1748 an attempt was made to subdue the Rohillas, but as the Vizier Sufdūr Jung was defeated in 1750, the aid of the Marattas was invoked, and the Rohillas submitted in 1751. A second invasion of India by Ahmed Shah Abdāli took place in this reign, and the Punjāb was ceded to him. Oudh may be considered as finally alienated from the crown of Delhi in 1753, to which province the Vizier Sufdūr Jung retired, leaving Ghāzi-ū-din paramount at the capital. The emperor plotted against the latter, but unsuccessfully, as he was himself deposed and blinded in 1754, a prince of the blood being placed on the throne by the title of (XI.) **Alumgir II.**, who reigned from 1755 to 1759. In 1756 a third invasion of India was carried out by Ahmed Shah Abdāli, whose governor of the Punjāb had been treacherously seized. Delhi was taken, and again became a scene of rapine, violence, and murder, while massacres and exactions took place in other cities of the empire. He returned to his own dominions in 1757, after having made arrangements for the protection of Alumgir against Ghāzi-ū-din. The latter called in the aid of the Marattas, who captured Delhi, and in 1758, under Raghoba, occupied the entire Punjāb, their intention being to conquer the whole of Hindūsthān. To prevent this, a general combination of the Mahomedan princes was effected, and the Marattas were, in 1759, driven with heavy loss across the Ganges. The same year Ahmed Shah Abdāli invaded India for the *fourth* time, and Ghāzi-ū-din, fearing the intercourse of Alumgir with Ahmed Shah, assassinated the emperor in November, 1759. In 1760 Ahmed Shah defeated the armies of Sindia and Holkar, and on 7th January, 1761, with the assistance of the Rohillas and the Nabob of Oudh, his army barely amounting to 100,000 men, defeated, at the celebrated battle of **Paniput**, the Maratta army, numbering nearly 300,000, under the command of Sudasheo Rao Bhao, cousin of Raghoba the Peishwa, who had exchanged duties with him. The Bhao was slain, and almost all the great Maratta chiefs were either killed or wounded; never was there a more complete defeat, and the destruction of this great Maratta host was felt to be a death-blow to their national greatness. Ahmed Shah withdrew from India after his victory, and took no further share in its affairs. The Mahomedan confederacy of princes dissolved of itself, and the Mogul empire from that time became, as regarded power and position, *extinct*. Out of its territories were formed other and independent kingdoms, such as the Dekhun, the Punjāb, Oudh, and Bengal. To quote the words of the Hon. Mountstuart Elphinstone:—"Its territory is broken up into separate states; the capital is deserted; the claimant to the name of emperor is an exile and a dependent; while a new race of conquerors has already commenced its career, which may again unite the empire under better auspices than before." From the date of this great struggle on the part of the Marattas for universal dominion throughout Hindūsthān, *Christian* rule in India may safely be said to take its rise. The English had now entered upon their career of conquest, and the man (the hero of Plassi) had arisen who was to lay the foundations of an empire in the East, destined in later times to extend its power throughout the entire length and breadth of the peninsula.

MEMORABLE EVENTS DURING THE REIGNS OF AHMED SHAH AND ALUMGIR II.

Marattas.

In 1748 Sahū, the grandson of Siwuji, died, but all substantial power had long since passed into the hands of the Peishwas, and in 1750 Ballāji Rao proclaimed an adopted prince sovereign of the Marattas, under the title of Rām Rājā, the Peishwa making Pūna his own capital. In 1752 the Marattas were induced, by promises of large Jagirs made by Ghāzi-ū-din Sūbhēdar of the Dekhun, to attack Salābut Jung, who was assisted by the French, but they were routed in every encounter, and bought off by Salābut Jung with similar concessions. In 1754-55 they levied contributions on a large scale in the Karnatik, and plundered Guzerat under Rugoonath Rao (Raghoba). In 1755 the Peishwa, conjointly with the English under Commodore James, sent an expedition against Konāji Angria, taking the strong fort of Sūverndrūg, and in the same year Gheriah, his chief port, was captured by Colonel Clive and Admiral Watson. In 1757-58 they assisted Ghāzi-ū-din, Ahmed Shah's minister, and under Raghoba planted their standards for the *first* time on the banks of the Indus, but brought back no booty with them. In 1758 they obtained by treachery the city of Ahmednuggur from the Sūbhēdar of the Dekhun, and by a subsequent treaty five of the most important fortresses in that country, as well as districts yielding a yearly revenue of not less than sixty laks. This was the zenith of their power, and their authority was acknowledged throughout a very great extent of India. The subsequent defeat of the armies of Sindia and Holkar in 1760, and the disastrous battle of Paniput in 1761, have been mentioned in the reign of Alumgir II. From that date the Maratta power was parcelled out between the Geikwar, the Rājā of Nāgpūr, Holkar, and

Angria.

Sindia. It is worthy of note that the **Pindarris** appeared, for the first time in history, on the side of the Marattas at the battle of Paniput.

English & French in Southern India.

The capture of Madras by the French in 1746 has already been mentioned, but from that year up to 1761, while the Mogul empire was rapidly approaching dissolution, very stirring events were occurring between the English and French for supremacy in Southern India, as also between the English and Native powers in the province of Bengal. In 1766 Anwar-ū-din, Nabob of the Karnatik, resenting the capture of Madras, sent an army of 10,000 men against a small French force, but he was miserably defeated, thus at once and for ever dissolving the spell which had hitherto kept Europeans in dread of native troops. The Nabob at once changed sides, and sought the French alliance. Fort St. David, another English settlement, was then besieged by Dupleix, but without success. The English in their turn laid siege to Pondicherri in 1748, but their efforts, too, were fruitless. Suspension of hostilities took place in consequence of the peace of Aix-la-Chapelle, and Madras was restored to the East India Company. In 1749 the English undertook an expedition, commanded by Major S. Lawrence, to Devi-Kote in Tanjūr (then governed by Prutāp Singh) to reseat his brother Sahūji on the throne; it ended in the Rājā paying all the Company's expenses of the war, ceding Devi-Kote, with the district around it, and pensioning Sahūji with 50,000 rupees a year. The genius of Clive first shone in this war. He had in 1744 arrived at Madras as a writer in the Company's service, but finding an opportunity of exchanging the pen for the sword, he joined the English army, and greatly assisted in restoring English influence in India. To further French interests, Dupleix obtained the liberation of Chunda Sahēb, and the latter, in consideration of being appointed Nabob of the Karnatik, agreed to aid Muzuffur, grandson of Nizām-ūl-Mūlk (Sūbhēdar of the Dekhun) against his uncle, Nazir Jung, who had assumed supreme authority. Anwar-ū-din, in resisting their joint invasion, was killed in July, 1749, leaving a son, Mohamed Ali, who fled to Trichinopoli, and implored the assistance of the English; meanwhile Nazir Jung, with the aid of the Pathān Nabobs of Kuddapa, Kurnūl, and Savanūr and an English force of 600 Europeans, entered the Karnatik, and defeated Mozuffur Jung and Chunda Sahēb, but was himself routed soon after, and killed by the Nabob of Kuddapa, whom he had accused of cowardice and treachery. Mozuffur Jung then (in 1750) became Nizām, but he, too, was struck dead with a javelin by the Nabob of Kurnūl. Bussy, who commanded a French force in aid of Mozuffur Jung, caused Salābut Jung, the third son of Nizām-ūl-mūlk, to be proclaimed Nizam, and Chunda Sahēb advanced to the siege of Trichinopoli, then garrisoned by the English. It was at this time that Captain Clive (the heaven-born general) carried out his expedition to Arkot, the capital of the Karnatik, which he took, and in it in 1751, with but 120 Europeans and 200 Sepoys, endured a siege of fifty days and the incessant assaults of 10,000 native troops and 150 Europeans. In 1752 the French were twice defeated by Major Lawrence; Chunda Sahēb was assassinated by Morari Rao, the Tanjūr general, and Mohamed Ali confirmed as Nabob of the Karnatik. In 1754 M. Godeheu, a French director who had arrived from Europe, negotiated a treaty with Mr. Saunders the governor of Madras, by which the French, independently of the Northern Sirkars held by Bussy, obtained a territory yielding 18 laks a year, while that secured by the English yielded but ten. To this treaty but little attention was paid, as war soon after broke out between France and England. Dupleix left India in 1754, and was in France consigned to poverty and neglect. Bussy maintained for a few years longer French influence in India, but by order of Count Lally, the recently-arrived governor-general of the French possessions in India, he took leave of the Dekhun in 1758, at a time when he had become the arbiter of its fate. In the same year Lally besieged Fort St. David, which was surrendered within a month, and its fortifications razed. He then attacked Tanjūr, but without success, and in 1759 besieged Madras, which he was unable to capture. In that year he suffered a defeat from Colonel Coote at Wandiwash, and subsequently all the French possessions in India were lost excepting Jinji and Pondicherri. In 1760 Coote laid siege to Pondicherri and took it on 14th January, when it was levelled with the ground. Lally returned to France, was thrown into the Bastille, and ultimately died by the hand of the executioner. With the loss of their settlements expired all hope of the French ever establishing an empire in India.

In Bengal.

In 1756 Ali Verdi Khān, the viceroy of Bengal, died, and was succeeded by his grandson, Surāja Dowla, a youth of but twenty years, but both cruel and profligate. Owing to a dispute with Mr. Drake, the governor of Kalkutta, the Nabob marched an army of 50,000 men to that city, the governor and the commandant (Minchin) both leaving the place without any instructions to the garrison, which, under Mr. Holwell, nevertheless, held out bravely for forty-eight hours, and then surrendered to the number of 146 persons. These were confined in a small room, since called the "BLACK HOLE," not twenty feet square, in one of the hottest nights of the most sultry season of the year; the consequence being that next morning only twenty-three were found alive. An expedition was sent from Madras in October of that year to retrieve this disaster. Kalkutta was re-captured by Colonel Clive in January, 1757, and the Nabob defeated, and on 9th February permission was given to fortify the town, and establish a mint, while a hint at compensation for losses was also held out. The French settlement of Chandernagore was taken, and a combination entered into among the Nabob's native officers to dethrone him, in which Clive joined. This had nearly failed, through the rapacity of a wealthy banker and favourite of the Nabob, named Omichund, who threatened to disclose the whole affair unless a special article were added to the agreement guaranteeing him 30 laks of rupees. This was acceded to, but inserted in a *false* treaty by Clive, to deceive Omichund, the real agreement containing no such stipulation. On 23rd June, 1757, Clive engaged the Nabob's army of 50,000 men at *Plassi* (forty miles south of Mūrshedabād) with 1,000 Europeans, 2,000 natives, and eight pieces of cannon, and entirely defeated it. On 29th June he entered Mūrshedabād, and raised Mir Jaffier, the Nabob's general, to the throne as Sūbhēdar of Bengal, Behar, and Orissa, two crores and twenty laks of rupees being paid by the new Nabob as compensation for the losses of the Company and of individuals, the fee simple of land around Kalkutta, and the Zemindari rights of the country to the south of Kalkutta being also secured to the Company. Surāja Dowla was soon after assassinated by Mir Jaffier's son. In the same year Clive quelled three revolts in Behar, Purneah, and Midnapūr. In 1759 Mohamed Ali Gohur, the heir apparent to the throne of Delhi, conjointly with the Sūbhēdar of Oudh, invaded Behar, and appeared before Patna, but finding that Clive was hastening to the rescue, fled at once from the province. For his services the Nabob conferred on Clive a jagir worth £30,000 a year; this was subsequently turned by the grantee to a noble purpose, and was known as "*Lord Clive's fund.*" In the same year a Dutch expedition of 700 Europeans and 800 Malay Sepoys from Batavia sent to Bengal to reinforce their settlement at Chinsura, was defeated, after which Clive, in February, 1760, embarked for England, Mr. Vansittart, a Madras civilian, succeeding him as governor of Bengal. A second invasion of Behar by the fugitive emperor of Delhi, Shah Alūm, supported by the Nabob of Oudh, took place in the same year, but he was again routed by Captain Knox with a mere handful of troops. The Nabob, Mir Jaffier, who had kept his army in arrears of pay, and was in other respects perfectly unfitted for administration, was deposed by the English, and his son-in-law, Mir Kossim, elevated to the dignity of Nabob in 1760-61, he ceding to the Company the three districts of Midnapūr, Chittagong, and Burdwān—making good all arrears, and bestowing a gratuity of twenty laks of rupees on his benefactors. He also, through the intervention of Colonel Carnac, paid homage to Shah Alūm at Patna in 1761, and by the promise of an annual payment of twenty-four laks, had the office of Sūbhēdar of Bengal, Behar, and Orissa conferred upon him, while the Dewani of the three Provinces was at the same time offered by the emperor to the Company. For the maintenance of order and the administration of justice, a mayor's court was established at Kalkutta in 1726, but this in 1753 was converted into a court of record, with higher powers.

NAMES OF NOTE DURING THE REIGNS OF MAHOMED SHAH, AHMED SHAH, AND ALUMGIR II.

Chin Kilich Khān (better known as Asof Jah and Nizām-ūl-Mūlk), Sūbhēdar of the Dekhun (1644-1748). A statesman of great experience and ability; he laid the foundation of the Nizam's dominion in 1724, making Heidurabād his capital.—**Bāji Rao Peishwa** (died 1740) a statesman and diplomatist of great judgment and extensive knowledge; he raised the Maratta confederacy to the highest position in India.—**Nadir Shah**, a Persian king noted for his invasion of India in 1739; he was assassinated in 1747.—**Ahmed Khān Abdāli**, chief of the Abdāli tribe of Afghans. Crowned king at Kandahar in 1747. He invaded India four times in succession, and commanded the Mahomedan army at the battle of Paniput in 1761.—**Colonel Coote** 1726-83), **Major Lawrence**, English military commanders.—**Bussy**, French general (1718-85). **Labourdounais** (1699-1755), Governor of the French settlements of Mauritius and Bourbon, and a military commander in India.—**Dupleix** (1698-1750), governor of the French settlements in India.—**Count Lally** 1702-66), governor-general of the French possessions in India.

MISCELLANEOUS MEMORANDA CONNECTED WITH THE MAHOMEDAN PERIOD.

Manners of the Mahomedans.

The early Mahomedans were stout and ruddy men, dressed in short tunics of thick cloth, and always in boots. In the time of Aurungzib they had become generally slender, dark and sallow, and wore long white gowns of the thinnest muslin, which spread out from the waist in innumerable folds, and scarcely showed the naked foot and embroidered slipper.

Government.

Among the Mahomedans the king's office was hereditary, and his power absolute. As a rule, they were generally easy of access to all parties who had complaints to make or petitions to offer. The Vizier, or prime minister, was in some cases an uncontrolled vice-gerent, in others only the chief among the ministers. The governors of provinces exercised, each within his jurisdiction, all the executive powers of the state, and most had under them some portion of the regular army, in addition to their local troops. A portion of the army was composed of men hired singly by the king, and mounted on his horses, but the greater number probably brought their own horses and arms. Land was assigned in lieu of pay for the first time, it is said, by Firuz Shah Toghlak.

Law.

There were two distinct classes of tribunals, those of the Kazis, which recognized the Mahomedan law alone, and had fixed rules of procedure, and those of the officers of government, whose authority was arbitrary and undefined. The powers of the Kazis varied in different reigns; at times the office was filled by men of celebrity, and their authority was respected, at others they merely performed marriages and registered and authenticated deeds. There existed no church government among the Mahomedans, any one who founded a mosque, left funds to maintain the priest (imām) and other persons required for public worship. The Moulvies were a class of graduates in law and divinity, from which not only were ministers of religion selected, but also judges and lawyers.

Fakirs.

The Fakirs were a numerous class of monkish devotees, who in some instances, by leading austere and religious lives, rose to the dignity of *saints*, (Pirs), and had disciples, by whom orders were formed, having their particular watchword and rites of initiation, and occasionally peculiarities of dress and observances. These saints were treated with the utmost reverence even by kings, and some managed to leave enormous wealth to their heirs. The most flourishing period for these holy men was the thirteenth and the beginning of the fourteenth centuries.

Religion.

The Shia religion (professed by the followers of Ali, the cousin and son-in-law of Mahomed) never made any progress in Hindūsthān, as it did in the Dekhun, where the Mahomedans were mostly Sūnnis (believers in the Kaliphs). Conversions of Hindūs to Mahomedanism were somewhat numerous on the first invasion of India by the followers of the prophet, owing mainly to the terror of the arms of the Mahomedans, and the novelty of their doctrines. The Hindūs were liable to a capitation tax (Jezzia) and to some other invidious distinctions, but were not molested in the exercise of their religion.

State of the people.

The condition of the people in ordinary times does not appear to have borne the marks of oppression. Every ryot is said to have possessed a good bedstead and a neat garden. The general state of the country is also thought to have been flourishing, as travellers, both Europeans and natives, speak highly of the well-built cities and towns they saw in different parts of the country, seated amidst beautiful gardens and orchards. That part of India still retained by the Hindūs was also represented as being prosperous, and Madura, in Southern India, was said to be as large as Delhi. The city of Bijāyanuggur is described as being exceedingly grand and extensive, and the pomp of the Rājā and the wealth of the inhabitants as equal to that of the palmiest days of Delhi or Kanouj.

Coinage.

Akbar is generally said to have been the first Mahomedan king who coined silver or gold money, but this appears to be an error, as coins of an earlier date have been found. The first princes used "*dinars*" and "*dirhems*," but these were subsequently changed for "*tankas*," which were subdivided into "*dāms*" or "*jitals*." The value of the dinar fluctuated in different districts from $2\frac{1}{2}d.$ to $9d.$ The tanka appears to be represented by the modern "*rupee*." Shir Shah changed the name of tanka to that of "*Rupeia*" or rupee, and this was adopted by Akbar, whose rupee was worth $1s.\ 11\frac{1}{2}d.$, and was divided into 40 dāms or peisas (copper), and the dām into 25 jitals (copper).

Mahomedan literature flourished mostly before the

reign of Akbar, and declined after his accession. The

Literature and Language. Hindūsthāni language is supposed to have made but little progress before the end of the twelfth century, and to have taken its present form during Teimūr's invasion. The pure local dialect in which Mahomedan poets are first presumed to have written was Hindi.

A Chronological Table showing the contemporaneous Sovereigns of England and Hindūsthān commencing from Mahmūd of Ghuzni and ending with Alumgir II.

England.	A.D.	Hindusthan.	A. D.
Saxon Line.		*House of Ghuzni.*	
Ethelred II.	978	Mahmūd	999
Edmond Ironside . . .	1016	Masāūd	1030
Edward the Confessor .	1041	Modūd	1040
		Abul Hassan	1049
		Abul Rashid	1051
		Ferokhzad	1052
Harold II.	1066	Ibrahim	1058
Norman Line.			
William I.	1066		
William II.	1087	Musāūd II.	1089
Henry I.	1100	Arslan	1114
Stephen	1135	Behram	1118
Plantagenet Line.			
Henry II.	1154	Khusru	1152
		Khusru Malik	1160
		House of Ghor.	
Richard I.	1189	Gheias-ū-din	1176
John	1199	Mahomed Ghori . . .	1202
		Slave Kings.	
		Kūtub-ū-din	1206
		Arām	1210
Henry III.	1216	Altamsh	1211
		Rukn-ū-din	1236
		Rezia Begum	1236
		Moiz-ū-din Behram . .	1239
		Ala-ū-din Masāūd . . .	1241
		Nasir-ū-din	1246
		Gheias-ū-din	1266

ENGLAND.		HINDUSTHAN.	
Plantagenet Line.	A. D.	*Slave Kings.*	A. D.
Edward I.	1272	Kei-Kobad	1286
		House of Khilji.	
		Jelal-ū-din	1288
		Ala-ū-din	1295
Edward II.	1307	Mubarik Khilji	1317
		House of Toghlak.	
		Gheias-ū-din	1321
Edward III.	1327	Mohamed Toghlak	1325
		Firuz Toghlak	1351
Richard II.	1377	Gheias-ū-din II.	1388
		Abubukur Toghlak	1389
House of Lancaster.		Nasir-ū-din Toghlak	1390
Henry IV.	1399	Mahmūd Toghlak	1394
		Syud Dynasty.	
Henry V.	1413	Khizir Khān	1414
Henry VI.	1422	Mubarik	1421
		Mohamed	1435
		Ala-ū-din	1445
House of York.		*House of Lodi.*	
Edward IV.	1461	Behlōl Lodi	1450
Edward V.	1483		
Richard III.	1483		
Tudor Line.			
Henry VII.	1485	Sekundur Lodi	1488
Henry VIII.	1509	Ibrahim Lodi	1517
		House of Teimūr.	
		Bāber	1526
		Humayūn	1530
Edward VI.	1547	Akbar	1556
Mary	1553		
Elizabeth	1558		
Stuart Line.			
James I.	1603	Jehāngir	1605
Charles I.	1625	Shah Jehān	1627
Commonwealth.			
Oliver Cromwell	1649		
Stuart Line (restored).			
Charles II.	1660	Aurungzib	1658
James II.	1685		
William III. & Mary II.	1688		
Anne	1702	Bahādur Shah	1707
House of Hanover.			
George I.	1714	Jehāndar Shah	1712
		Farokhsir	1713
		Mahomed Shah	1719
George II.	1727	Ahmed Shah	1748
George III.	1760	Alūmgir II.	1755

THE CHRISTIAN PERIOD FROM A.D. 1761 *UP TO THE PRESENT TIME.*

A STAGE of Indian History has now been arrived at, when the English began to play an important political part in the country. At the end of 1761 Shah Alum, the emperor of Delhi was a fugitive, and possessed only of nominal power. The great Sūbahs or provinces of the empire had become independent. Bengal was under a Nabob, Mir Kossim, of English creation. In Madras the East India Company had but recently finished a successful war with France for supremacy in southern India, and had raised Mahomed Ali to the dignity of Nabob of the Karnatik. A new adventurer had turned up in Maisūr, formerly one of the provinces of the Hindū kingdom of Bijāyanuggur, but which since 1564 had become independent under Hindū princes of its own. This was Heidur Naik, born of an humble family, but who after forty-seven years of complete obscurity, laid, in 1755, the foundations of a fortune which six years later made him master of the kingdom of Maisūr (Mysore). On the western coast the English power was small and contracted. Among the Marattas, Mahdū Rao had, in 1761, succeeded his father Ballaji Rao as Peishwa, and was preparing for a war with Salābut Jung, the Sūbhēdar of the Dekhun. The history of the following thirteen years (1761-74), at the end of which the first governor-general of India was appointed, will therefore be considered under the separate heads of the three Presidencies of *Bengal*, *Madras*, and *Bombay*.

BENGAL (A.D. 1761 TO 1774).

In 1762 Mr. Vansittart was governor of Bengal and Mir Kossim the Nabob. The latter removed his seat of government to Monghir (320 miles from Kalkutta), and with the assistance of an Armenian, known as Gurghin Khān, formed a large and efficient army, reduced the expenses of his government, discharged all his pecuniary obligations with the English, and set to work to make himself independent of them. He despoiled several of the great provincial officers, among others, Rāmnaryen, the governor of Patna, and this with the connivance of the English. In 1763 he abolished all transit duties throughout the province, in consequence of their great abuse by the Company's servants, and it was through the intemperate and unscrupulous conduct of one of them, Mr. Ellis, that war was declared in the same year against the Nabob. Several actions were fought in the months of July and August, and Mūrshedabād was taken. Enraged at his losses, the Nabob massacred his English prisoners and then proceeded to Patna, which was captured by the English in November, and Mir Kossim, four months after the rupture began, fled to the Nabob vizier of Oudh, Sūja-ū-dowla, for protection. In 1764 the emperor of Delhi, the Nabob of Oudh, and Mir Kossim marched to Patna, which in May they attacked vigorously, but were repulsed, though not without difficulty, and compelled to retire to Buxar for the rains. It was in 1764 that the first Sepoy mutiny among the Company's troops took place, arising from a refusal of their demands for large donations and increased pay. Major Munro, then in command, had twenty-four of the ringleaders blown away from guns, and discipline was restored. In October, 1764, the important battle of Buxar was fought, followed by the capture of Luknow, and a second action at Korah; these demolished the power of the Nabob vizier, who surrendered himself to General Carnac, and made the English masters of the entire valley of the Ganges, from the Himalayas to the sea. Mir Jaffier was again installed as Nabob, but died in January 1765, and his death was hastened, it is said, by the pecuniary importunities of the council, who had found the making of Nabobs during the past seven years the most lucrative of employments. Mr. Vansittart had resigned in November, 1764, and his place was filled by Mr. Spenser, who resigned it in May, 1765, to Lord Clive, specially sent out by the Court of Directors to retrieve the Company's affairs in India, then in the charge of a government justly described as "headstrong and corrupt, and lost to every sense of honour." He arrived as commander-in-chief, and president and governor of Bengal, with great powers, and at once commenced the work of reformation. In the first place he enforced the execution of the covenants with the civil servants, abolishing the receipt of presents, and in June, 1765, left for the Upper Provinces, where he pensioned the Nabob of Mūrshedabād with fifty-three laks of rupees a year, and restored the province of Oudh to the Nabob vizier, excepting the two districts of Korah and Allahabād, which were given to the emperor, from whom, in consideration of these, and the annual payment of twenty-six laks of rupees, Lord Clive received on 12th August in due form, on behalf of the Company, the Dewani of Bengal, Behar, and Orissa, that is to say, the government of 25,000,000 of people, and an annual revenue of four krores of rupees. The abolition of "double batta" to the army, announced by Lord Clive to cease from the 1st January, 1766, produced a mutiny among the officers, headed by Sir Robert Fletcher, and 200 of them resigned their commissions on the same day, but this formidable conspiracy was effectually quelled by the vigour and resolution of Clive in a fortnight. He devised a plan for covering the expense of paying the civil servants adequately, by establishing a monopoly of salt, betel-nut, and tobacco, but this lasted only two years, and a commission of 2½ per cent. on the gross revenue of the province was afterwards substituted for it. Lord Clive resigned in January, 1767, and returned to England the same year, and after much mental and bodily suffering, put an end to his existence in 1774. He was succeeded in the government by Mr. Verelst, whose rule was one of comparative tranquillity. The administration was nominally vested in the Nabob, in whose name the revenue was collected, and justice administered by native officers, the former being checked by English supervisors or collectors appointed in 1769, but the power and rapacity of the Company's servants introduced endless intrigue and oppression. It was at this time that the great majority of rent-free tenures was created, and forty laks of annual revenue was thus alienated from the resources of the state. In 1769 Mr. John Cartier succeeded Mr. Verelst as governor, and it was during his rule (1770) that there occurred, owing to a deficient rain-fall, the great famine which swept away one-third of the population of the Lower Provinces. In 1772 Mr. Cartier resigned, and was succeeded by the celebrated Warren Hastings, subsequently (1774) appointed the first governor-general of India. He arrived in India in 1750, and had, by the usual system of seniority, advanced to the council board in the time of Mr. Vansittart, whose views he steadily supported. He was subsequently appointed second in council at Madras, and thence elevated to the governorship of Bengal. He was in 1772 called upon to introduce a complete revolution in the entire system of administration, civil, criminal, and fiscal, and this was commenced by his removing the revenue business, and treasury from Mūrshedabād to Kalkutta, which thus became the capital of Bengal. The lands were farmed out for five years, the charge of civil and criminal justice, for which he compiled a simple code of regulations, was entrusted to European officers, and courts of appeal were established at Kalkutta. All these changes were effected in six months. Meanwhile in England, parliamentary interference was being loudly called for in the affairs of India. The machinery of the India House, constructed for the management of trade, was altogether unsuited to the administration of government. The East India Company in London consisted of a number of shareholders, or proprietors of stock, having votes according to the amount of stock they held, an owner of £500 stock possessing one vote, of £1000, two votes, and so on in proportion. Out of the proprietors twenty-four directors were chosen, who, with a chairman and deputy chairman, carried on the business of the Company. Stock was therefore purchased, not for investment only, but chiefly for power and influence. In 1771 the crown claimed the sovereignty of the possessions obtained by the arms of its subjects, which was of course disputed by the Company, but a compromise was effected, by which the latter were to retain the territorial revenues of India, but to pay to the British nation forty laks of rupees a year. Financial difficulties, however, pressed heavily on the Company. There was a deficit in the revenues, and a debt of upwards of $2\frac{1}{4}$ millions sterling, of which $1\frac{1}{4}$ was in London, and the remainder at Kalkutta. A loan from the public was sought for, and in 1772 a select committee of the Commons was appointed, which in 1774 ultimately produced the Regulating Act, otherwise called the New Charter (Act 13, Geo. III. cap. 63), by which a million sterling was lent to the Company—the qualification of a single proprietor's vote raised from £500 to £1000—no individual to have more than four votes, and six directors only to retire annually. The governor of Bengal was to be

East India Company.

Regulating Act.

governor-general on a salary of £25,000 a year, with four councillors at £10,000 each. A crown court was to be established at Kalkutta, with a chief justice at £8000, and three puisne judges at £6000 each a year.

Rohilla War.

In 1773 Mr. Hastings concluded a treaty with the vizier of Oudh, by which he engaged to assist the latter with an English force in destroying the Rohillas, a powerful Afghān confederacy on the borders of Oudh (founded in the reign of Mahomed Shah, and composed mostly of Eusof-zeis), and for this he was to receive forty laks of rupees, and two laks a month for the services of the English contingent. In consequence of the emperor seeking Maratta protection, and ceasing to be a free agent, the two districts of Korah and Allahabād, previously made over to him in 1764, were sold to the vizier for fifty laks, and the subsidy of twenty-six laks, also settled upon the emperor out of the revenues of Bengal, Behar, and Orissa, was abolished. In April, 1774, the Rohillas under Hafiz Rehmut Khan were defeated by the allied army, and the campaign at once brought to an end, the brunt of the engagement falling on the British contingent commanded by Colonel Champion. One chieftain alone, Fyzūlla Khān, was permitted to retain any power in Rohilkund. To him was given Rampūra, and some Jagīrs, of the annual value of fifteen laks of rupees. This war was, it is admitted, inconsistent with the plainest dictates of common justice and even of sound policy, but the treasury at Kalkutta was empty, and the vizier's offer seemed to be the best suited for replenishing it. On the 19th October, 1774, the judges of the supreme court, and the new members of council (General Clavering, Colonel Monson, and Mr. Phillip Francis), landed at Kalkutta, and on the 20th the new government, comprising Mr. Hastings as governor-general, with four members of council, was duly inaugurated by proclamation.

MADRAS (A.D. 1761 TO 1774).

In 1761 Mr. George Pigot was governor of Madras, and Mahomed Ali, the ally of the English, the Nabob of the Karnatik. In 1763 Mr. Robert Palk succeeded Mr. Pigot as governor, and the Nabob, who had previously been called upon to pay up fifty laks of rupees towards the expenses of the late war with France, instigated the Madras government to attack the Tanjūr state as a means of raising the sum demanded of him, but an adjustment was finally agreed to, and another unjust war prevented. In this year Nizam Ali, who had assassinated his brother Salābut Jung, the Sūbhēdar of the Dekhun, invaded the Karnatik with a large army, but retreated on the approach of the English troops. The Delhi emperor's "*firman*" was afterwards (1765) received by Lord Clive, releasing the Nabob from all dependence on the Nizam, and at the same time an imperial grant of the Northern Sirkars was obtained; but the Madras government, disregarding this, entered in 1766 into a treaty with the Nizam, agreeing to hold the latter territory as a tributary under him at eight laks a year, to give an immediate donation of five laks, and, moreover, to furnish, when necessary, two battalions of infantry and six pieces of cannon. It was this treaty which afterwards involved the Madras presidency in a war with Heidur Ali Khān, the ruler of Maisūr. A brief notice of the rise of this remarkable man has already been given, and it will now suffice to say that in 1761 he had, by his skill both in diplomacy and war, become the master of the entire kingdom of Maisūr. In 1763 he invaded the territory of Bednūr, and took the capital, then one of the wealthiest cities in the Dekhun. In 1765 he was defeated in two general actions by the Marattas, who invaded his dominions under Mahdū Rao

Heidur Ali.

Peishwa, and he only obtained peace by a cession of territory and the payment of thirty-two laks of rupees. In 1766 Heidur invaded Malabar, reducing both the Nairs and the Zamorin of Kalikut into subjection. In the latter part of that year a confederacy of the Marattas and the Nizam was formed against Heidur, and into this the Madras government was drawn by its previous treaty with the Dekhun Sūbhēdar, and compelled to furnish a contingent under Colonel Smith. The Marattas were bought off by Heidur by a payment of thirty laks, and in May, 1767, when the British force entered Maisūr, it was found that the Nizam had changed sides, having received a payment of twenty laks, and a promise of six laks of tribute. The combined Maisūr and Dekhun armies then advanced against the English troops, but they were defeated by Colonel Smith at the battles of Changama and Trinomalli, and as the Nizam's capital was threatened by a force under Colonel Peach from Bengal, a treaty was concluded by him on the 23rd February, 1768, with Mr. Bourchier, the governor of Madras, on nearly the same terms, and quite as humiliating to the Company as the previous one. In the meantime Heidur was busy on the western coast for seven months, in repelling the advance of an English expedition from Bombay, which had destroyed his fleet and captured Mangalūr and Honore (Honāwur), but was compelled afterwards to abandon the former town under disastrous circumstances. In this he was successful, and then returned to prosecute the war in the eastern districts, where the English, under Colonel Smith, had taken nearly one-half of his dominions and eight of his principal forts. Heidur's overtures for peace were not listened to, but the tide of success now turned against the English, and the Maisūr ruler, early in 1769, recovered all the districts he had lost. On the 29th March he appeared before Madras, to the astonishment of the bewildered council, and on the 4th April a treaty was concluded on the very moderate terms of a mutual restitution of conquests, and an assurance of mutual assistance in case of either party being attacked. In 1770 Mr. Josias Dupré succeeded Mr. Bourchier as governor, and it was in that year that Admiral Sir John Lindsay arrived at Madras with the power of a king's minister-plenipotentiary to the court of the Nabob, Mahomed Ali. The mission lasted only two years, but its effects were most mischievous, as the policy advocated was directly contrary to that pursued by the Madras government. It brought about a war between Heidur and the Marattas, in which the application for aid by the former, in terms of the treaty of 1769, was evaded by the English, and this Heidur never forgave or forgot. In 1771, at the instigation of Mahomed Ali, the Madras government engaged in war with the Rājā of Tanjūr, which resulted, in October of the same year, in the extortion of fifty laks from the Tanjūr state as compensation for peace. In 1773 a second attack was made on this small kingdom, though its injustice was fully recognized by the Madras council, and it ended in the deposition of the Rājā and the cession of his country to the Nabob. The Court of Directors disapproved of these proceedings, the Madras governor, Mr. Alexander Wynch was dismissed from his post, and the Rājā restored to his kingdom.

BOMBAY (A.D. 1761 TO 1774).

Bombay was at this time (1761) the smallest, as regarded territory, of all the three Presidencies, and its wealth was mainly derived from commerce. Its importance had been, in 1759, somewhat increased by the delivery to the English on the part of the Siddi, Ahmed Khān, of the fleet and the castle of Surat. During the governorship of Mr. Charles Crommelin (1760 to 1769) nothing happened worthy of record excepting the fact of an expedition being fitted out in 1768 at Bombay against the naval power of Heidur Ali Khān, the ruler of Maisūr. The result has already been mentioned (see page 89). In 1769 Mr. Thomas Hodges succeeded Mr. Crommelin as governor, and to him in 1771 succeeded Mr. William Hornby, during whose rule the government took, for the first time, a serious part in the affairs of the Marattas.

Marattas.

The incursions of this restless people were checked for a time by the battle of Paniput, but in 1769 a large army numbering 300,000 horse and foot, under Visaji, the Peishwa's general, and accompanied by the great chiefs, Sindia and Holkar, was fitted out for plundering Hindūsthān. They invited the Delhi emperor, who had continued to reside at Allahabād, in the quiet enjoyment of his pension, to return to his old capital, and as he was naturally desirous of mounting the throne of his ancestors, he threw himself on Maratta protection, and was installed at Delhi on 25th December, 1771. Rohilkund was then ravaged, and vast plunder appropriated by the victors, but Mahdū Rao, Peishwa, died in November 1772, and the emperor, who had long repented the step he had taken, tried to rid himself of his protectors, but was totally defeated, and required to cede to the Marattas his two districts of Korah and Allahabād, but this the Kalkutta government would not allow. Naryen Rao, a younger brother of Mahdū Rao, succeeded the latter as Peishwa, but he was assassinated after a short reign of nine months, with the connivance, it is said, of his uncle Rugunath Rao (or Raghobà) who took the vacant office. In 1772 the nominal revenue of the Maratta empire was about ten krores of rupees, the amount actually realized did not, however, exceed seven krores, of which four were appropriated by the Geikwar, Bhonslē, Holkar, Sindia, and other chieftains. The Peishwa, with their assistance, could bring into the field not less than 100,000 fine cavalry, and a proportionate strength of artillery and foot. A circumstance now occurred which eventually led to negotiations with the English on the part of Raghoba, and this was the fact of Naryen Rao's widow being delivered of a son in April, 1774, who was at once installed as Peishwa, under the title of Mahdū Rao II. To establish himself in the government of Pūna, Raghoba solicited from the Bombay council the aid of a British force, which was granted in September, 1774, on the proviso that he advanced fifteen or twenty laks of rupees, and ceded Salsette (Sashti) and Bassein (Wusāi) in perpetuity to the Company. Raghoba declined to give up Salsette, but the Bombay government, hearing that a Portuguese expedition was fitting out at Goa to recover their former settlements, took forcible possession of the island at the latter end of 1774. The towns of Broach and Tanna had both previously been taken in 1773.

Names of Note.—**Lord Clive** (1725—1774), the founder of English dominion in India; called by Pitt "the heaven-born general," and by the natives "the daring in war." General **Smith** and General **Forde** military commanders. **Mir Kosim**, Nabob of Bengal. **Mahdu Rao**, Peishwa (died 1772). **Morari Rao**, Maratta military commander.

(I.) WARREN HASTINGS (Governor-General, 1774-85).

Governors of Madras.		*Governors of Bombay.*	
Alexander Wynch	1773-5	William Hornby	1771-85
Lord Pigot	1775-7	Rawson Hart Boddam	1785-
Whitehill	1777-8		
Sir Thomas Rumbold	1778-80		
Whitehill	1780		
Charles Smith	1780-1		
Lord Macartney	1781-5		

Appointment.—Entered upon his duties as the first

Governor-General of India in October, 1774. Was born in 1732 at Daylesford, in Worcestershire, and arrived in India as a writer in the East India Company's service in 1750. Served as Governor of Bengal from 1772 to 1774.

Resignation.—Resigned on 1st February, 1785, after a most eventful administration as Governor of Bengal, and Governor-General of India for thirteen years. He had, in 1776, owing to dissensions with his council, tendered his resignation, but afterwards retracted it. He died at Daylesford in August, 1818.

Character.—Was distinguished for great administrative abilities, and in private life was of high principle and unsullied probity. His conduct in the Rohilla war and his treatment of Cheyte Singh and the Begums were open to opprobrium, and led to the impeachment which has made his name so celebrated. Lord Macaulay said of him—"We cannot regard without admiration the amplitude and fertility of his intellect, his rare talents for command, for administration, and for controversy, his dauntless courage, his honourable poverty, his fervent zeal for the interests of the state, his noble equanimity, tried by both extremes of fortune and never disturbed by either."

Wars.—I. With the Marattas in 1775 in support of Raghoba, who on 6th March concluded a treaty, known as the "*Treaty of Surat,*" by which 3,000 British troops were to be furnished him on a payment of eighteen laks a year, and Salsette and Bassein ceded to the Company. In May 1775, the battle of Arras was fought, and the Marattas defeated by Colonel Keating. Their navy also was completely crippled. The Geikwar of Baroda then changed sides, and agreed to assist Raghoba with men and money. By this campaign the Company had obtained a territorial revenue of twenty-four laks a year, but the Kalkutta council stepped in, disallowed the "Treaty of Surat," and sent Colonel Upton to carry on negotiations which ended in the "*Treaty* of Purundhur," signed on the part of the Marattas on 1st March, 1776, by Sukaram Bappū and Nānā Furnavis. By it "(*a*) all engagements between the Bombay government and Raghoba were annulled, the latter to retire to the banks of the Godaveri on a pension of 3 laks a year; (*b*) the British army to quit the field; (*c*) Salsette to be retained by the Company if the Governor-General wished it, but all other acquisitions to be relinquished; (*d*) the claim on the Broach revenues conceded, with twelve laks of rupees towards the expenses of the war." In August the decision of the Court of Directors was received approving of the "Surat Treaty," on which Raghoba was invited to Bombay, and 10,000 rupees a month settled upon him. Another despatch afterwards received from the court regretted the sacrifices made by the "Purundhur Treaty," but allowed a renewal of the alliance with Raghoba in case of any infraction on the part of the Pūna regency. In 1778 a French agent, one St. Lubin, was received with honour at Pūna, and Choul, near Bombay, was given to the French by the Marattas. In the same year a revolution took place at Pūna in favour of Raghoba, supported by Holkar, Moroba Furnavis, and Sukaram Bappū, but a counter-revolution occurred in July, restoring Nānā Furnavis again to power, upon which a new treaty was made with Raghoba by the Company, and an expedition under Colonel Egerton, consisting of 4,000 men, sent in November to Punā, to reinstate Raghoba. It terminated disastrously in the convention of Wurgaon, drawn up in January, 1779, by which all acquisitions made since 1773 were sacrificed, to save the British army from destruction. Raghoba had previously surrendered himself to Sindia, who granted him a jagīr of twelve laks of rupees in Bundelkund. Another large force, under Colonel Goddard, from Bengal, reached Surat in January, 1780, and the Wurgaon convention was repudiated by both the Governor-General and the Bombay government. Raghoba escaped from Sindia, and fled to Surat, where he remained with Colonel Goddard. Negotiations with the Marattas were again tried, but being unsuccessful, war was renewed early in 1780. Ahmedabād was captured by the English in February, and both Sindia and Holkar were routed on the 2nd and 14th of April. The strong fort of Gwālior was stormed and taken by Major Popham in August. A confederacy formed in 1779 by the Nizam, Heidur Ali, and the Maratta chiefs, to expel the English from India, began its operations in the following year. Bassein was taken on 11th December, 1780, by Goddard, and the following day the Marattas, under Ramchunder Gunnēsh, were defeated by Colonel Hartley at Dugaud in the Kōnkun. In 1781 Goddard advanced upon Pūna, but he was vigorously attacked by Holkar, and compelled to fall back upon Bombay. In March, 1781, Sindia was signally routed by Colonel Carnac, and in October he signed a treaty, by which he regained his territory west of the Jumna, with the exception of the fort of Gwālior, which was reserved for the Rāna of Gohud. On 17th May, 1782, a treaty, known as that of "**Salbye**," between the Company and the Maratta Regency, was negotiated by Sindia, by which—"(*a*) all territory acquired by the British since the treaty of Purundhur was restored; (*b*) Futteh Sīngh Geikwar was replaced in his original position at Guzerat; (*c*) Raghoba to be allowed three laks of rupees a year, and live where he chose; (*d*) Heidur Ali to give up all his conquests in the Karnatik and all his prisoners within six months, failing which to be attacked by the Peishwa." II. In consequence of a declaration of war between France and England in 1778, Pondicherri was captured by a force under Sir Hector Munro in October of that year, and Māhē, a small French settlement on the Malabar coast, was taken in March, 1779. It was this latter capture, combined with a march of English troops without Heidur's permission through the province of Kurpa, that induced him to join the confederacy of 1779, and enter into a war (III.) with the Company in July, 1780. At first an English force under Colonel Baillie was totally destroyed on 10th September at Perambaukum, but the energetic measures of Hastings soon retrieved this disaster, and Sir Eyre Coote was sent to take the command-in-chief of the Madras army. In arrangement with the Rājā of Berar in 1780, a Bengal detachment under Colonel Pearce was sent by land on 9th January, 1781, to join the Madras troops in repelling Heidur Ali. Half of them perished from cholera, but 2,000 of the Rājā's horse joined it, and so completed its strength. The citadel of Arkot fell into Heidur's hands in 1781, but Wandewash was bravely defended, and the fortified town of Karangolli taken. In July, 1781, Heidur was defeated by Coote at Porto Novo, and in August at Pollilūr, and once again in September at Solingur. It was now, too, that the Dutch, against whom England had declared war early in 1781, lost their settlements of Sadras and Pulikat, and Negapatam itself was captured on 12th November, together with a large quantity of military stores. In 1782 Colonel Braithwaite suffered a defeat from Tippū, Heidur's son, in Tanjūr, but this was soon after counterbalanced by a success at Tellicherri in February, which stirred up the Nairs to resistance, and created a violent reaction in Kūrg. In conjunction with the French, who sent an expedition to India in 1781-82, Heidur captured Kuddalūr and the important port of Permakoil, and though the action at Arni in June, 1782, was in favour of the English, it was not attended with any direct advantage. On the Malabar coast a Bombay force under Colonel Humberstone had achieved some successes, but later in 1782 it moved back to the coast, closely assailed by Tippū. Heidur died on 7th December, and was succeeded by his son Tippū. He returned to the western coast in March, 1783, to oppose General Mathews, who had taken the towns of Mirji and Honore, destroyed several Maisūr ships of war, and had also captured Bednūr, which was, however, subsequently surrendered to Tippū, together with the town of Mangalūr, after a brave resistance of nine months, under Colonel Campbell. The veteran French General Bussy had landed in April, 1783, at Kuddalūr, and thither a strong English force was despatched under General Stuart to besiege him, but all military operations between the two powers ceased on the news of a peace between England and France. Meanwhile a powerful force under Colonel Fullarton was penetrating into the heart of Maisūr; the fortress of Palghāt was captured on 15th November, and Koimbatūr occupied on the 26th, and an immediate advance was about to be made on Seringapatam, when orders were received to suspend operations, and relinquish all the districts occupied. The Madras Council were entering into negotiations with Tippū, who for a time cajoled them, and they afterwards, in March, 1784, signed the disgraceful treaty of *Mangalūr*, on the basis of a mutual restitution of conquests. IV. In 1781 a rupture took place with the Rājā of Benares, Cheyte Singh, in consequence of his being placed in arrest by Hastings for not having obeyed a requisition made upon him for 2000 horse and 5 laks of rupees. For this delinquency he was fined 50 laks of rupees. The province revolted, but the Raja's troops sustained a succession of defeats, and Bidgegur was captured with a booty amounting to 40 laks of rupees. This on the strength of a private letter from Hastings was divided amongst the victorious troops. Cheyte Singh remained at Gwālior for twenty-nine years. His nephew was raised to the throne, and the tribute augmented from 22½ to 40 laks a year. Hastings had in 1780 for similar reasons caused Fyzūlla Khān to be dispossessed of his jagirs, but seeing his error he restored them to the Rohilla chieftain, and released him from all obligation of furnishing troops in consideration of a payment by him of 15 laks of rupees.

Memorable Events.—Hastings met with opposition from the three new members of his Council at their first meeting on 20th October, 1774, and as they formed a majority, the government of India at once passed into their hands. In 1775 they interfered to such an extent in the affairs of Oudh, that the presence of the English brigade alone saved that country from a revolution. The inferior position of Hastings in the Council naturally produced a host of accusations against him, the chief of which were two grave charges of bribery preferred by one Nundu Kumar, a wealthy but disreputable and intriguing Hindū. The majority of the Council, comprising Francis and his friends, found the Governor-General guilty of having illegally received 3,40,000 rupees, which they determined he should repay. A counter-charge of conspiracy was made by Mr. Hastings against Nundu Kumar, and shortly afterwards a previous charge of forgery was renewed against him by one Mohun Persaud. This latter crime was established on the clearest evidence by the Supreme Court and Nundu Kumar was hanged in the presence of thousands of his countrymen. After his death facsimiles of the seals of all the most eminent personages in Bengal were found in his cabinet. By the death in September, 1776, of Colonel Monson, Hastings' authority was restored in his Council. Another of the new members, Sir John Clavering, also died in 1777. In 1780 the disputes between Hastings and Francis resulted in a hostile meeting in which the latter was wounded; he returned to England at the close of that year. A new settlement of the land revenue was made by Warren Hastings in 1777, but by order of the Court of Directors, who could see no necessity for such an arrangement, it was fixed for one year only. By the former system the country had become impoverished, and the Company had in five years lost by remissions and irrecoverable balances nearly 2½ krores of rupees.

Madras.

In 1775 Lord Pigot became Governor of Madras, and about 1776, in accordance with the orders of the Court of Directors, he restored the Rājāh of Tanjūr to his throne. In the same year he was violently removed from his government for unconstitutional conduct, by a majority of the Council, but was subsequently directed to be re-instated by the Court of Directors. He died in May, 1777 before their order reached Madras, after a confinement of eight months. Mr. Whitehill who succeeded him officiated but six months, resigning the government to Sir Thomas Rumbold, who also incurred the displeasure of the Court of Directors. They passed the severest censure on his conduct in his dealings with Basalūt Jung, the Nizam of the Dekhun, and in other matters, and both he and the members of Council were dismissed from their posts. Published papers and correspondence have however since shown that as regards Sir Thomas Rumbold, these charges were based on erroneous information and partial investigation. Mr. Whitehill again assumed the Government but was suspended by the Governor-General for persistence in retaining Guntūr, after receiving orders to restore it. In 1781, owing to pressure of events in the Karnatik, the Nabob was compelled to resign the revenues for five years, taking only *one-sixth* for his personal expenditure and for his creditors. In 1784 it was determined to pay off the debts of the Nabob of Arkot, which had been for years a great source of demoralization at the Madras Presidency, and 12 laks of pagodas were annually appropriated to this object, until the amount (5 krores) was liquidated.

Between the years 1775 and 1780 it was found that the Supreme Court (under Sir Elijah Impey), intended to protect the natives from the oppression of Europeans, had, by interfering in every department of the state, paralyzed the whole system of government. Petitions were addressed to Parliament praying for a redress of these intolerable nuisances. The Governor-General himself in 1780 resisted this violence and quieted the Supreme Court by making Sir Elijah Impey chief judge of the Suddur Court, an arrangement which brought about the recall of the judge, but it subsequently led to a more distinct definition, by Act of Parliament, of the functions of the Supreme Court.

Supreme Court.

The transaction in connection with the spoliation of the Begums of Oudh is one that has brought great odium on Hastings' name. The Begums were the wife and mother of the late Nabob of Oudh, and on the representation that they had abetted Cheyte Singh in his rebellion, with troops and money, Hastings yielded to the solicitation of the Vizier for the spoliation of the Princesses, and his consent was duly embodied in a treaty. 76 laks of rupees were extorted at various times, and paid over to the Company. For the barbarities practised on the Begums and their servants by the Nabob, Hastings cannot be held personally answerable, but the stain has nevertheless clung to him. His proceedings were severely condemned by the Court of Directors, and in 1784, on their requisition, he restored the Jagīrs to the Begums through the agency of the Vizier of Oudh, and then resigned his office to his successor, Mr. Macpherson, the senior member of Council, embarking for England in February, 1785.

Begums of Oudh.

On the 20th of June of that year he was impeached by the British Parliament on twenty-two charges connected with his administration of India, but *three* only were of serious import,—the first Rohilla War—Cheyte Singh—and the Begums of Oudh. His trial terminated on 23rd April, 1795, in a complete and honourable acquittal. It cost him 10 laks of rupees, and reduced him to comparative poverty, but an annuity of £4000 was subsequently granted him by the Court of Directors.

Impeachment of Hastings.

In 1783 owing to the pecuniary embarrassments of the Company, two Acts of Parliament were passed for their relief, and Mr. Fox, then at the head of the Coalition Ministry, brought in his famous India Bill providing for (*a*) a transfer for four years of the powers of government of the Company to a board of seven commissioners, to be nominated at first by the Parliament, and afterwards by the Crown; (*b*) that the Company's trade be managed by nine assistant directors, to be chosen eventually by proprietors of India Stock. The bill passed the Lower House but was thrown out by the Lords.

Fox's India Bill.

Mr. Pitt, who was placed at the head of the new ministry, then brought in his India Bill, on 13th August, 1784. The principal provisions were, (*a*) the appointment of a Board of Commissioners, composed of six members of the Privy Council, with power to control all acts, operations and concerns relating to the revenues and civil and military government of India; (*b*) that all letters sent to, and received from, India, be submitted to the Board, and all despatches and orders of the Board be implicitly obeyed; (*c*) that a committee of secrecy, consisting of three directors, be constituted; (*d*) that the Court of Proprietors be restricted from interfering with the Board's decisions; (*e*) that a schedule of the property of every officer returning from India be given in; (*f*) that a separate and august tribunal be established in England for trial of great delinquents. Mr. Dundas was appointed the first President of the Board of Control, and held the office for sixteen years.

Pitt's India Bill.

At the close of Warren Hastings' administration, the English possessions in India were:—the **Bengal** *Presidency*, comprising Bengal, Behar, Orissa and Benares; the **Madras** *Presidency*, Madras, with a Jagir around it, and the northern Sirkars; the **Bombay** *Presidency*, the islands of Bombay and Salsette, Broach, Ahmedabād and Bassein (Wusāi).

Names of Note.—**Sir Philip Francis** (1740-1818); **Sir Elijah Impey,** Chief Justice of Bengal (app. 1774). **Sir Eyre Coote** (1726-83). **Colonel Goddard, Major Popham,** military commanders. **Heidur Ali,** ruler of Maisūr (1702-82); **Raghoha,** Maratta Peishwa.

As a temporary arrangement only, Mr. (afterwards Sir John) Macpherson, the senior member of Council, assumed the government of India on Mr. Hastings' departure. He held the office but twenty months, resigning it to Lord Cornwallis in September, 1786. Mr. Macpherson applied himself with great energy to financial reforms, and effected reductions exceeding a krore of rupees. Lord Macartney, the Governor of Madras, had previously been offered the Governor-generalship in 1786, but through over solicitation on his part, he was passed over.

II. EARL (AFTERWARDS MARQUIS) CORNWALLIS

GOVERNOR GENERAL (A.D. 1786-93).

Governors of Madras.		*Governors of Bombay.*	
SIR ARCHIBALD CAMPBELL	1786-9	RAWSON HART BODDAM	1785-8
JOHN and EDW. HOLLAND (provisional) .	1789-90	ANDREW RAMSAY. .	1788
GENERAL MEDOWS .	1790-2	GENERAL MEDOWS .	1788-90
SIR CHAS. OAKLEY, Bt.	1792-3	SIR R. ABERCROMBIE	1790-

Appointment.—Made in February, 1786, and Lord Cornwallis entered upon his duties on 12th September. He had previously been employed in the American war, and had filled several important posts, both military and diplomatic. In 1786, he also received the appointment of Commander-in-Chief of India, in addition to that of Governor-General.

Resignation.—In 1793, when he embarked at Madras for England. His administration of seven years was greatly occupied with the war with the Maisūr Government, then under Tippū Sūltan. (Lord Cornwallis' second assumption of the Governor-Generalship in 1805, as successor to Lord Wellesley, will be noticed in its proper place, see page 123.)

Wars.—I. In 1790, with Tippū, Sultan of Maisūr, who had attacked Travankore (Tiruvankodu), in December, 1789, on the plea of the Rājā refusing to cede to him the towns of Kranganūr and Ayahkotah, lately purchased from the Dutch. This act he disavowed in the following year. A tripartite treaty was then concluded in 1790, between the East India Company, the Marattas, and the Nizam, for jointly reducing Tippū. Its provisions were, (*a*) the two latter states to join the British army, if required, with 10,000 horse, for which they were to be reimbursed; (*b*) a British contingent to accompany these troops; (*c*) all conquered territories to be equally divided among them; and (*d*) after peace with Tippū, if he attacked either of the contracting parties, the others to join in punishing him. General Medows commanded the Madras forces, and a Bengal division under Colonel Hartley, sent by land, joined it in November, while a Bombay army under General Abercrombie, co-operated on the Malabar coast. Owing to the desultory movements of Medows, Lord Cornwallis took the field in person, early in 1791, captured Bengalūr (Bangalore), on 21st March, and was joined by the Nizam's horse in April. On 13th May, when at Artikera, and within a short distance of Seringapatam, the capital, Tippū engaged the English army and was entirely defeated. This victory could not be followed up, owing to the scanty stores with the British troops, and Lord Cornwallis was constrained to retreat. On 24th May, he was joined by a Maratta force under Hurri Punt, with a supply of provisions and draught cattle, but it was too late in the season to resume operations, and the army continued its retreat to Bengalūr. Early in 1792, the campaign was re-opened with a finely-equipped army, joined by the Nizam's force of 8000 men, and a small body of Hurri Punt's Marattas. On 6th February, Seringapatam was besieged, on 16th, General Abercrombie joined with 6000 men, and the capital was on the point of being taken, when Tippū, on the 23rd, agreed to the severe terms prescribed by Lord Cornwallis, viz., (*a*) to cede half his territories; (*b*) to pay 3 krores of rupees towards the expenses of the war; and (*c*) to give up two of his sons as hostages. To the Company there fell the district of Dindigul in the south, and the Bara Mehal in the east, including some important passes into Maisūr, besides Malabar, a large strip of fertile territory on the western coast (which was annexed to Bombay), the whole comprising about 24,000 square miles. On 19th March, this treaty was definitely settled. II. War with France, on the declaration by that power in 1793 of war with England, when Pondicherri, and other French settlements in India, were at once taken possession of by the British.

Memorable Events.—The conduct of Lord Cornwallis in the Maisur war was censured in 1793 in the House of Commons, but it subsequently ratified all his measures, including the acquisition of territory. The King also conferred upon him the dignity of a Marquis.

During the first three years of his administration, the Governor-General set about correcting several abuses in the public service. Official depredation was still rampant, and small salaries and large perquisites were still the rule. All jobbing agencies, contracts and sinecures were abolished, and in 1788 liberal salaries were given to the Company's civil servants. In 1788, the number of European soldiers in India was 12,000, and of native Sepoys 58,000. The command of a regiment was then considered to be worth about 80,000 rupees (£8000) a-year.

As the Regulating Act of 1773 gave the Governor-General only a single vote in Council, rendering him liable to be over-ruled by his colleagues, Lord Cornwallis refused, with this incumbrance, to take up the office. A Bill was, therefore, passed in 1786, enabling the Governor-General, and the Governors of the various Presidencies to act, when necessary, in opposition to the opinion of their Councils.

In February, 1788, the "**Declaratory Act**" was introduced by Mr. Pitt into Parliament, with the view of declaring the meaning of the Act passed in 1784; the object was to place the Indian army on the same establishment as the king's. It encountered much opposition, and the Minister found it necessary to make great concessions, and add several conciliatory clauses to it.

Judicial Reforms.

It was during Lord Cornwallis's administration that great reforms were effected in the judicial institutions of the Bengal Presidency. Financial and judicial functions were separated, and the collector confined to fiscal duties. Civil Courts were established in the districts and in the principal cities, and four Courts of Appeal were constituted at Kalkutta, Dakka, Mūrshedabād, and Patna. For criminal justice, circuit judges were appointed, and Zillah judges were invested with magisterial power. The rules of 1781 (drawn up by Sir Elijah Impey), were altered in 1793, mainly by Mr. (afterwards Sir George) Barlow, a civil servant of eminence, into an elaborate volume of regulations, too full, however, of formalities of procedure, and thus unsuited to an oriental people.

Permanent Settlement.

The permanent settlement in 1793 of Bengal and Behar has rendered Lord Cornwallis's administration of India memorable. It had been found, that owing to the uncertainty of tenure then prevailing, the revenue was steadily diminishing, and the country becoming impoverished and exhausted. The Court of Directors, in their letter of 12th April, 1786, directed that all revenue engagements should be made with the old Zumindars for a period of ten years, after which, if satisfactory, they might be declared *permanent.* These Zumindars were, in the first instance, agents employed by the Government in collecting the revenue from the ryots or cultivators, and for their trouble received a certain percentage on the collections. By degrees this office, as is the tendency in India, became hereditary; the powers of these collectors were increased, they kept up a military force, had the control of the police, adjudicated rights, and at length became in effect *the masters* of the district, and assumed the title and dignity of Rājā. They were nevertheless capable of being ousted out of their offices when others offered more for the lands than they were prepared to give. After numerous investigations as to the value of the lands, the nature of the tenures, &c., which resulted in but little true information being elicited, the Government determined to confer a proprietary interest in the soil on some one class, and they selected the Zumindars, and bestowed it on them. The Zumindar was restricted from enhancing the rents of the "independent talukdars," and of two other classes of renters, who paid fixed sums, but the ryots were left to his mercy, the great mistake of the settlement being, that no clear or defined rules were drawn up for *their* protection, and it was only 66 years afterwards, that an Act (X. of 1859) was passed with this object by the then Governor-General in Council. Mr. Shore, at the time the best revenue authority in India, strongly opposed the settlement being made a permanent one, but all opposition was useless, and the "Permanent settlement of Bengal and Behar" was promulgated at Kalkutta, on 22nd March 1793. It was supposed to be the only remedy for the numerous evils with which the country was then afflicted, but it is generally admitted that, though conceived in the highest spirit of benevolence, the permanent settlement has been altogether one-sided in its action, and has, in a measure, failed as a revenue institution.

Renewal of the Charter.

In 1793, the East India Company's Charter expired, but it was renewed for another 20 years, on the grounds, that if the trade were thrown open generally, the Company would be unable to pay its debts,—that the growing commerce of India would be checked,—and that it would lead to the colonization of the country, and so ensure its loss to England. Private trade to the extent of 3,000 tons a year was permitted, but the grant was so hampered with restrictions, as to be practically useless.

Sindia.

After the Treaty of **Salbye** (1782), Māhādāji Sindia became an independent chief, and, in 1784, taking advantage of a favourable opportunity of pushing forward his ambitious schemes in Hindūsthān, secured such influence and authority at the Court of Delhi, as to obtain for the Peishwa, the title of Vukil-ūl-Mutlūk (Regent of the Empire), and for himself that of Deputy-Regent, while the Provinces of Agra and Delhi were assigned to him on the payment monthly of 65,000 rupees for the emperor's expenditure. A powerful Mahomedan party was, however, soon formed against him; and when he proceeded in 1787 to despoil the Rājpūts, he was attacked and defeated. On the 24th April, 1788, he was again defeated by Ismāil Beg, near Agra, but, in the following June, he gained a signal victory under the walls of that city. Meanwhile Delhi became once more a scene of spoliation. A Rohilla chieftain, the infamous Ghūlam Khādir, let loose his soldiery for two months on the unhappy city, blinded the emperor, and committed terrible atrocities. Sindia soon after advanced upon Delhi, re-seated the emperor, and put Ghūlam Khādir to a cruel death. Sindia's successes were mainly owing to a well-disciplined force of 18,000 regular infantry, 2,000 regular, and 6,000 irregular cavalry, trained and officered by Europeans, of whom Count de Boigne was the chief. In June 1790, he defeated the Rājpūts at Pātun, and again in September 1791 at Mairta, when Ajmīr was given up by the Rājā of Jodhpūr, and peace granted to the other Rājās on the payment of a moderate tribute. In June 1792, Sindia arrived at Pūna, where, in the following month, he invested, with much splendour, the young Peishwa, Mahdū Rao II., with the office and title of "Vukil-ūl-Mutlūk," previously granted by the Delhi Emperor. In the same year, his disciplined army under De Boigne, defeated Holkar's forces, and this success made Sindia absolute in Hindūsthān, and an object of dread and anxiety at the Pūna Durbar.

Madras.

A treaty was concluded with the Nabob of the Karnatik in 1792, the chief provisions of which were, (*a*) that an annual subsidy should be paid to the British troops entrusted with the defence of the Karnatik, certain districts being given in pledge; (*b*) that in the event of any war on the coast, the Governor-General might assume the entire government of the Karnatik, a fifth of the revenue being reserved for the Nabob; (*c*) the Nabob was not to enter into any negotiation or political correspondence with any European or native power without the Company's consent.

(III.) SIR JOHN SHORE (AFTERWARDS LORD TEIGNMOUTH,) GOVERNOR-GENERAL (A.D. 1793—98).

Governors of Madras.		*Governors of Bombay.*	
SIR CHARLES OAKLEY, Bart.	1792-4	SIR ROBERT ABERCROMBY	1790-4
LORD HOBART	1794-8	GEORGE DICK	1794-5
MAJOR-GEN. HARRIS (Pro.)	1798	JOHN GRIFFITHS	1795
		JONATHAN DUNCAN	1795-

Appointment.—Succeeded Lord Cornwallis as Governor-General on 28th October, 1793. He had previously been in the Company's Civil Service, in which he rose to a high position, and was admitted to be one of the best revenue authorities of his day.

Resignation.—On 25th March, 1798, a short time after his being raised to the peerage as Lord Teignmouth.

Character.—He displayed much honesty, talent and industry in his high office, and in circumstances of great delicacy and embarrassment conducted himself with temper and ability, but British influence in India was greatly weakened during his rule by his adherence to the *non-interfering* policy advocated by the Court of Directors.

Wars.—Owing to the neutrality policy carried out by Sir John Shore the East India Company became involved in no war with any of the Indian powers during his administration, but a mutiny of a very serious character took place among the Bengal officers of the Company's army in 1795-96, and this was only put down by the grant of very liberal concessions on the part of the Government. The demands of the mutineers were that, (*a*) no reduction should take place in the Company's regiments and no augmentation in the King's troops; (*b*) promotion to go by seniority; and (*c*) all allowances (including double batta) should be restored. In May, 1796, the new regulations for the army arrived from England, but they pleased neither party. They were modified by the Governor-General, and the following concessions made: (*a*) arrears of batta (7 laks) granted unasked; (*b*) arrears of brevet rank gratuitously bestowed, and allowances to officers of all grades so increased as to entail a permanent annual charge of seven laks.

To these concessions the British Government had eventually to submit. Sir John Shore was superseded, and Lord Cornwallis appointed Governor-General on 1st February, 1797, but owing to the weakness displayed by the Board of Control, he resigned the office in disgust on the 2nd August following.

The Nizam.

In 1795 the Nizam of the Dekhun was attacked by the Peishwa with an army of 130,000 horse and foot and 150 pieces of artillery. As Tippū intended to assist in crushing the Nizam, the latter applied for assistance to the Governor-General in terms of the treaty of 1790, but Sir John Shore left him to his fate. On 11th March he was defeated by the Marattas at Kurdla, and on 13th he purchased peace by ceding territory valued at 35 laks a year, paying an indemnity of 3 krores of rupees and surrendering his Prime Minister, Mushir-ūl-Mūlk, to his enemies.

Marattas.

Mention has already been made of the war between the Marattas and the Nizam in 1795. In the following October the young Peishwa, Mahdū Rao II. died, by throwing himself from the terrace of his palace. He left the succession to his cousin Bāji Rao, and though this arrangement was sought at first to be altered by the Minister Nāna Furnavis, Bāji Rao II. after numerous complications, was on 4th December, 1796, placed by him on the Maratta throne. A scene of confusion and intrigue followed the accession of this prince. Nāna was in 1797 seized and confined in the fort of Ahmednuggur, and Pūna was given up to plunder and violence to supply exerted himself in putting down the custom of infanticide, then very rife in that part of India.

Missionary Enterprise.

In 1799 other Protestant Missionaries (Messrs. Marshman and Ward) joined Messrs. Carey and Thomas at Kalkutta, but as the East-India Company would not countenance their exertions in the work of conversion, they found an asylum in Serampore, at that time a Danish settlement. Mr. Carey was appointed by Lord Wellesley a professor in the college at Fort William. In 1798 the Church Missionary Society was instituted at Madras.

Names of Note.—**Vittul Punt** (Sindia's prime minister), died 1804. **Nana Furnavis** (Maratta statesman), died 1800. **Tippū** (Sultan of Maisūr), 1753-99. **General Wellesley** (afterwards **Duke of Wellington**), 1769-1852; **General Harris** (1759-1829); **General Hartley**; **Sir David Baird** (1757-1829); **M. Raymond** (1755-1798); **Count de Boigne** (1751-1830); **Colonel Barry Close**; military commanders.

(V.) MARQUIS CORNWALLIS, Governor-General (A.D. 1805).

Governor of Madras.		*Governor of Bombay.*	
Lord W. C. Bentinck	1802	Jonathan Duncan	1795

Appointment and Death.—Appointed in 1805 and landed at Kalkutta on 30th July of that year. Died while on his way to the Upper Provinces, at Ghazipore near Benares on 5th October 1805 from old age and an enfeebled constitution.

Character.—He was distinguished for sterling integrity of character and had gained the esteem of all classes. During his first tenure of office as Governor-General he displayed great vigour and decision, and in all his actions was guided by a proper spirit of justice and moderation.

During the brief space of a little over two months in which Lord Cornwallis held office, nothing of any importance was effected. The line of policy he had intended to pursue was laid down in his September despatch to Lord Lake. It was altogether opposed to Lord Wellesley's system of subsidiary alliances, and was of a peaceful and conciliatory nature. He disbanded a large body of irregular troops, and paid up all arrears due to them. He proposed to restore to Holkar all his dominions, to conciliate Sindia by ceding certain districts to him, and to remove the Mogul emperor nearer Kalkutta, but before Lord Lake's answer could be received the Governor-General had died.

(VI.) SIR GEORGE H. BARLOW, GOVERNOR-GENERAL (A.D. 1805-7).

Governor of Madras.		*Governor of Bombay.*	
LORD W. C. BENTINCK	1802-7	JONATHAN DUNCAN	1795-

Appointment.—Sir George Barlow succeeded Lord Cornwallis as Governor-General in October, 1805, and was confirmed in office in February, 1806. He had previously been a civil servant on the Bengal establishment, and his knowledge and experience of the country and its people were considered to be very great.

Resignation.—After an administration of nearly two years he resigned his office in July, 1807 to Lord Minto, and took up the Governorship of Madras, to which he had been appointed.

Character.—He was zealous in his duties and shewed great official aptitude and industry, but his administration was of a timid nature. He had assisted in carrying out Lord Wellesley's views in India, but as these were distasteful to the Court of Directors, he adopted in a great measure the non-interfering policy put forward by his predecessor Lord Cornwallis.

out India, intended not only to make the Company a paramount power, but to secure the tranquillity of the country, showed this in an eminent degree. He has not inaptly been termed the "Akbar of the Company's dynasty."

Wars.—I. With Tippū Sūltān of Maisūr in 1799, in consequence of his having proposed an alliance with the French to expel the English from India. In 1798 an army was assembled at Madras in anticipation of the Sultan's designs, and on 3rd February, 1799, a British force of 20,802 men, together with the Nizam's army of 20,000 horse and foot, advanced into Maisūr, under the command of General Harris. A Bombay division of 6,420 troops, under General Stuart, was put in motion simultaneously from the Malabar Coast. On 6th March, Tippū engaged an advanced post of this division, under General Hartley, at Sidāsir, but the main body coming up in time, Tippū was defeated, and returned to Seringapatam. On 27th March, Tippū encountered the English force under General Harris at Malavelli, where he was again routed. In this battle Colonel Wellesley (afterwards Duke of Wellington) greatly distinguished himself. On 6th April, after having crossed the Kāvēri at Sosilla, General Harris appeared before Seringapatam, and the siege commenced on the 17th. As it was reported on 3rd May that but two days' provisions remained in the English camp, an assault was determined upon for the following day, and in a few hours the capital of Maisūr, garrisoned by 20,000 men, and defended by 287 pieces of ordnance, fell into the hands of the English. Tippū was killed in the assault, and his body was found under one of the gateways of the fort. At the time of his death he was 46 years of age. The prize-money amounted to about one krore of rupees (one million sterling), and this was divided, though unequally and unfairly, among the army. A new Maisūr kingdom was created, and a child of the ancient Hindū dynasty was placed on the throne, he receiving districts yielding 14 laks of pagodas yearly, and being allowed a military force, disciplined and commanded by British officers, at a cost of 7 laks of pagodas. Of the remaining districts the East India Company took territory, including the capital, of the annual value of 777,000 star-pagodas, out of which 240,000 were assigned for the maintenance of Heidur and Tippū's families at Vellūr. To the Nizam was assigned districts of the annual value of 600,000 star-pagodas, but charged with certain payments, while territory yielding 263,000 star-pagodas yearly, was offered to the Peishwa, though he had taken no part in the war, provided he admitted the mediation of the British Government in all disputes with the Nizam, and excluded the French from his dominions. This being refused, the district was divided between the Company and the Nizam. The only opposition which followed the Maisūr settlement was from Dhūndia Wāg, a freebooter, who had been released from confinement on the taking of Seringapatam. With a body of desperate men he plundered several towns and villages; but in September, 1800, after an energetic pursuit, was completely defeated, and killed in action, by Colonel Wellesley. II. In 1801 an expeditionary force of 4,000 Europeans and 5,000 volunteer Sepoys, under General Sir David Baird, was sent to co-operate with the English army in Egypt. It landed at Kosseir in June, reached Cairo on 10th August, and encamped at Rosetta on 27th, but was not brought into action, owing to the capitulation of the French general. The troops ultimately reached Suez, where they embarked for India on 5th June, 1802. III. In 1803 with Doulut Rao Sindia and the Rājā of Nāgpūr, who opposed the conditions of the treaty of Bassein, made in 1802: their armies conjointly amounted to 100,000 men (a portion of which had been disciplined under French officers), with a fine train of artillery. To oppose them, British troops, numbering in all 55,000 men, were despatched in separate divisions, the principal being under the command of General Wellesley and Colonel Stevenson in the Dekhun, and General Lake in the north of India. On 12th August, Ahmednuggur was captured by General Wellesley, and all Sindia's territories south of the Godaveri subsequently taken. On 23rd September the Maratta army of 50,000 men was routed at Assaye, by the same general, with but 4,500 troops. The town of Burhānpūr was captured on the 16th, and the strong fortress of Asirgarh on the 21st October, after which an armistice was granted to Sindia on 23rd November. General Wellesley then turned his attention to the Rājā of Nāgpūr, whose province of Kuttak had been previously occupied by Colonel Harcourt. On 28th November the battle of Argaon was won by General Wellesley, the fort of Gawulgarh captured by Colonel Stevenson on the 15th December, and the British army was advancing on Nāgpūr when the Rājā sued for peace. The treaty of **Deogaon** was then entered into and signed: it stipulated that "(*a*) Kuttak be ceded to the Company; (*b*) the districts of Berar, west of the Wurda, be given to the Nizam; (*c*) all differences with the Nizam to be referred to the British Government, and all Frenchmen and Europeans of any nation at war with England be excluded from the Nāgpūr dominions." In the north, Sindia suffered severely. The fortress of Aligarh was captured by General Lake on 29th August, 1803; this was followed on 11th September by a victory at Delhi, and on 15th the blind and aged Mogul Emperor, **Shah Alūm**, was released, and made over to the protection of the British Government. On 17th October, Agra was captured, and the booty, amounting to 17 laks of rupees, promptly distributed among the officers and men of General Lake's army: on 1st November the hard-fought battle of Laswari took place, thus completing, in the short space of twelve weeks, the full humiliation of

Sindia. Broach, his only sea-port, had been previously taken by Colonel Murray, and all his territory in Guzerat occupied. He then signed the treaty of **Sirji Anjengaon**, by which "(*a*) he ceded all his territories in Hindūsthān, lying in the Doāb, between the Ganges and Jumna, as also those north of the Rājpūt principalities of Jeipūr and Jodhpūr, together with the fort and district of Ahmednuggur in the Dekhun, and Broach, with its dependencies in Guzerat; (*b*) relinquished all claims on the Peishwa, Nizam, the Geikwar, and the East India Company, and recognized the independence of those rājās and feudatories in Hindūsthān (a list of these was furnished him) with whom General Lake had concluded treaties, &c.); and (*c*) agreed to refer all disputes with the Peishwa to the British Government." Two districts to the north of the prescribed limits were, however, restored to him, the fort and district of Ahmednuggur were made over to the Peishwa.

IV. With Yeshwunt Rao Holkar in April, 1804, on account of his insolent demands, and for invading the territories of the Rāja of Jeipūr, an ally of the British Government. Holkar's army numbered 60,000 horse and 15,000 foot. On 16th May Rampūra, Holkar's stronghold in the north was taken by Colonel Dow, but the disastrous retreat of a single native brigade of troops under Colonel Monson, who had been sent on the eve of the rainy season in pursuit of Holkar had a bad effect on the prestige and influence of the Company. It was attacked on 10th July by the whole of Holkar's army at the Mokundra Pass, between Kotah and Nimuch. In October, Holkar besieged Delhi, but the British Resident Colonel Ochterlony defended the place so bravely that the Maratta forces were drawn off, and the guns and infantry sent into the Bhurtpūr districts, the cavalry accompanying Holkar into the British territories. On 13th November the former were utterly defeated by General Fraser in the vicinity of Dig, in the Bhurtpūr district, the fort of which was captured on 23rd December. On 17th November Holkar himself was surprised by General Lake at Futtēghur, his troops cut up, and he himself compelled to beat a hasty retreat. All his forts in Malwa and the Dekhun had been taken, and Lake, early in January, 1805, proceeded to invest Bhurtpūr, but the fort remained uncaptured, notwithstanding four assaults and a loss of 3200 men in killed and wounded. In April a treaty was concluded with the Bhurtpūr Rājā, by which he agreed (*a*) "to pay 20 laks of rupees in four instalments towards the expenses of the war, the fort of Dīg remaining with the English till performance of conditions and (*b*) to give up some territory previously received from the English." Owing to the repeated failures before Bhurtpūr, Sindia, Holkar, Amir Khān, and the Rājā of Bhurtpūr again plotted against British rule and the former chief marched an army towards the fortress: the alliance was subsequently broken up, owing to dissensions between Sindia and Holkar. At this juncture Lord Cornwallis landed at Kalkutta (30th July) and assumed charge of the government.

Memorable Events.—The state of India on Lord Wellesley's assumption of the Governor-Generalship in 1798, was one of peculiar difficulty. Zemaun Shah, grandson of Ahmed Shah Abdāli (the conqueror of Paniput) threatened an invasion of India from the north. Tippū Sūltān in the south was burning to take his revenge on the English. The Nizam possessed a formidable French force of fourteen battalions under M. Raymond. Sindia was supreme at both Pūna and Delhi, and had a well trained and highly disciplined force of 40,000 men raised by De Boigne. The European officers of the company's army were in a state of insubordination, and the public credit was at a very low ebb. When he resigned his high office, he had added to the Bengal Presidency, the Upper Doāb, Delhi, Agra, Hurriāna, Sāharunpore, Mirūt, Aligarh,

Etāwah, Kuttak, and Balasūr. Madras had also received a large addition of territory, and Bombay acquired Broach in Guzerat. The Mogul Emperor at Delhi had also become a pensioner of the company. At the end of 1804-5 the Indian revenue amounted to £15,403,409, and the debt to £25,626,631.

One of the first acts of the Governor-General was to extinguish the large French force then in the pay of the Nizam, and this was accomplished without the loss of a single life. He proposed to the Nizam and to the Peishwa (Bāji Rao) in 1799 to substitute a disciplined *subsidiary* force for their own turbulent and unruly soldiery. This was refused by the Peishwa, but after some vacillation accepted by the Nizam and four battalions of British troops, in addition to the two formerly in his service, took the place of the French force. In lieu of a money payment of 40 laks on their account, districts previously obtained from Maisūr, and yielding 63 laks of annual revenue, were ceded in perpetuity to the company. The Nizam died in 1803, and was succeeded by his son, Sekundur Jah.

Embassy to Persia.

During Lord Wellesley's administration an imposing embassy was despatched to Persia in 1800, under Captain (afterwards Sir John) Malcolm to establish British influence in Central Asia, and prevent Zemann Shah's threatened invasion of India. This latter object had already been effected by a native envoy, Mehndi Ali, previously sent to the Persian Court. It resulted in the conclusion of a treaty, of both a political and commercial nature, between the two countries.

Suddur Court.

The Suddur Court at Kalkutta, the highest *local* Court of Appeal, was reconstructed, the Governor-General and Council being divested of their judicial functions, and an able judicial officer appointed as President. Mr. H. T. Colebrooke, a civil servant and a profound Oriental scholar, was selected for this office.

College at Fort William.

Lord Wellesley founded a college at Kalkutta on a princely scale for the purpose of teaching young civil servants, the laws, literature, and languages of the people of India. This institution was ordered to be abolished by the Court of Directors in 1802, though afterwards retained on a reduced scale for Bengal civil servants only. It gave rise to the foundation soon after of Haileybury College in England for the instruction of students of the Indian Civil service.

Private Trade.

The Governor-General gave great encouragement to free trade between the ports of India and London in India-built ships, and was decidedly of opinion that a well-organized system of such intercourse was indispensable to the interests both of the company and the nation. To this the Directors of the East India Company were entirely opposed, and Lord Wellesley's proceedings in this matter were severely condemned.

It was during Lord Wellesley's rule that Kalkutta was greatly improved in appearance; to him, the Government House, the residence at Barrakpūr, some colleges and other edifices owe their erection.

During the years 1803-5, the disputes between Lord Wellesley and the India House were frequent, and the Governor-General's policy and government were alike denounced and humiliated. Two slight efforts at an impeachment on account of his proceedings in Oudh and the Karnatik were made in 1806 but ended in nothing. Thirty years afterwards his great and brilliant services were recognised by a grant of £20,000, and an order for his statue to be placed in the India House.

In January, 1799, Mr. Cherry, the British Resident at Benares, as well as some other Europeans were murdered by Vizier Ali, who had been displaced from the Viziership of Oudh by Sir John Shore and pensioned at Benares. Detachments were sent against Vizier Ali, who was at length delivered up by the Rājpūt Rājā of Jeipūr, with whom he had taken refuge. The reigning Vizier of Oudh, Saādut Ali, who was unwilling to pay for an additional military force, pressed upon him by the British Government, proposed to abdicate, but afterwards abandoned all intention of doing so. Upon this there ensued a discussion lasting two years, when on 10th November, 1801, a treaty was signed by the Nabob, by which he ceded to the Company districts yielding 135 laks yearly, retaining for himself territory bringing in a little more than 1 krore of rupees in revenue. The safety of Oudh was thus secured by a powerful British force, not only from invasion from the north but from Maratta inroads as well.

Oudh.

Tuljāji, the Raja of Tanjūr having adopted one Surfoji, a youth of promise, educated by the Missionary Schwartz, died in 1786. Objection was taken at first to Surfoji, and the late Rājā's half-brother, Amīr-Singh, was placed on the throne, but his misconduct and the perfectly unexceptionable character of the adoption having been afterwards recognised, Surfoji was reinstated by Lord Wellesley. As there were debts due, the Company assumed the administration of this state, allowing the Rājā 1 lakh of pagodas yearly as well as one-fifth of its net revenue. Its independence thus expired 150 years after its foundation by Shahji, the father of Siwuji.

Tanjūr.

On the death of the Nabob, Omdut-ul-omrah, the throne of the Karnatik was offered to his *reputed* son on the proviso that the British Government should exercise all civil and military power, the late Nabob and his father having been engaged in a clandestine correspon-

The Karnatik.

dence with Tippū in violation of the treaty of 1792. As these conditions were refused, it was offered on the same terms to Azim-ul-omrah, the deceased abob's brother, who accepted it. The Karnatik was thus in 1801 annexed to the Madras Presidency, and one-fifth of its revenues assigned to the nominal Nabob for himself and his family.

The Marattas.

Nāna Furnavis, the great Maratta statesman, died in 1800. He is reported to have possessed humanity, veracity, and honesty of purpose, qualities very rare among orientals, and with him it was also said, "had departed all the wisdom and moderation of the Maratta government." Among the Maratta chieftains who played an important part during Lord Wellesley's administration was Yēshwunt Rao Holkar, the illegitimate son of Tokaji Holkar, commander of the army under the Regent Aylah-Bāi, the widow of the son of the first founder of the family Mulhar Rao. Aylah-Bāi died in 1795 and Tokaji in 1797. Yēshwunt Rao had fled to Nāgpūr after the defeat and death of his brother Mulhar Rao by Sindia, but within two years he managed to raise an army of 70,000 men, with which he laid waste the province of Malwa, and defeated Sindia's army in 1801, taking Ujein the capital. He was however in turn routed by Sindia on 14th October, 1801, and his own capital Indore captured and sacked. Recovering from this heavy blow, he in 1802 moved down with a force on Pūna, ostensibly to claim the Peishwa's protection against Sindia, but really to avenge the death of his brother Vittoji, whom Bāji Rao II. had cruelly put to death in 1801. Notwithstanding the aid from Sindia of ten battalions of foot and a large body of cavalry in addition to his own army Bāji Rao was defeated by Holkar at Pūna on 25th October, 1802, and fled to Bassein. Holkar then placed a nephew of the Peishwā on the throne and after a time gave up the city of Pūna to indiscriminate plunder.

Meanwhile the important treaty of **Bassein** was concluded between the British Government and Bāji Rao on 31st December, 1802, providing that "(*a*) a British force should be stationed in the Peishwa's territories and that districts in the Dekhun yielding 26 laks yearly (afterwards exchanged for districts in Bundelkund yielding 36 laks) be assigned for their support; (*b*) the Peishwa to entertain no European belonging to any nation at war with England and to engage in no hostilities or negotiations without the Company's consent; (*c*) to refer all his claims on the Nizam and the Geikwar to the Governor-General's arbitration; and (*d*) to guarantee to his Southern Jagīrdars the full enjoyment of all their rights." This treaty greatly offended Sindia, Holkar, and the Nāgpūr Rājā, whose plans were thus thwarted by Lord Wellesley's policy, and a coalition was formed among them to frustrate it. The Peishwā himself even repented of his act after he had signed it. Holkar retired from Pūna in 1803 leaving 1500 troops with Amrut Rao, Bāji Rao's brother, who hearing of General Wellesley's advance, had resolved to fire the city, but the general arrived in time to save it. Bāji Rao entered his capital on 13th May, 1803 surrounded by British troops. In August of that year war ensued between the British Government and Sindia allied with the Nāgpūr Rājā (see Wars III.) during which Holkar engaged in predatory expeditions in Hindūsthān.

Geikwar.

The system of subsidiary alliances was also extended to the dominions of Anund Rao Geikwar in 1800. He was the eldest son of Futteh Singh, who died in 1792, and the grandson of Damaji Geikwar who died in 1768. Five battalions of troops were sent to Anund Rao and districts yielding between 11 and 12 laks yearly were assigned for their support. Major Walker was appointed Resident at the Court at Baroda, and not only did he improve the financial resources of this state, but he successfully the means of defraying the cost of Sindia's army at that city. Māhādāji Sindia died in February, 1794, and had bequeathed to his successor, Dowlut Rao, a youth of thirteen and his grand-nephew, besides an excellent native army, a territory extending from the Sutlej to Allahabād, two-thirds of Malwa, and the finest provinces in the Dekhun.

Oudh.

It was during the administration of Sir John Shore that a change was made in the Oudh succession. In 1797 the Nabob Vizier died, worn out with excesses, and the succession was transferred to his reputed son Vizier Ali, but as it was subsequently found that all the late Nabob's children were illegitimate, the throne was offered in 1798 to his brother Saādut Ali, subject to the following conditions: (*a*) the British troops in Oudh to number 10,000 with an annual payment on their account of 76 laks of rupees; (*b*) the fort of Allahabād to be made over to the English; (*c*) the Nabob to maintain only 35,000 troops, and to enter into no negotiation with any foreign power without the consent of the British Government. To these Saādut Ali consented, and on 21st January, 1798, he was proclaimed Nabob Vizier of Oudh.

Madras.

Mahomed Ali, the Nabob of the Karnatik, died in 1795, after a reign of nearly fifty years, and was succeeded by his son Omdut-ūl-Omrah. Owing to the indebtedness of this prince, the country was fast going to ruin, and it was from disputes with the Supreme Government on this question that the Madras Governor, Lord Hobart, was recalled by the Court of Directors in 1797.

Education.—In 1795 a Sungskrut College was established at Benares for the encouragement of native learning. A Madrissa (Mahomedan College) had previously been founded by Mr. Hastings at Kalkutta in 1781.

Missionary Societies.—It is worthy of note that the first Protestant Missionary Society at Kalkutta was founded during this administration; the missionaries were Messrs. Carey and Thomas, who arrived in India in 1794. Madras had however been the first in the field, having set on foot a mission so early as 1726. Kiemander the Lutheran missionary had established himself at Kuddalūr in 1750, thence he removed in 1758 to Kalkutta, and in 1770 erected a church in which he preached the Gospel to the heathen.

Names of Note.—**Māhādāji Sindia,** (died 1794), "a man of great political sagacity and considerable genius, of deep artifice, restless ambition and implacable revenge," **Mahomed Ali,** (died 1795,) Nabob of the Karnatik.

(IV.) EARL MORNINGTON (AFTERWARDS MARQUIS WELLESLEY) GOVERNOR-GENERAL (A.D. 1798—1805).

Governors of Madras.		*Governor of Bombay.*	
LORD CLIVE . . .	1798-1802	JONATHAN DUNCAN . .	1795-
LORD W. C. BENTINCK	1802-		

Appointment.—Made in 1797, and Lord Mornington arrived at Kalkutta on 17th May, 1798. Was born in Ireland in 1760, and had, previously to his appointment as Governor-General, been for four years a member of the Board of Control.

Resignation.—In July, 1805. Was recalled by the Court of Directors on account of his lavish expenditure of public money, and his great schemes of conquest and extension of empire. He had previously (in 1802) resigned office, but was solicited to remain another year. He died on 26th September, 1842, in his 83rd year.

Character.—Lord Wellesley displayed much vigour and energy in his administration, and he possessed a peculiar genius for creating and consolidating an empire. His policy of establishing subsidiary alliances through-

Wars.—I. With Yēshwunt Rao Holkar, who still exhibited a vigorous and daring spirit, and had collected a force of about 12,000 horse and 3,000 foot with 30 guns. Failing to secure the assistance of the Jeipūr Rājā, he fled in 1805 to the Punjāb whither Lord Lake followed him. Runjit Singh (then 25 years old) who was at the time laying the foundation of the great Sikh kingdom, refused all aid to Holkar, and this compelled him to sue for peace. A treaty of the most lenient kind was entered into with Holkar in January 1806, by which (*a*) "all his dominions south of the Chumbul, including Rampūra, were restored to him, the British Government engaging not to interfere with any of the Rājās or dependants of the Holkar family south of it, and withdrawing their protection from the states west of the Jumna, with whom alliances had been formed two years before; (*b*) not to entertain Europeans in his service without the permission of Government." By this treaty British protection was withdrawn from the Rājās of Jeipūr and Būndi, and both were left to the tender mercies of Holkar, who speedily extorted 18 laks from the former prince, and did not in fact scruple to violate every article of the treaty he had signed. On his return to his own dominions Holkar exhorted the other Maratta princes to make head against their common enemy, the English, but none responded to the call. II. In July, 1806, occurred the first Sepoy mutiny at Vellore (Vellūr), a fortress distant about ninety miles from Madras, where Tippū Sūltān's family and adherents resided. The garrison consisted of about 370 Europeans of the 69th Regiment and 1500 Sepoys of the 1st and 23rd Madras Regiments, many of the latter being Maisūr Mahomedans. The Sepoys mutinied on 10th July, and massacred thirteen English officers and a large number of European soldiers, but Colonel Gillespie, with a portion of the 19th Dragoons speedily arrived from Arkot, nine miles distant, and saved the survivors. Between three and four hundred of the mutineers were killed, seventeen were hanged and a large number were dismissed the service. The cause of the mutiny was attributed to innovations made in the dress of the Sepoys by Sir John Cradock, the Commander-in-chief, as well as to complicity and intrigue on the part of the members of Tippū's family; the latter were removed without delay to Kalkutta, and both the Madras Governor, Lord Bentinck, and Sir John Cradock were recalled by the Court of Directors.

Sindia.

Memorable Events.—In 1805 a new treaty was entered into with Sindia, after he had allowed the English Resident to leave his Court unmolested. By it, (*a*) "the former treaty of **Anjengaon** was confirmed, (*b*) Gohud and the fort of Gwālior were restored to him on his agreeing to pay 3 laks from their revenues to the Rānā. (*c*) Pensions were settled on himself, his wife and his daughter, (*d*) the Chumbul was made the boundary of the two states, and the British Government were to enter into no treaties with the Rājas of Udipūr, Jodhpūr, or with Sindia's tributaries, the chiefs in Mālwa, and Mēwar, (or Marwar), and (*e*) Sindia never to admit Sirji Rao Ghātkē into his counsels." This treaty was ratified on 25th December, 1805.

Nizam.

During the years 1806-7 the Nizam evinced a desire to dissolve his connection with the East-India Company, and began to intrigue with Sindia and Holkar, but Mir Alum, his minister being unfavourable to this scheme, and fearing for his life, fled to the British Presidency. Sir George Barlow at once directed the Nizam to restore Mir Alum to his office and further banished all who were hostile to the British alliance.

Peishwa.

In like manner he refused, though at the instance of the Court of Directors, to modify the treaty of **Bassein**, as it would supply means to the Marattas of prosecuting designs hostile to British interests, and revive their ancient influence and power.

Revenue and Debt.

Sir George Barlow was enabled by the cessation of war to reduce the annual expenditure of the empire; the previous yearly deficit was converted into a surplus, which lasted with a few variations till the first Burmese war in 1823. In the year preceding Lord Wellesley's arrival the Indian revenue was eight krores (£8,000,000), and the debt 17 krores (£17,000,000); when he left India the former had increased to fifteen and a half krores, and the debt to 31 krores.

(VII.) VISCOUNT (AFTERWARDS EARL) MINTO, GOVERNOR-GENERAL (A.D. 1807-13).

Governors of Madras.		*Governors of Bombay.*	
WILLIAM PETRIE (Provisional)	1807	JONATHAN DUNCAN.	1795-1811
SIR GEO. H. BARLOW.	1807-13	GEORGE BROWN . .	1811-12
		SIR EVAN NEPEAN .	1812-

Appointment.—In 1806, landed at Kalkutta in July, 1807. He was a well-trained politician, and had previously been President of the Board of Control.

Resignation.—Lord Minto was suspended in 1812, but he did not resign his office to his successor, Lord Moira, till October, 1813, in which year he returned to England. He died shortly afterwards at Malta in the sixty-third year of his age.

Character.—He was a statesman of sound judgment, mild and moderate in his views, but without any deficiency of firmness. His previous duties in the Board of Control had given him an enlarged comprehension of Indian questions; though of a conciliatory disposition, he never dreaded responsibility, and displayed, when occasion required, great promptitude and decision.

Wars. I. In 1809 Amir Khān, a predatory robber, and the recognised chief of the Patans, who had in ten years gradually created a principality yielding a yearly revenue of fifteen laks, attacked the Nāgpūr territory in the name of Holkar, with a force of 40,000 horse and 24,000 Pindāris, and though the Rājā was only an ally of the Company, the Governor-General ordered two armies into the field for the defence of his kingdom. Amir Khān was twice defeated by the Nāgpūr army under Sādik Ali ; a British force took his capital, Indore, and would have extinguished him had not the troops been recalled by Lord Minto. II. In the same year there occurred a mutiny in the Madras army, partly caused, it is believed, by an abrupt order of Sir George Barlow, the Governor, with reference to the abolition of the "*tent contract*," by which commanding officers drew a fixed monthly allowance for providing their men, when in the field, with camp-equipage. The dissatisfaction was general, and when the Governor further suspended several officers of rank for having promoted a memorial to the Governor-General, setting forth the grievances of the Madras army, the mutiny broke out. The troops at Jālna and Heidurabād, and the Company's European regiment at Masulipatam (Machlīpatanam) conceived the idea of marching on Madras and seizing the Government, but the only collision which occurred was at Seringapatam, where two battalions of Sepoys had an encounter with the king's troops. At this crisis Lord Minto arrived at Madras in 1810, and by conciliation and firmness restored tranquillity. A general amnesty was granted, excluding those only who had taken a leading part in the disaffection. This mutiny ultimately led to the recall of Sir George Barlow by the Court of Directors. III. In 1810 an expedition was fitted out at the three Presidencies for the capture of the French islands of Bourbon and Mauritius, the former was taken by Colonel Keating in July, and the latter by General Abercromby on 1st December. The island of Java was also reduced in 1811, Lord Minto accompanying the expedition as a volunteer.

On 4th August the troops, numbering 6,000, under the command of Sir Samuel Auchmuty, disembarked and occupied Batavia; on 26th the Dutch entrenched camp at Cornelis was carried, and on 16th September the Dutch General Jansens gave himself up, and surrendered to the English Java and all its dependencies.

Holkar.

Memorable Events.—After Yeshwunt Rao Holkar's return to his own dominions in 1806, a mutiny occurred among his troops, who proclaimed a little boy, Khundeh Rao, his nephew, as their sovereign. This child as well as his brother Kāshi Rao was soon after poisoned by Holkar, and this double murder is supposed to have induced fits of insanity, from which he died on 20th October, 1811.

Bundelkund.

During Sir George Barlow's administration, the province of Bundelkund, owing to the non-interfering policy then in vogue, was overrun by a number of military adventurers, and the forts held by chieftains who were always at feud with each other. As certain districts in this province were held by the English for the support of the subsidiary force with the Peishwā, Lord Minto in 1807 determined to interfere, and suppress all intestine disorder. The two forts of Ajigarh and Kalinjer, the strongholds of the banditti which infested the country, were taken, and peace was restored to that part of India.

Sikhs.

The Sikh community, since the battle of Paniput in 1761, had been gradually enlarging itself in the Punjāb. Churrut Singh, the head of one of their twelve fraternities or "*misils*," encroached on his neighbours, and this was followed by his successor, Māhā Singh, who died in 1792, leaving a son Runjīt Singh, who increased his power over the different chiefs in the Punjāb, and in 1806 extended his conquests to the Sutlej. South of this river is Sirhind, with several independent Sikh States, such as Puttiāla, Jhind, and Keithul. These he wished to annex, but the Sirhind chiefs in 1808 sought the protection of the British Government, and Lord Minto sent Mr. Charles Metcalfe, a Bengal civilian, with an embassy to Runjīt Singh to frustrate his intentions. Runjīt nevertheless occupied Sirhind, compelling nearly all the chieftains to acknowledge his authority. A British army was therefore assembled under Colonel Ochterlony, and Runjīt was directed to restore all the districts he had taken. It ended in a treaty, concluded on 25th April, 1809, by which Runjīt was restricted to his territory on the north of the Sutlej, and agreed to keep from all encroachments to the south of it, and this he observed with scrupulous fidelity.

Kābūl.

An embassy was sent in 1808, under Mr. (afterwards the Honourable) Mountstuart Elphinstone, to Shah Sūjah the ruler of Afghānisthān, to form a defensive alliance against a French invasion then apprehended. No treaty was effected, as Shah Sūjah was soon after driven from his throne, and had to seek refuge across the Indus. From the same alarm of a French invasion Lord Minto despatched Colonel Malcolm in 1808 again to Persia, but on the Shah refusing to allow him to advance to Teherān, and insisting on his negotiating with his son, then at Shiraz, Colonel Malcolm declined to go any further, and returned to Kalkutta. In 1809 Sir Harford Jones proceeded to Persia as ambassador, while Colonel Malcolm was again sent there from India on a second embassy. In March a treaty was made by which—" (*a*) Great Britain engaged to pay £100,000 a year, as a subsidy, so long as the Shah was at war with Russia, and to provide arms, artillery, men, and officers; (*b*) The Shah to assist in repelling any attempt made by the French to invade the Company's territories." The two embassies cost thirty-eight laks of rupees, and ended in both envoys being superseded by Sir Gore Ouseley, appointed as ambassador from England.

Persia.

Sir George Barlow, the Governor of Madras, appears to have made himself very unpopular in his Presidency, first in 1808, by unjustly removing Mr. Sherson, a civil servant from his situation, and afterwards prosecuting him, and again by an unwarrantable interference with the Karnatik Commission, appointed by Act of Parliament to inquire into the debts of the Nabob, for which the Company was responsible.

Madras.

It was during Lord Minto's administration that piracy was suppressed for a time on the Arabian coast, by the despatch, in 1809, of an expedition to take Ras-el-Keima, their stronghold, as well as other towns of inferior note. The piratical ports on the Malabar coast, belonging to the Kolapūr and Sāwunt Wari chiefs, were also surrendered under certain provisoes.

Piracy suppressed.

Towards the end of Lord Minto's rule in 1812, the Pindāris, a class of the lowest freebooters, began to attack British territory. They had, in the time of Aurungzib, accompanied for the sake of plunder the Maratta armies in their various expeditions, numbers of them engaging in the service of both Holkar and Sindia. Though poorly armed they were all mounted, and managed to make marches of from thirty to forty miles a day. When plundering villages they committed the most unheard-of atrocities on the wretched inhabitants. In 1808 the principal Pindāri leaders of note were Dost Mahomed and Wassil Mahomed (sons of a former chief, Hirun), Chetū and Kurrim Khān. Chetū possessed five districts, made over to him by Sindia ; his head quarters were at Nimar, among the hills lying between the Nurbudda and the Vindaya range. Kurrim Khān also obtained lands from Sindia, and by gradual encroachment created in 1806 a principality yielding 16 laks of rupees

The Pindāris.

in revenue. Up to 1812 the Pindāris had confined their depredations to Malwa, Rajpūtāna and Berar, but in that year they, for the first time, under the leadership of Dost Mahomed, entered the Company's district of Mirzapūr, plundered it and then disappeared. The Governor-General hesitated to take any effectual steps towards punishing these miscreants, from a dread of exciting a new Maratta war, and their extirpation was thus left to his successor, Lord Moira.

Permanent Settlement.

The permanent settlement, introduced by Lord Cornwallis in 1793, became, up to the end of Lord Minto's rule in 1813, the means of ejecting most of the old Zumindars who had, by the settlement, been declared sole proprietors under certain provisoes, and it had introduced others in their stead, who, though wealthy, were strangers to the ryots. The condition of the cultivator had deteriorated, and this was greatly hastened by Reg. VII. of 1799, which permitted the Zumindar to distrain summarily and without any limitation. This, coupled with the system of sub-letting introduced with the permanent settlement, greatly contracted the cultivated area of the Province, and both impoverished and depopulated the country. By Reg. V. of 1812 the Zumindars were allowed to form any engagements they pleased with their ryots, except with those who had possessed fields twelve years before the introduction of the settlement, and they naturally made this an engine for illegal exactions and extortion in the matter of rents. The infliction of a permanent settlement on those provinces in the North-west, either ceded or conquered during Lord Wellesley's administration, was greatly desired by him as well as by his successors, Sir George Barlow and Lord Minto, but it was specially prohibited by the Court of Directors in 1813, and periodical settlements made instead. Neither was the permanent settlement extended to Madras, because no Zumindars could be found there.

General (afterwards Sir Thomas) Munro partly introduced the Ryot-wari system, the chief characteristics of which were, that the government was regarded as the absolute proprietor of the land, and a settlement was made by it with the ryot from year to year, the assessment being equal to one-third of the produce. The fields were distributed among the villagers by the head man, and where the crops of any particular fields failed, the whole village was assessed to the extent of ten per cent. on the deficiency.

Ryot-wari System.

The provisions laid down in the time of Lord Cornwallis for both civil and criminal jurisprudence failed also in part. To so great an extent was litigation carried on during Lord Minto's rule, that additional courts had to be established, and the cost of judicial establishments was raised in fifteen years from thirty to eighty laks a year. The Mūnsiffs also were increased both in number and pay. Magistrates were unable sometimes to take up cases for months together, while the "Daroga," or head police-officer of a district, a new creation from 1793, and, as usual, inadequately paid, indemnified himself by extortion, and reaped a harvest from every crime. Dacoity (or gang robbery) had greatly increased throughout the country, and was followed by persons who were agriculturists and mechanics *by day*, but "dacoits" at night under professional leaders.

Civil and Criminal Jurisprudence.

The renewal of the Company's Charter occupied the attention of both the Court of Directors and the Board of Control several years before the expiry of the act, the main question at issue being the opening of the out-ports to import trade, to which the India House raised the gravest objections. Both manufactures and commerce had greatly increased since 1793,

Charter Bill of 1813.

as while the imports of Indian textile fabrics had fallen from three and a-half krores (£3,500,000) a year to half a krore, the export of Manchester cottons to India had increased from 7,000 rupees a year to ten laks (£100,000). The India bill of 1813 was introduced by Lord Castlereagh into the House of Commons on the 22nd March, its chief provisions being:—"(*a*) The continuance for a further period of twenty years of the government of British India by the Company, with liberty to pursue their trade; (*b*) The whole British nation to be admitted to the import and export trade, but no private vessel to be above 400 tons in burden; (*c*) The exclusive China trade to be restricted to the Company; (*d*) Europeans to be permitted to go to India on obtaining a license from either the Court of Directors, or Board of Control, but the local Indian authorities at liberty to cancel it at their discretion; (*e*) Provision to be made out of the revenues for public instruction, and for an ecclesiastical establishment in India." To this bill great opposition was made by the Court of Directors, and the evidence of Warren Hastings (then in his eightieth year), Lord Teignmouth, Mr. C. Grant, Colonels Malcolm and Munro, and of numerous other witnesses, was adduced in their favour. Even Lord Wellesley abandoned his former opinions and pleaded for the Company's exclusive trade, but all was in vain. The bill passed, and struck the first blow at the Company as a monopoly, and Indian commerce was at last opened out to English capital and enterprise.

Indian Trade.

From 1800 to 1810 the average annual value of goods imported into India from England, was about £8,500,000, and that exported from India to England nearly £3,000,000. They consisted mainly of tea, raw silk, piece-goods, sugar, pepper, saltpetre, indigo, and cotton. The Company's fleet numbered 104 ships, ranging from 500 to 1,200 tons each, and manned by 7,000 seamen.

The export of raw silk in 1750 from Bengal was only 80,000 lbs.; in 1770 it was 320,000 lbs.; owing to great improvements having been effected, it rose in 1785 to 576,175 lbs., but in consequence of the cheapening of English cotton goods it decreased in 1805 to 300,000 lbs. In 1786 about 245,000 lbs. of indigo were exported to England, but in 1795 it rose to 2,644,700 lbs., and in 1810 to 5,520,870 lbs. The finest indigo was produced in the Bengal districts of Jessore and Kishnagur. In 1790 but 100 or 200 tons were exported from Bengal, in 1807 it amounted to over 5,000 tons. The Indian revenue in 1809-10 was £15,525,055, and the debt £28,897,742.

Names of Note.—**Sir James Mackintosh**, Recorder of Bombay (1765-1832). **Yēshwunt Rao Holkar**, a powerful Maratta chieftain (died 1811). **Mir Alūm**, the Nizam's prime minister (died 1808). **Reverend Henry Martyn** (1781-1812).

(VIII.) EARL MOIRA (AFTERWARDS MARQUIS HASTINGS), GOVERNOR-GENERAL (A.D. 1813-23).

Governors of Madras.		*Governors of Bombay.*	
GEN. J. ABERCROMBY	1813-14	SIR EVAN NEPEAN	1812-19
RT. HON. H. ELLIOTT	1814-20	HON. MOUNTST. ELPHINSTONE	1819-
SIR THOMAS MUNRO	1820-		

Appointment.—Made in 1813, and he arrived at Kalkutta on 4th October of that year. Lord Hastings at the same time held the post of Commander-in-chief of India. He was fifty-nine years old when he became Governor-General, and had previously served in the army, and in great public and political stations.

Resignation.—In January, 1823, when he made over his office to Mr. John Adam, the senior member of Council. On his return to Europe an attempt was made to grant him £5,000 a year for twenty years, but it was unsuccessful. He had previously received £10,000 in

1819, at the close of the Maratta war. In 1824 he was appointed Governor of Malta, but died on 29th November, 1825.

Character.—He was zealous and able, of great vigour of mind and decision, and possessed a very kindly disposition. In the performance of his duties he was very assiduous, labouring, it is said, between seven and eight hours a day for nine years. Though not possessing, perhaps, the political genius of Lord Wellesley, he nevertheless showed administrative talent of a high order, and greatly consolidated British power in India. In person he was tall and commanding.

Wars.—I. With the Rājā of Nipāl, whose subjects, the Gūrkhas, had in 1812 committed several depredations in the British districts of Gorukpūr and Tirhūt, and though threatened by Lord Minto with reprisals unless the districts were given up, had refused to do so. Borrowing two krores of rupees from the Nabob of Oudh, Lord Hastings in 1814 assembled an army of 30,000 men with 60 guns, which was to penetrate the hilly and difficult country of Nipāl simultaneously in four separate divisions. The first, under General Wood, was repulsed at the stockade of Jitpore on 14th January, 1814, and forced to retreat. The second, commanded by General Gillespie, failed miserably in October, 1814, in an attack on the fortified position of Kalunga, where the commander fell mortally wounded. The third, under General Marley, 8,000 strong, also suffered reverses. This division did little or nothing during the war. The fourth, under General (afterwards Sir David) Ochterlony, was more successful. On 1st November, 1814, he captured the fort of Nālāgur, and by April, 1815, had taken all the Gūrkha fortresses except Maloun. Meanwhile Almora, the capital of Kumaon, fell on 27th April to Colonel Nicolls, upon which the fort of Maloun was surrendered to Ochterlony by Umur Singh, the Gūrkha general. After an unsuccessful attempt to negotiate a treaty, the war was renewed, and Mukwānpore, fifty miles only from the capital, Katmandū, was taken by the same commander. Negotiations then took place in earnest, and a treaty was signed on 2nd March, 1816, by which—"(*a*) the Nipāl Rājā agreed to resign all claims on the hill Rājās west of the Kāli river; (*b*) To cede the belt of low lands called the 'terrāi;' (*c*) To restore the territory of Sikkim and receive a British resident." Unlike other Indian treaties this has always been faithfully observed by the Gūrkhas. The Nipāl war lasted about eighteen months, and cost fifty-four laks of rupees.

II. In 1816 an insurrection took place at Bareilly in the North-West provinces, owing to the imposition of a house-tax for the support of the municipal police, which was resisted by the Rohilla population. A conflict ensued between them and the Government troops, in which the former lost 400 killed, besides a large number wounded. About the same time the strong fortress of Hattras, on the borders of Rohilkund, belonging to a Zumindar named Dyaram, who refused to admit any government servant into his town, was reduced in a few hours.

III. With the Peishwā (Bāji Rao II.) on 5th November, 1817, mainly through his minister, the notorious Trimbukji Danglia, by whom a general confederacy against the Company's government was organized in 1815. This man was also instrumental in the murder that same year, at the sacred city of Punderpūr, of Gungādhur Shāstri, the Geikwar's minister, sent to Pūna to settle with the Peishwā about the renewal of the lease of the Ahmedabād district, and upon other questions then at issue between the two states. The resident, Mr. Mountstuart Elphinstone, finding on enquiry that Trimbukji was a guilty party in the murder, requested him to be given up, which, after some hesitation, was done on 25th September, 1815, and the minister was confined at

Tanna, whence he escaped in September, 1816. After this Bāji Rao's hostility became so apparent that the resident demanded the surrender of Trimbukji within a month, and also of three fortresses as a security; the former was not forthcoming, but the latter were made over as requested. On 5th June, 1817, the Peishwā signed a treaty whereby—"(*a*) he agreed to renounce Trimbukji for ever, and to give up the character of supreme head of the Maratta Empire; (*b*) To dismiss all foreign agents, and refer all matters in dispute to the Company's government; (*c*) To resign all his rights to Saugor and Bundelkund; and, (*d*) In lieu of the auxiliary force he was bound to maintain of 5000 horse and 3000 foot, to cede territory yielding twenty-four laks a year." On 5th November, 1817, the Peishwā plunged into hostilities, but his army was easily and speedily defeated at the battle of Kirki by Colonel Burr with the small force at his disposal. On 17th November the city of Pūna surrendered to General Smith, and thus fell the power of the Peishwā just one hundred years after its first establishment by Ballāji Vishwanath in 1717. On 1st January, 1818, was fought the battle of Korigaon near Pūna, in which a British force of one infantry battalion, 300 irregular horse, and 24 artillerymen with two small guns, under Captain Stanton, kept at bay the whole army of the Peishwā, 25,000 strong. The Peishwā fled thence to the Karnatik, followed up by General Smith, who defeated him at Ashti on 19th February, 1818; he escaped, but afterwards delivered himself up to Sir John Malcolm, near Mhow, in the following May. He was subsequently pensioned on eight laks of rupees a year at Bithūr near Kaunpore (Kanhpūr). His dominions, excepting a portion yielding fifteen laks a year, which was created into a principality for the Rājā of Sattara, a descendant of the family of Siwuji, were incorporated into the Company's territories.

IV. With Appa Sahēb, Rājā of Nāgpūr, on 26th

November, 1817. Lord Hastings, on 27th May, 1816, had made a subsidiary alliance with the Regent, Appa Sahēb, nephew of the reigning Rajā, Persaji, who was idiotic, blind and palsied. This treaty provided—"(*a*) that 6,000 infantry, a regiment of cavalry, and some artillery should be supplied to the Nāgpūr state at an expense of 7½ laks a year; (*b*) The Rājā not to enter into any foreign negotiation without the consent of the British Government." On 1st February, 1817, the Rājā was found dead, and on inquiry it was ascertained he had been strangled by Appa Sahēb's orders. He had also engaged in secret correspondence with the Peishwā, Bāji Rao, and on 26th November, 1817, Mr. Jenkins, the Resident, and about 1350 rank and file, were attacked at Sitābuldi by the Rāja's entire army, numbering 18,000 men, but the latter were completely defeated. Terms were afterwards dictated to Appa Sahēb, who on 16th December, agreed—"(*a*) to deliver up his ordnance and stores; (*b*) to disband his Arabs at once, and afterwards his other troops, and then repair to the Residency till the terms of the treaty were arranged." As he still harboured hostile designs against the British Government, the Rājā was placed in confinement, but he managed to escape by stratagem when on his way to Allahabād, whither he was being taken. He fled to the Jodhpūr Rājā, who refused to befriend him, but he subsequently obtained refuge at Lahore, and died a pensioner on Runjīt Singh's bounty. Persaji, the next heir, was raised to the throne of Nāgpūr.

V. With Holkar, on 16th December, 1817. On Yēshwunt Rao's death, in 1811, his favourite concubine, Tūlsi Bāi, adopted a son of his, and ruled the country herself as Regent, but the state was distracted with two factions, the Marattas and the Patāns, and was rapidly becoming completely disorganised. Hearing of the Peishwā having risen in arms in 1817, the chiefs decided on a war with the English, and suspecting Tūlsi

Bāi of a leaning towards a British alliance, they beheaded her on 20th December. The next day (21st), Sir Thomas Hislop engaged Holkar's army at Mehidpūr, and defeated it, taking sixty-three guns and a large quantity of stores. A treaty was soon after concluded at Mundesūr, by which cessions of territory were made, not only to the Company but to other chiefs also, and Holkar's power thus became irretrievably broken.

VI. With the Pindāris, in 1817-18. When Lord Hastings arrived in India, it was calculated that there were 50,000 of these freebooters in Central India subsisting on plunder. In September, 1815, after assembling in great force under Chetū, at Nimar, they in October attacked the Nizam's territories, returning with an immense booty. In February, 1816, they plundered the northern Sirkars, sacking the civil station of Guntūr, and disappearing as usual with astonishing celerity—339 Company's villages were plundered, 182 persons killed, 500 wounded, and 3,600 tortured, the entire loss of property being estimated at 25 laks of rupees. In 1816-17, they attacked the Company's district of Kimedi, burning a portion of the town of Ganjam, while another body overran the Nāgpūr and Heidurabād territories. The Pindāris having managed to break through a force of 32,000 British troops besides the Nāgpūr, Nizām's and Pūna contingents, it was determined to use the most rigorous efforts to suppress them, and Sindia was requested to co-operate in this measure, which he reluctantly promised to do on certain conditions. The Pindāris were gradually hemmed in by eight different armies, so arranged as to converge on their haunts. Kurrim Khān was defeated by General Donkin, his elephants, standards, &c. captured, and the other chiefs surrendered one after the other. Kurrim Khān was placed on an estate in the Gorukpūr district—Wassil Mahomed poisoned himself while under restraint at Ghazipūr, and the notorious Chetū, after being hunted out of his old haunts and deserted by all, was devoured by tigers in a dense jungle in which he had hidden himself. The Pindāris were thus extirpated and their bands utterly extinguished. In conjunction with this war, and those waged against Holkar and the Peishwā, numerous forts—among them Talneir, Malligaon, and Asirgarh, mostly garrisoned by Arab mercenaries—were subsequently captured.

VII. On 26th March, 1819, owing to the misconduct of Barmulji, the Rao of Kutch, the Bombay Government took Bhūj, his capital, and placed his son, Rao Desal, on the throne in his stead. Treaties were formed with the new government, as also with two of the Amirs of Sindh.

VIII. In September, 1819, an expedition was despatched from Bombay to attack Ras-el-Keima, in Arabia; it was occupied, and the Sheik promised to abstain from piracy and other barbarous customs. Another Arab tribe, the Beni-bu-ali, were also reduced by Sir Lionel Smith. In 1820, the town of Mocha, in the Red Sea, where the English agent had been ill-treated, was bombarded, and nearly reduced to ashes.

Memorable Events.—On Lord Hastings' assumption of the Governor-Generalship in 1813, Holkar's government was in a state of anarchy, the Gūrkhas were encroaching on British territory, Sindia and Amir Khān were busy in Rājpūtāna promoting their own individual aggrandisement, the Peishwā was anxious to throw off the British yoke, and the Pindāris were spreading desolation throughout an immense extent of territory. At its close, the Gūrkhas had been defeated, the power of the Marattas irretrievably broken, the Pindāris extirpated as a predatory body; twenty-eight actions had been fought in the field, 120 forts captured, and the greater portion of the Peishwā's dominions annexed to British territory.

Rise of Gūrkha power.

The country of Nipāl was colonized by a band of Rājpūts as early as the fourteenth century; one of the chiefs, Prithi-Naryun, in the eighteenth century, subdued the others, and after founding a dynasty died, in 1771, leaving the succession to a grandson, who, being put to death in 1805, his son, an infant, was proclaimed Rājā. A Gūrkha army was subsequently defeated by the Emperor of China, to whom they were compelled to pay tribute. They afterwards entered the Punjāb territory, and engaged in an unsuccessful war with Runjīt Singh on the upper Sutlej. Still later, between 1809 and 1813, they encroached on British territory, taking more than 200 villages, and laying claim to the districts of Būtwal and Seoraj, which brought about the war of 1814.

Bhopāl.

The small principality of Bhopāl, which was so nobly defended in 1813 by Vizier Mahomed against the conjoint forces of Sindia and the Nāgpūr Rājā, who had eventually to raise the siege, is situate in Malwa, in the valley of the Nurbudda, and was founded by an Afghān favourite of Aurungzib. It was this state that assisted General Goddard in his march across Central India in 1778.

Sindia.

In 1817 Sindia was requested to co-operate with the English against the predatory associations then in force, and, as a proof of his sincerity, to admit British garrisons temporarily into his two fortresses of Hindia and Asirgarh. An advance had to be made upon Gwālior, his capital, to hasten his determination, and on 5th November 1817, he signed the treaty required of him.

Treaties of Alliance.

In 1817-18 a series of alliances were formed with the states of Mālwa and Rājpūtāna, to protect them from a repetition of the oppressions to which they had been subjected. About nineteen princes entered into this arrangement, beginning with the Kotah chief, Zalim Singh, and ending with the Jeipūr Rājā. Nearly all these treaties were signed within the short space of four months.

The Nizām.

The Nizām's dominions had, from 1808 up to 1820, been administered by Chandū Lāll, a Hindū, and such was the mismanagement, that life and property were everywhere insecure. In 1820, Sir Charles Metcalfe, the Resident, exerted himself to arrest the progress of desolation, and with such good effect, that no less than 300 villages were speedily re-peopled, and cultivation resumed and extended. The large banking house of Palmer and Co. had been established at Heidurabād in 1814, and in times of difficulty had made many advances at high rates of interest to the Nizam's government. In 1820, it was found by the resident that a loan sanctioned by government, though under false representations, of sixty laks by Palmer and Co. to the Nizam, had not *all* been paid into the Heidurabād treasury, but a portion (eight laks) kept back by the firm in the shape of a bonus to the directors. This was represented to the supreme government, as also that the firm was all-powerful, and superseded the Resident's authority. The transaction was condemned by Lord Hastings in Council, and the debt owing to Palmer and Co. liquidated by capitalizing the annual payment of seven laks due to the Nizam on account of the northern Sirkars, after which the firm became insolvent. The undue interest Lord Hastings manifested in Sir Thomas Rumbold, one of the directors, is considered to be the only speck in his Indian administration, and the India House afterwards passed a vote of censure in the matter, stating, that though no corrupt motives were imputed to the Governor-General, he had lent the Company's credit for the sole benefit of Palmer and Co.

Sikhs.

Runjit Singh, who had previous to 1810 successfully formed and disciplined several regular battalions of infantry, in that year besieged Mūltān, but he had to retire with loss. In 1812, he got possession of Attok, and in 1814 invaded Kāshmir, but without success. In 1818 he subdued the Prince of Mūltān, and took Pēshāwur with his disciplined army, and in 1819 conquered Kāshmir.

Lord Hastings' military preparations in 1817 against the Maratta powers and the Pindāris were on a grand scale, the armies of the three Presidencies numbering 116,000 infantry and cavalry, with 300 guns. These preparations were intended to provide against any adverse contingency that might arise. It was in the same year that an epidemic, since known as cholera, broke out at Jessore in Bengal, and in November attacked Lord Hastings' army. For ten days the camp was like a hospital, and, including camp-followers, the force lost nearly 20,000 persons.

Revenue Settlements.

In 1820, under orders from the Court of Directors, the Ryotwāri system was fully established in the Madras Presidency under the supervision of the Governor, Sir Thomas Munro, who abolished several useless rules and practices formerly in connection with it. A system of fraudulent sales of land had taken place for some years in the North-West Provinces, instigated by the Bengāli officials, which Rājās and bankers did not scruple to join. By it many of the Zumindars were ousted from their lands and reduced to pauperism. Representations of this systematic plunder were made in 1827 to the Supreme Government, who appointed a special commission to examine into the matter, when some redress was made, but the relief afforded was not general. The same nefarious traffic, coupled with the high price of salt and over-assessment, produced an insurrection in Kuttak in 1818, which was not put down without some trouble. An equitable administration was afterwards introduced and the assessment reduced forty per cent. since which this province has enjoyed perfect tranquillity.

Financial and Territorial Increase.

At no former period were the finances in so flourishing a condition as at the close of Lord Hastings' rule. The increase of annual revenue was equal to six krores (£6,000,000), while that of expenditure was four krores (£4,000,000), leaving a clear annual surplus of two krores, besides ten krores in the treasuries. In 1822-23 the Indian revenue was £19,645,000 and the Indian debt £29,382,600. All the Peishwā's dominions excepting the Sattara Principality were annexed to the Bombay Presidency.

Singapore.

By the treaty of Paris in 1815, Java was restored to the Dutch, but a new British settlement, to command the China seas, was formed in the Malay States. This was the island of Singapore, obtained by Sir Stamford Raffles from the Rājā of Johore in September, 1819. Its subsequent importance as an entrepôt of trade has fully justified the wisdom of its selection, and Singapore is now one of the most thriving commercial cities in the East.

Lord Hastings was the first Governor-General to encourage education among the natives. Numerous vernacular schools were opened in the neighbourhood of Kalkutta by Mr. May (a missionary), Dr. Carey, and others, and on 31st May, 1818, the first native newspaper in India, the *Sumachar Durpun* ("Mirror of News,") was issued by the Serampore missionaries. The first English newspaper published in India was *Hickie's Gazette*, at Kalkutta, in 1781, but it was soon after suppressed by Government. The *Bombay Gazette*, established in 1789, and the *Bombay Courier*, in 1791, follow next. The *Bengal Hurkaru* was issued in 1802. At Madras the earliest English newspapers were the

Courier and *Gazette*, both published in 1814. In 1815 the Education Society was established at Bombay, and the Elphinstone Institution in 1819, and at Kalkutta the Hindū College was opened in 1821.

During Lord Hastings' rule, numerous roads, bridges, and light-houses were constructed, canals restored, and churches and chapels built in the three Presidencies. So restricted however were means of communication in the interior, that in 1823, while rice was selling in the Khāndēsh districts at fifty pounds for eight annas (one shilling), only four pounds were procurable for the same sum at Pūna. The docks at Bombay were greatly improved, and many fine vessels built there.

Trade.

The annual exports of India piece goods to Great Britain from 1771 to 1793 were, on an average, £1,250,000 in value, and from 1793 to 1806 a little over £2,000,000. After this they decreased and ceased altogether, owing to the cheapening of Manchester fabrics.

Ecclesiastical.

In 1814 Dr. Th. F. Middleton was appointed the first Anglican Bishop of Kalkutta. At that time there was an Archdeacon at each of the other Presidencies, fifteen chaplains in Bengal, twelve at Madras, and five at Bombay. On 15th December, 1820, the Bishop founded a Missionary College at Kalkutta. He died on 8th July, 1822, and was succeeded by the celebrated Dr. Reginald Heber.

Names of Note.—**Honourable Mountstuart Elphinstone**, Governor of Bombay, 1779-1859. **Sir John Malcolm**, afterwards Governor of Bombay, and author of History of Persia, Memoirs of Central India, &c., 1769-1833. **Sir Stamford Raffles**, founder of Singapore, 1781-1826. Statesmen, **General Gillespie**, died 1814. **Sir David Ochterlony**, 1758-1825. **Sir Tho. Hislop**, Commander-in-Chief of Madras. **General Smith**, and Captains **Stanton** and **Fitzgerald**, military commanders; **Chetū** and **Kurrim Khān,** Pindāri freebooters, **Umur Singh,** a Gūrkha general; **Vizier Mahomed** of Bhopal; **Gungādhur Shāstri,** the Geikwar's minister, assassinated 1815; **Tūlsi Bāi,** regent of Holkar's territories, beheaded in 1817.

On the resignation of Lord Hastings, Mr. Canning, who had been President of the Board of Control, was appointed Governor-General, but as his presence was required in the English cabinet, the choice fell ultimately on Lord Amherst. Till this nobleman's arrival in India, the reins of government were held by Mr. John Adam, senior member of council, whose brief administration of seven months was chiefly distniguished for his persecution of Mr. Silk Buckingham, the editor of the *Kalkutta Journal*. For certain strictures upon the editor of a rival paper, Mr. Buckingham's license was revoked, and he was deported from India. Mr. Adam enjoyed the reputation of exemplary integrity, distinguished ability, and indefatigable zeal. He died on his passage to England on 4th June, 1825.

(IX.) VISCOUNT (AFTERWARDS EARL) AMHERST OF ARAKAN, GOVERNOR-GENERAL (A.D. 1823-28).

Governors of Madras.		*Governors of Bombay.*	
SIR THOMAS MUNRO .	1820-27	HON. MOUNTST. ELPHINSTONE . . .	1819-27
HON. S. R. LUSHINGTON	1827-	SIR JOHN MALCOLM .	1827-

Appointment.—Made in 1822, and he arrived at Kalkutta on 1st August, 1823. He had previously been sent on an embassy to China.

Resignation.—March 10th, 1828. He left India earlier than he had expected, on account of his son's illness, resigning the government to the senior member of council, Mr. Butterworth Bayley, who performed the duties *ad interim* until the 4th of July, when Lord Bentinck took up the Governor-Generalship.

Character.—Lord Amherst was active and persevering, and gifted with a liberal disposition. The gross misconduct, however, of the Burmese war, the length of time it was protracted, and its heavy cost, created a strong feeling against him in England, and rendered his administration, in a financial point of view, calamitous.

Wars.—I. With the Burmese, in February, 1824. So far back as 1753 Alompra, a man of obscure birth, had founded a new dynasty at Ava. In 1766 the Tenasserim provinces, and in 1787 the province of Arakan, were both conquered and annexed to the Burmese empire. In 1798, nearly 30,000 Arakanese, having sought refuge from Burman oppression in the British district of Chittagong, their surrender was demanded by the Burman governor, under threat of an invasion, and the British Government then thought it necessary to protect their frontier. In 1822 both the kingdom of Assam and the district of Munipore were annexed to Burmah by Muhā Bundūla, their great national hero, and Lord Amherst, finding all efforts to maintain peace were fruitless, declared war in February, 1824. The expedition, comprising 11,000 European and native troops under Sir Archibald Campbell, was unfortunately planned to proceed to Rangoon as the rains commenced. It arrived there on 11th May, and occupied the town, but the natives had deserted it, and all supplies being intercepted, and the rains setting in, the army had to remain inactive in quarters for six months, during which time it suffered severely from the unhealthy climate and the want of proper provisions. Meanwhile a small British post on the Chittagong frontier had been attacked and routed on 17th May by a Burmese army, but a large force was speedily sent to the frontier, and this checked any further advance of the enemy. In August, Martaban, the capital of the Tenasserim provinces, was occupied by the British, and in October the stockade of Kaik-lu was taken. Between the 7th and 15th December the Burmese army, 60,000 strong, under Bundūla, was routed at Kokien, and he retired to Donabew, forty miles up the river. In 1825 Assam, with its capital, Rungpore, was taken from the Burmese by Colonel Richards. After the failure of two expeditions to advance on Ava by way of the eastern districts, arising mainly from the difficulties of the country and the pestilential climate, a move was made by Sir Archibald Campbell up the river towards Ava from Rangoon on 13th February, 1825, and after the reduction of numerous stockades, Prome was occupied on 25th April. Several attacks were made on the British position during November by the Burmese, but without any success. A treaty was signed on 3rd January, 1826, but as it was not ratified, the fortified position of Mellown was attacked and taken, and on 19th January a further advance was made towards the capital. The king was induced to make one more effort to repel the invaders with an army of 16,000 men, but this, too, was totally routed in February, and the British troops moved forward to Yandabū, only forty miles from Ava. The treaty of **Yandabū** was then signed on 24th February; by it—"(*a*) the Burmese king ceded Assam, Tenasserim, and Arakan to the East India Company; (*b*) agreed to pay one krore of rupees towards the expenses of the war in four instalments; and (*c*) to admit a British minister at Ava." The Burmese war cost thirteen krores of rupees (£13,000,000), and the ceded provinces were poor and unremunerative, but *now* the hill-slopes of Assam are covered with tea-plantations, rice is largely exported from Akyāb in Arakan, and Mūlmein in Tenasserim is the great outlet for the export of teak and other timber.

II. A Sepoy mutiny occurred in 1825 at Barrakpūr. The Bengal Sepoys of the 10th, 26th, 47th, and 62nd regiments, quartered there, hesitated to embark for

Burmah, owing to a curtailment of their extra allowances, and to a report having been spread abroad of the invulnerability of the Burmese. As the 47th, with portions of the 10th and 62nd regiments, still persisted in showing an insubordinate spirit, they were surrounded on 1st November by two European regiments and a battery of artillery—fired upon, and a large number cut down. The ringleaders were executed, and the number 47 of the Bengal regiment erased from the army list. The mutiny was suppressed by this sharp remedy, and no reluctance was afterwards shewn to proceed to either Arakan, Pegu, or any other portion of the Burmese empire.

III. With Dūrjan Sāl, nephew of Buldeo Singh (late Rājā of Bhurtpūr), in 1825. As he had usurped the throne, and confined the young Rājā, a child of six years, a force of 16,000 men and 100 guns was at once assembled by Sir David Ochterlony, the British representative in Malwā and Rājpūtāna to punish him. Differences however taking place between Sir David and the Supreme Government, the former resigned his appointment, and died soon after at Mirūt brokenhearted. On 10th December, 1825, Lord Combermere, the Commander-in-chief appeared before the fort of Bhurtpūr, which had years before baffled all the efforts of Lord Lake. It was built of mud, was five miles in circumference, and stood in a plain surrounded by a ditch fifty-five feet deep and 150 feet broad. One of the bastions having been blown up, an assault was made, and the fortress taken on 18th January, 1826. The loss of the enemy was 4,000 in killed, and the entire stores, arms, and ammunition fell into the hands of the victors. The fortifications were demolished, and forty-eight laks of rupees distributed as prize-money among the troops. Dūrjan Sāl and his family were taken prisoners and confined in Benares, while the boy Rājā was placed on the throne. The capture of this formidable fortress diffused a feeling of awe throughout India, and greatly strengthened the power of the British Government.

Memorable Events.—During Lord Amherst's administration ten krores of rupees (£10,000,000) were added to the public debt, mainly through the Burmese war, which was very costly. Towards the close of his rule, the Governor-General made a progress through the North-West provinces, holding stately Durbars for the reception of native princes. He was the first Governor-General who selected Simla, on the Himalayan mountains, as a summer retreat, and he proceeded there in 1827.

Burmese.

The Burmese soldiers had few firearms, but were mostly armed with swords and pikes. They were very expert in constructing stockades, and entrenching themselves in pits, each of which contained two men, with supplies of rice, water, and fuel. With the Burmese army was a corps of warriors called the "Invulnerables," who wore short hair, and were tattooed on the arms and legs. Three young women of high rank accompanied the Shan division of the army on horseback, and inspired the troops with courage; they were believed to possess the power of rendering bullets harmless.

Kolapūr.

In 1826 some disturbances took place between the Bombay Government and the Rājā of Kolapūr, but the questions pending with that state were arranged satisfactorily in January of that year, without recourse to actual hostilities.

Bombay.

In May, 1824, the Recorder's Court at Bombay (established in August, 1798) was raised to the dignity of a Supreme Court, the recorder, Sir Edward West, being appointed chief justice, with two puisne judges to assist him.

Dr. Reginald Heber was Bishop of Kalkutta from 1823 to 1826, in which latter year he died in the Madras Presidency, while visiting Tanjūr and Trichinopoli.

He was succeeded by Dr. J. T. James, who died in July, 1828. Numerous churches, colleges, roads, bridges, lighthouses, and other public works, were, during Lord Amherst's rule, constructed in different parts of India. Churches were erected at Kalkutta, Dum-Dum, Mirūt, Kaunpore, Dakka, and Burdwān in Bengal, and at Bombay, Pūna, Surat, and Kirki, in the Bombay Presidency. Natives of India were allowed to sit as jurors for the first time in 1827.

Names of Note.—**Sir Thomas Munro**, Governor of Madras, (died 1827)—"Europe never produced a more accomplished statesman, nor India a more skilful soldier." **Mr. Jenkins**, Resident of Nāgpur. **Dr. Reginald Heber**, Bishop of Kalkutta (1783-1826). **Dowlut Rao Sindia**, Māhārājā of Gwālior (died 1827). **Bundūla**, a celebrated Burmese general, and the national hero of his country, (killed in battle 1825).

(X.) LORD W. C. BENTINCK, GOVERNOR-GENERAL (A.D. 1828-35).

Governors of Madras.		*Governors of Bombay.*	
HON. S. R. LUSHINGTON	1827-32	SIR JOHN MALCOLM	1827-30
GEN. SIR FRED. ADAM	1832	GEN. SIR T. S. BECKWITH	1830-31
		EARL OF CLARE	1831-35
		SIR ROB. GRANT	1835

Appointment.—Made in 1828, and he arrived at Kalkutta on July 4th of that year. In March, 1833, he received the appointment of Commander-in-Chief, in addition to that of Governor-General. He had previously held the office of Governor in the Madras Presidency from 1802 to 1807.

Resignation.—In March, 1835, on account of his health. He left Kalkutta the same month, and on his return to England became a member of Parliament for Glasgow. He died at Paris 17th June, 1839.

Character.—Lord Bentinck was able, zealous, energetic,

and of great integrity, and these qualities were fully shown in his attempts to improve the country, advance the moral and social condition of its people, and develop its commercial and agricultural resources.

Wars.—With the exception of the conquest of Kūrg, and an insurrection among the Koles, a hill tribe in the south-west of Bengal, the general tranquillity of India was not disturbed during Lord Bentinck's administration. Owing to the cruelties and oppression practised by Vera Rājundra Wūdier, the Rājā of Kūrg, whose father had been a steady ally of the English, he was in April, 1834, declared to be unfit to reign, and a large force under Colonel Lindesay was sent to occupy his territories. The troops met with little opposition, except at a few stockades, which had been erected to defend Mudgherri, the capital, but these, as also the Rājā himself, were taken in April, 1834, and the latter sent to Benares. The prize money, amounting to thirteen laks, was distributed among the troops, and the province of Kūrg annexed to the Madras Presidency.

Memorable Events.—Lord Bentinck was very unpopular at the commencement of his administration, as, owing to the great expense of the Burmese war, he had to carry out a system of retrenchment in both the civil and military services. Land revenue, alienated from the state by fraudulent deeds, was recovered to the extent of thirty laks a year, and the hill province of Kachar, on the north-east frontier of Bengal, was annexed in 1832. For the administration of justice Amins' and Suddur Amins' Courts were established, as also courts of appeal at Allahabād for the benefit of the North-west provinces, where a new settlement, simple in plan, was introduced in 1832. A stamp duty was imposed—Sutti was forbidden by proclamation in 1830—great efforts were also made to root out female infanticide among the Rājpūts and the Khonds of Orissa, and the department established for putting down "Thugs" or organized gangs of murderers, who made it their business to worm themselves into the confidence of unsuspecting travellers, and then strangle them for the sake of their wealth. Native education was promoted, and the Kalkutta medical college established in 1835, and many offices under government were opened out to the educated natives of the country.

Sindia.

Dowlut Rao Sindia, dying in March 1827, without male heirs, his widow, Bāiza Bāi, became Regent. She adopted a youth named Jhudkū Rao, who on coming of age desired to wield the sovereignty himself, but this the Regent was not willing to allow. Application was then made by the young prince to the Governor-General for his support, but he refusing to interfere, Jhudkū Rao, in July, 1833, made an attempt to seize the supreme power, but failed. Soon after a strong party in the state proclaimed the young prince their sovereign. Bāiza Bāi fled to Dholpūr, but finding opposition useless, surrendered. She was allowed a revenue of ten laks of rupees, and took up her residence at Futtēgarh.

Jodhpūr.

As Maun Singh, the Rājā of Jodhpūr, who had been restored to power by the Governor-General through a subsidiary alliance, had allowed his stipulated tribute to fall into arrears, and had also engaged in several very equivocal proceedings, a force of 10,000 men was assembled at Nussirabād, with the object of compelling an unqualified submission. The Rājā at once sent envoys to the British Resident at Ajmir to plead his attachment to the government, when he was requested to deliver up at once all criminal refugees, whom he had sheltered, and pay the expenses of the force collected at Nussirabād to overawe him. This, after some hesitation, was acceded to.

The Rājpūt state of Jeipūr was disturbed during Lord Bentinck's rule by its minister, Jota Rām, who was strongly suspected of having murdered the Rājā. He was removed, but in June, 1835, an emeute took place at the capital, in which Mr. Blake, an officer attached to the Residency, was murdered. Jota Rām, having been found guilty of instigating this crime, was sentenced to death, but this was afterwards commuted to exile and imprisonment.

Jeipūr.

In 1811 the government of Maisūr was assumed by the Rājā, then sixteen years old, but in consequence of a continuous system of misrule the people, in 1830, broke out into open revolt. This was quelled by a British force, and in 1832 the management of this fine province was taken in hand by the East India Company, the Rājā being amply provided for.

Maisūr.

The post of resident at Delhi seems to have been one of great difficulty and even danger. In March, 1835, Mr. Frazer, the acting Resident, was shot dead by a hired assassin. On investigation it was found that the murder had been instigated by the Nawāb of Ferozpūr, who, with the assassin, one Kurrim, was condemned and executed.

Delhi.

This state, during Lord Bentinck's administration, had, owing to misgovernment, presented a deplorable picture of misery. In 1831 the Governor-General had advised the Rājā to adopt certain reforms, and though, in 1834, authorized by the Court of Directors to assume the government of Oudh, Lord Bentinck merely continued to urge the adoption of improvements on the Rājā.

Oudh.

On 13th June, 1833, the new Settlement of India Bill was introduced into Parliament by Mr. Charles Grant (afterwards Lord Glenelg). Its principal provisions were:—"(*a*) The Government of India to be entrusted to the Company till 1854; (*b*) The China trade to be thrown open to all, and the right of trading

Settlement of India Bill.

and of purchasing lands in India to be granted to all British subjects, the Company to close its commercial concerns, all its debts being charged to the Indian revenues; (*c*) Legislative powers to a certain extent to be vested in the Governor-General; (*d*) No native, or British subject, resident in India, to be disabled from holding office by reason of colour, birth, or descent; (*e*) Slavery to be abolished; and (*f*) Two additional bishops (for Madras and Bombay) to be created, the Bishop of Kalkutta to be metropolitan." The Bill became law on 28th August, 1833, having been accepted by both the Court of Directors and the proprietors of India stock. One of the subsequent arrangements of the new settlement was the constitution, in 1833, of a Legislative Council in India.

In 1833 a dispute took place between the Government of Bombay and the judges of the Supreme Court at that Presidency, in consequence of the resistance offered at Pūna to a writ of Habeas Corpus issued by the latter. The Governor, Sir John Malcolm, was determined not to allow such writs to extend into the interior. As this discussion involved some of the highest prerogatives of the Court of King's Bench, reference was made to the Privy Council, who decided that writs of "Habeas Corpus" did not extend to natives without the immediate local bounds of the island of Bombay.

Opium.

Much discontent as well as injury to the revenue had taken place, owing to the exorbitant duties levied upon opium, the produce of Rājpūtāna, when passing through the Company's territories. This led to its being smuggled into Sindh, and through the Portuguese ports of Diu and Damaun. At length the system of granting licenses or passes for its transit to Bombay was hit upon, and this in some degree remedied the difficulty.

It was during Lord Bentinck's administration that Lieutenant (afterwards Sir Alexander) Burnes undertook a tour of exploration through the countries of Central Asia, proceeding by way of the Indus through Sindh, then very little known to the English. In February, 1832, a treaty of commerce was concluded between the Company and the Mirs of Sindh. Three routes were also attempted by steamers from England to India—the first, by the Cape of Good Hope, which effected but little saving in time—the second, from Bombay through the Red Sea, Egypt, and the Mediterranean, by Lieutenant Waghorn—the third, by the Euphrates and Persian Gulf, by Captain Chesney. The second was found the most practicable, and a line of packets was established. The navigation of the Ganges by steamers was also commenced during Lord Bentinck's rule.

Indian Trade.

From 1792 to 1830, the amount of annual revenue derived from opium ranged from £180,000 to £800,000, but in 1835 it rose to £1,399,000. The opium from Patna, in Bengal, was considered the finest in quality. In 1833, on the renewal of the charter, all the Company's extensive filatures of silk were sold to private persons. Before 1820, there were but few commercial houses at the Indian ports, but after that year other firms were established with a large amount of capital. The Company's annual imports from 1818 to 1827, were 2¼ millions in value, while the "private" trade amounted to 5½ millions sterling. The annual value of exports for the same period was, Company's £1,900,000, and "private" a little over 8 millions. In 1830, a commercial crisis took place at Kalkutta, when many houses failed—six of the largest for £15,000,000.

Famine.

There occurred a terrible famine in 1833, by which 50,000 persons perished in September at Luknow, in Oudh; at Kaunpore, 1,200; and at Guntūr, 250,000 people died, besides 74,000 bullocks, 159,000 milch cattle, and 300,000 sheep and goats. The direct loss to government by this visitation exceeded five million pounds sterling.

Māhāb-lēshwur.

In 1828, the sanitarium of Malcolm Peth, on the Māhāblēshwur hills, in the Bombay Presidency, was founded by Sir John Malcolm, hence its name. It is 4,500 feet above the level of the sea, and affords a pleasant retreat during the hot season for the Governor of Bombay and other high officials.

Public Works.

During Lord Bentinck's government, the following public works were carried on: Four iron suspension bridges, 86 bridges of masonry, 70 different roads, 412 tanks, 113 wells, 107 ghāts, 15 serāis for travellers, and 9 iron chain bridges for Kumaon. In Bombay, the Town Hall and Kolāba Observatory were completed in 1830. In the same year the Agri-horticultural Society of Western India was established, and in 1832 the Bombay Geographical Society was founded. The Agra Bank was established on 1st July, 1833.

Ecclesiastical and Educational.

Dr. John M. Turner succeeded Dr. James as bishop of Kalkutta in 1829, but he, dying on 7th July, 1830, Dr. Daniel Wilson was appointed his successor in April 1832. He employed himself actively in visiting the numerous stations of his large Indian diocese. In 1834, the new charter brought two more bishops into India,—Dr. Daniel Corrie, archdeacon of Madras, as bishop of that Presidency, and Dr. Thomas Carr, archdeacon of Bombay, as bishop of Bombay. In 1830, Dr. Duff opened the General Assembly's school in Kalkutta, on Christian principles, and it soon rivalled the Hindū College in the number and qualifications of its students. Rammohun Roy, one of the most active promoters of the Hindū College, and a Hindū of distinguished literary attainments, was sent by the Delhi emperor to England, to represent his case to the government there, but failed in his mission. He was versed in Persian, Arabic, Sungskrut and English. In after life he adopted Monotheism as his religious creed, and died at Bristol in 1833.

Lord Bentinck made several progresses in India during his rule. In 1828 he visited the North-West Provinces, and in 1829 the Straits and Eastern Settlements. In October, 1831, he met Runjīt Singh, the Māhārāja of Lahore, at Rūpur, and in 1832 again proceeded to the Upper Provinces, meeting the Rājpūt princes at Ajmīr. In 1833 he visited Delhi and Ajmīr, returning to Kalkutta in February of that year.

Names of Note.—**Sir Charles** (afterwards **Lord Metcalfe**, statesman (1785-1846). **Rammohun Roy** (1780-1833). **Bāiza Bāi**, the Regent of the Gwālior State.

On Lord Bentinck's resignation in March, 1835, **Sir Charles** (afterwards **Lord**) **Metcalfe** became Governor-General *provisionally* till March, 1836. The Court of Directors had appointed Lord Heytesbury, but on the Whig ministry returning to power, before that nobleman could sail to his destination, the appointment was cancelled. Sir Charles Metcalfe had previously held important and trustworthy posts under the Indian government, and during his short rule as Governor-General he became popular by removing the restrictions to which the press had previously been subjected. He returned to Europe in 1837, resigned the Company's service, and was appointed Governor of Jamaica in 1839. Subsequently he became Governor-General of Canada, but was forced by disease to resign that post in November, 1845. On his return to England he was raised to the peerage as Lord Metcalfe, and died on 12th September, 1846.

(XI.) VISCOUNT (AFTERWARDS EARL) AUCKLAND, GOVERNOR-GENERAL (A.D. 1836-42).

Governors of Madras.		*Governors of Bombay.*	
SIR FRED. ADAM . .	1832-36	SIR ROB. GRANT . .	1835-38
LORD ELPHINSTONE .	1836	JAMES FARISH (Pro.) .	1838-39
		SIR J. RIVETT, CARNAC	1839-41
		G. W. ANDERSON (Pro.)	1841

Appointment.—Made in 1835, and he landed at Kalkutta on 20th March, 1836. Lord Auckland had previously been President of the Board of Trade, Master of the Mint, and first Lord of the Admiralty.

Resignation.—On 28th February, 1842, after a calamitous administration of six years. He left India on 12th March following, and afterwards joined the Whig administration. He died on 1st January, 1849.

Character.—Pacific, and by nature amicably disposed, he was ill-fitted for the troublous times into which he was thrown. He gave his attention, as far as possible, to the advancement of native education, and was eager to carry out schemes of social improvement, but his administration of six years was mainly occupied with the disastrous campaign in Afghānisthān.

Wars.—I. With the Khūnd Rājā of Gumsūr in 1836, who displayed a refractory spirit. The Rājā soon submitted, and Gumsūr and other forts were speedily occupied, but several insubordinate chieftains offered resistance, trusting to their fastnesses and jungles. The troops suffered severely in this desultory warfare in an unhealthy country, but the chief fortresses were at length taken and demolished, and the Khūnds subdued.

II. With Dost Mahomed Khān, Amir of Afghānisthān, in October 1838. In 1812, a revolution occurred in that country, which compelled the reigning prince, Shah Sūjah, to abandon his throne, and seek shelter at first in Lahore, and afterwards in British territory, and it ended in Shah Mahmūd becoming the sovereign, with Futteh Khān Barukzye as his vizier. This minister was put to a cruel death by the king in 1818, on which Mahomed Azim Khān, his brother, took up arms, and placed Ayūb, a brother of Shah Sujāh, on the throne. In 1823, Afghānisthān had become a prey to civil wars, and the empire was parcelled out into petty principalities. It was at this time that Dost Mahomed, a brother of Futteh Khān, appeared upon the scene, having taken possession of Kabūl, and by treachery, accompanied with murder, he in 1825 obtained supreme power in Afghānisthān. In 1836, Kabūl was again in a state of anarchy, and the efforts made by Dost Mahomed to levy money caused several revolts. Runjīt Singh, taking advantage of this, captured Peshāwur, and in the same year, Captain (afterwards Sir Alexander) Burnes, was sent on a mission of a commercial nature to Dost Mahomed, but all attempts at negotiation were fruitless. In December, 1837, a Persian army advanced upon Herat, then ruled by Kamran, Shah Mahmūd's eldest son, but it was repulsed with loss, and the siege raised in September, 1838. Lord Auckland, after concluding in June, 1838, a tripartite treaty with Runjīt Singh and Shah Sūjah, issued in October of that year his grand manifesto, in which he determined to espouse by force the cause of Shah Sūjah, and reinstate him on the Afghān throne. A British force from Bombay was prepared to ascend the Indus, but as it was found that the Mīrs of Sindh were unwilling to let it pass through their territory, their seaport town, Kurrachi, was taken on 2nd February, 1839, and this led to a treaty, by which the Mīrs agreed to pay £300,000, maintain an auxiliary force of 4,000 men, pay a tribute of one-half of their revenue, and acknowledge the sovereignty of the East India Company. In March, the army reinforced by a Bengal division, reached Shikarpūr, and soon after set out, under Sir John Keane, for the Bolan pass, which was found obstructed by the Bilūchis, led on by the Khān of Khilāt. It arrived at Quetta on 26th March, and after great privations occupied Kandahar on 25th April, and here Shah Sūjah, on 8th May, was installed as king with much ceremony. On 27th June, the army advanced on Ghuzni, and on 23rd July, this celebrated fortress was successfully stormed, the governor, Heidur Khān, a son of Dost Mahomed, being taken prisoner. A further advance was then made on Kābūl, whither also another British column, under Colonel Wade, was also marching. After having forced its way through the formidable Kheibur pass, twenty-eight miles in extent, Sir John Keane's army reached the capital on 6th August, and Colonel Wade's division the same place on 3rd September. Dost Mahomed fled to Bokhāra, and Shah Sūjah was enthroned, after which the main body of the troops returned to India by the Kheibur pass and Peshāwur, Mr. M'Naghten remaining as Envoy, as well as a detachment under General Elphinstone, for the protection of the new sovereign. The disaffected Afghān chiefs were but partially subdued, and on 15th October Khilāt was successfully stormed by General Willshire, and the governor, Mehrāb Khān, slain. It was soon found that Shah Sūjah was unpopular, and this incited Dost Mahomed to fresh exertions, in order to expel the English from Afghānisthān. Escaping from the king of Bokhāra, he levied troops and offered some opposition, but to the surprise of everyone, on 3rd November 1840, after the fight at Purwān, he surrendered himself to the British envoy, by whom he was sent with his family to Lūdiāna. The campaign in Afghānisthān being considered at an end, Lord Auckland was created an earl, Sir John Keane raised to the peerage, Mr. M'Naghten and Colonel Pottinger made baronets, and Colonels Wade and Thackwell, and Captain Burnes knighted. In October 1841, everything appeared tranquil, but on 2nd November following, an insurrection broke out suddenly at Kabūl, promoted, it was supposed, mainly by Akbar Khān, the favourite son of Dost Mahomed. Sir Alexander Burnes and other British officers were murdered; the Afghāns took the forts in the vicinity of the British cantonments; several small detachments in the districts were cut to pieces, and, on the arrival at Kabūl of Akbar Khān, on 22nd November, many chiefs, hitherto friendly to Shah Sūjah and the English, at once changed sides. Negotiations were then attempted, and it was agreed that the British troops should leave Afghānisthan, taking with them Shah Sūjah if willing, and that Dost Mahomed was to be allowed to return to Kabūl. Shah Sūjah, knowing that his countrymen never observed treaties, rejected the convention altogether. The winter had now set in with great severity, and the demands of the Afghāns were daily becoming more and more exorbitant. On 23rd December, while holding a conference with Akbar Khān, Sir William M'Naghten was murdered by that chief. Captain Trevor met the same fate, and other officers were made prisoners. Major Pottinger, who then became British envoy, managed to patch up a convention on very humiliating terms, and on 6th January 1842, commenced the retreat of the British army, numbering, with camp-followers, about 15,000 men, exposed to continual attacks from the Afghāns, compelled to deliver up their women and children as hostages, and suffering dreadfully from hunger, thirst, and cold. It ended in one officer only, Dr. Brydon, being able to reach Jellālabād in safety, to tell the disastrous tale. In four days 12,000 men, including camp-followers, were lost, the army suffering mostly in the terrible passes through which their route to India lay. General Sale, at Jellālabād, General Nott at Kandahar, and the garrison at Khilāt-i-Ghilzi, still maintained their positions, but at Ghuzni, the troops under Colonel

Palmer surrendered to the Afghāns on 6th March 1842. Preparations were going forward in India to send relief to the beleaguered garrisons, when Lord Ellenborough arrived in Kalkutta, and assumed the reigns of government on 28th February, 1842.

III. On the 22nd January, 1839, an English expedition took possession of the town of Aden, at the entrance of the Red Sea. A treaty for its peaceable surrender had previously been made with the Sultan of Lahēj, who held it, but this was resisted by his nephew. A sharp fight then took place with the Arabs, who were defeated. In 1840 they made several desperate attacks upon the place, and were again repelled with great slaughter, as they neither took nor gave quarter. The spot was considered to be a convenient position as a station for regular steam communication between England and India.

Memorable Events.—A disturbance took place in Oudh in July, 1837, on the death of the king of that country. He had previously acknowledged two youths, Keiwān Jāh, and Mūnah Jaun, as his sons, but the adoption being irregular, the British Government determined to vest the succession in Nussir-ū-Dowlah, the eldest surviving uncle of the monarch, on the proviso that he should sign such a treaty as the Governor-General might dictate. On the king's death the queen dowager, with an armed force of 2,000 men, attempted to place Mūnah Jaun on the throne, but the resident, Colonel Low, at once called up his troops and opened fire upon the insurgents, who were, with the Begum, made prisoners. Two other aspirants to the throne appeared in the persons of two nephews, but their claims, according to the principles of the Sūni sect, were declared to be untenable.

Oudh.

In 1820 the Rājā of Bhopal died, and his widow, Sekundur Begum, assumed the government, adopting her nephew as the heir to the throne. Disputes afterwards arose

Bhopal.

between her and her nephew, and they both appealed to arms, but through the mediation of the British Government the youth ascended the throne, the Begum retiring to a Jagir. The Rājā died soon after, leaving the succession to his daughter, then six years old.

Sattara.

In 1839, during the Afghān war, the Rājā of Sattara, having taken a share in hostile negotiations, in gross violation of the treaty entered into by him, and refused to dismiss the minister who was supposed to have urged him to this act, was deposed, and his brother Appa Sahēb made ruler in his stead. A conspiracy was also discovered in the Dekhun, headed by the Nizam's brother, in which the Nabob of Kurnāl was found to be implicated. The Rājā of Jodhpūr, too, also showed a refractory spirit. A force was sent against both these chieftains, and their designs at once suppressed.

Sikhs.

Runjīt Singh died on 30th June, 1839, and was succeeded by his son Kurruk, who died after an inglorious reign of about twelve months. His son Nao Nehāl succeeded him, but he was killed by a stone which fell on him when passing under a gate at Lahore. Shir Singh, the unacknowledged son of Runjīt, who was addicted to drunkenness and debauchery, was then (1841) proclaimed king through the influence of Dyan, a favourite of Runjīt.

Tea Trade.

In 1827 the introduction of the tea plant into India occupied some attention, and in 1834 active measures were taken to carry on its cultivation. Plants and seeds were obtained from China, and in 1838 those reared in Kumaon had produced seed. The tea plant had been found growing "*wild*" in Assam, and in 1837 samples prepared from this kind were sent to Kalkutta and favourably reported upon. Chinese plants were also introduced into that country, and a company called the

"Assam Company" was formed to carry on tea cultivation.

The trade in cotton may be said to have commenced from 1788, when about 500,000 lbs. were shipped to England. Up to 1810 the export of this article greatly fluctuated in quantity, and from that year to 1812 varied annually from 694,000 lbs. to 27,375,000 lbs. with prices ranging from 8*d.* to 3*s.* per pound. From 1817 to 1840 it varied from 12¼ millions to 75¾ million pounds, and prices from 2⅞*d.* to 1*s.* 4*d.* per pound. Experimental culture of exotic varieties of cotton was begun in 1840, in the Madras and Bombay Presidencies, by planters brought by the government of India from the Southern States of America.

Cotton.

The great trigonometrical survey of India, which was commenced in 1800 during Lord Wellesley's administration by Colonel Lambton, had in the year 1841 advanced to the completion of the whole Indian arc from Cape Komorin to the Himālayan mountains.

During Lord Auckland's administration the full liberty of the press was confirmed, the civil courts augmented, and the use of the vernacular languages permitted in schools and courts of justice. The Chamber of Commerce at Bombay was established in 1835, that at Madras in 1836. The order of "British India" for native officers was introduced at Madras by Lord Elphinstone in 1837, and he opened the University there in April, 1841. At Bombay the munificent Parsi merchant, Jamsetji Jijibhoy, was knighted in 1842; his charities exceeded £60,000, and he expended £30,000 in the translation of useful works into Gujirathi. The Parsi community in Bombay had now become both numerous and influential, and bore a high character for industry, peacefulness, and intelligence. The word "*Parsi*" is derived from the name of the province of ancient Persia, "Pars"

Parsis.

or "Fars," from which they originally came. They are in fact the remnants of the "Guebres," or fire-worshippers of Persia (*followers of Zerdūsht* (*Zoroaster*), who were defeated at the great battle of Nahāvand in A.D. 651, by the Kaliph Omar, when a portion left Persia, and, as is ascertained from a poem called the *Kissah-i-Sanjān* (written by Behram in A.D. 1599), arrived in India about A.D. 717. Diu, on the Kattiawar coast, was the first place touched at, and here they remained nineteen years; thence they proceeded to the coast of Guzerat, settling at Sanjān, twenty-four miles south of the Portuguese settlement of Damaun. In time they increased in numbers, residing chiefly at Nowsari, Surat, Ahmedabād, and Bombay; at present they are most numerous in the last-mentioned city. There are a few practical points in connection with their religion which are worthy of notice. They will eat nothing cooked by a person of another religion; they object to beef and pork; marriages are only contracted with persons of their own caste and creed; their dead are not buried, but exposed on iron gratings in their "*Dokmas,*" or temples of silence, to be devoured by birds; the bones are subsequently placed in a subterranean cavern.

Ecclesiastical.

Dr. Corrie, Bishop of Madras, died on 5th February, 1837. He was so much beloved that a grammar-school was founded in the city of Madras to perpetuate his memory. He was succeeded by Dr. Trevor Spencer, who arrived in India on 21st October, 1839. The progress of missionary labour was not very marked during the first twelve years of the present century, only 161 Hindūs having been converted to Christianity. Ten years afterwards the number rose to 403, in 1832 to 647, and up to 1842 this had increased to 1,055.

Names of Note.—**Sir Wm. NcNaghten**, Resident at Kabūl (murdered in 1841); he had previously been appointed Governor of Bombay. **Sir Alex. Burnes**

(1805-41). Generals, **Sir Robt. Sale** (1782-1845), **Nott** (1782-1845), **Pollock** (b. 1786). Major **Eldred Pottinger** (1811-43), Captain **Arthur Conolly**, military commanders. **Runjit Singh**, Māhārājā of Lahore (1780-1839).

(XII.) VISCOUNT (AFTERWARDS EARL) ELLENBOROUGH, GOVERNOR-GENERAL (A.D. 1842-44).

Governors of Madras.		*Governors of Bombay.*	
LORD ELPHINSTONE	1836-42	G. W. ANDERSON (Pro.)	1841-42
MARQUIS OF TWEEDDALE	1842	SIR GEO. ARTHUR, BART.	1842

Appointment.—Made in 1841, and he landed at Kalkutta on 28th February, 1842. Lord Ellenborough had previously been President of the Board of Control under the Tory administration.

Resignation.—Lord Ellenborough was, in July, 1844, removed from his office by the Court of Directors, the government of India being provisionally conducted by Mr. W. W. Bird, till the arrival of his successor, Sir Henry Hardinge. He left for Europe on 1st August, 1844, and was afterwards raised to the dignity of an earl.

Character.—Lord Ellenborough was very desirous of obtaining military glory, and this sentiment seems to have prevented his doing much towards the internal improvement of India. He was wanting in steadiness and constancy, and his administration showed no marked or consistent course of policy. He nevertheless possessed great energy and talent, and his indefatigable industry and indomitable resolution were generally appreciated.

Wars.—At the time Lord Ellenborough assumed the Governor-Generalship, the Afghān war was still going on, there being two British garrisons in that country, one at Jellalabād and the other at Kandahar. In April, 1842, the former, under Sir Robert Sale, was relieved by

General Pollock. Orders for retreating from Afghānisthān were at first issued by the Governor-General, but the then state of Kabūl encouraging an advance, Generals Nott and Pollock were allowed to act as they thought best. Shah Sūjah had previously, in April, 1842, been assassinated, and his son Futteh Jung made ruler by Akbar Khān. On 11th September General Pollock defeated 16,000 Afghāns at Tezin, and on 15th entered Kabūl, where, two days afterwards, General Nott, the defender of Kandahar, joined him, having on his way taken Ghuzni on 5th September and destroyed its fortifications and citadel. Akbar Khān's European prisoners, numbering about eighty men, eleven women, and nineteen children, whom it was that chieftain's intention to sell as slaves, managed to bribe Sāleh Mahomed Khān who was in charge of them, and they were met on the 17th September by Sir Richmond Shakespeare with some native irregular horse, and on 20th by General Sale.

After destroying the great Bazar and several mosques and houses at Kabūl, that city was abandoned on 12th October, and the British army returned to India through the Kheibur Pass, though not without meeting with obstruction, bringing with them the gates of the temple of Somnath, captured by Mahmūd of Ghuzni some eight centuries before. On 25th October, 1842, Dost Mahomed and his family, together with all Afghāns then in India, were permitted to return to their country, and the war in Afghānisthān was thus brought to a successful termination.

II. With the Mīrs of Sindh, in 1842. This province, which had, with a few intermissions, been a constituent part of the Mahomedan dominions from the time of the Ghuzni dynasty to the end of that of Teimūr, became in 1740 a dependent portion of the Persian empire under Nādir Shah, and was governed by the Kulhora race, which, about the year 1786, was displaced by a Bilūch tribe, the Talpūrs, of the Shiah sect, under the leadership of Mir

Futteh Ali. He assigned portions of the conquered territory to his relations, whence arose the states of Kheirpūr and Mīrpūr, but retained the larger portion, containing the capital, Heidurabād, for himself. In 1836 the Mīrs became tributary to Runjīt Singh, the Mahārājā of Lahore. In 1838, a British resident, Colonel (afterwards Sir Henry) Pottinger, was stationed at Heidurabād, with the reluctant consent of the Mīrs, and various treaties were made with them. In December, 1840, Major Outram, being then Resident, the chief Mīr, Nūr Mahomed, died, and as a portion of the yearly subsidies, promised by the Mīrs for defraying the expenses of the British force in Afghānisthān, remained unpaid, Sir Charles Napier was sent to Sindh in September, 1842, and invested with the chief military and political power in that province. On his approach Mīr Rūstum Khān of Kheirpūr fled to Emāmghur, a fort in the desert, which Sir Charles Napier speedily destroyed on 9th January, 1843. On 14th February the Mīrs signed a treaty, relieving themselves from the payment of the subsidy, but surrendering Kurrachi, Tatta and three other towns, with a strip of land on each side of the Indus, and allowing the right of cutting wood for the steamers on the river banks. Meanwhile plots were formed by them against the Resident, and an attack was made in February, 1843, on the British Residency near Heidurabād by 8000 Bilūchis with six guns, which resulted in the Resident abandoning the place. On the 17th February Sir Charles Napier, with 2800 men of all arms and twelve guns, attacked the Mīrs' army of 22,000 men, strongly posted at Miāni, six miles from Heidurabād, and gained a complete victory over them. It resulted in the surrender of Heidurabād and of six of the Mīrs. As, however, Shir Mohamed of Mīrpūr still remained unsubdued, he was on 24th March encountered and defeated by Sir Charles at Dubba, four miles from Heidurabād. Sindh then became a British province and

Sir Charles Napier its first governor. Mir Ali Mūrad of Kheirpūr, who had remained faithful to his engagements, received an accession of territory, slavery was abolished, and the Indus declared open to the navigation of the world. The captive Mīrs were removed at first to Bombay and afterwards to Kalkutta.

III. With the Gwālior State, in 1843. After the death of Dowlut Rao Sindia in 1827, his widow adopted Jeiāji Rao, a child of eight years old, and the deceased chief's nearest relative, while Māmā Sahēb, his maternal uncle, was appointed regent. Through the intrigues of the Māhārāni (Queen Mother), the Regent was compelled to withdraw from Gwālior, the chief power falling into the hands of Dādā Khāsji Walla, but his presence there being pronounced injurious by the British Resident, his removal was demanded, to which the Māhārāni yielded a reluctant assent.

To obtain guarantees for the future security of the country, British troops, under Sir Hugh Gough and accompanied by the Governor-General, were marched into the Gwālior districts in December, 1843, and, as all attempts at negotiation were fruitless, the British army, 14,000 strong with forty guns, attacked the Maratta force of 18,000 men with 100 guns at Māhārājpūr on 29th December, and defeated it after a severe struggle. On the same day General Grey obtained a brilliant victory over another force of 12,000 Marattas near Punniar, twelve miles from Gwālior, and these combined successes soon induced the Gwālior Durbar to sue for peace. The Maratta army was disbanded, and on 17th January, 1844, a treaty was entered into, the chief provisions of which were—"(*a*) the administration of the Gwālior government by a council till the Māhārājā attained his 18th year; (*b*) the increase of the British contingent force in Sindia's territories, and (*c*) the payment of twenty-six laks owing to the British Government, and of an annual allowance of three laks of rupees to the Māhārāni."

Memorable Events.—The Mīrs of Sindh were very fond of hunting, and the banks of the Indus were in several places allowed to remain covered with thick wood or jungle, where they might indulge in the pleasure of slaughtering the game preserved in these forests. These spots were known as "*shikargahs*" or hunting grounds.

Lord Ellenborough does not appear to have cared about securing the good opinion of the Court of Directors, and misunderstandings arose, which eventually resulted in his being recalled by the Court. Public works languished during his administration, but slavery and lotteries were abolished. The office of Lieutenant-Governor of the North-west Provinces was made by Lord Ellenborough, and Mr. (afterwards Sir George) Clerk, was the first incumbent. In 1843, the Seal College was opened at Kalcutta. In 1841-42, the Indian revenue was £16,834,000; in 1843-44, it rose to £18,284,000. The Indian debt during the same two periods was £34,378,000, and £37,640,000 respectively.

In July, 1843, the Bank of Madras was opened. In 1844, a mutiny took place in the 47th Madras native infantry while proceeding to Bombay by sea for service in Sindh. Several regiments of the Bengal native army, among which the 7th cavalry, and the 4th, 34th, 64th, and 69th native infantry were conspicuous, also shewed a mutinous spirit, by refusing to proceed to the same province, on the plea that they lost the extra allowances granted while on active service in an enemy's country.

In 1844, the Lutheran and German missionaries began their labours in the Madras Presidency. At Bombay, the Jamsetji Jijibhoy Hospital and the Grant Medical College were both founded in 1843; and in that same year the first vessel of the Peninsula and Oriental Company was despatched to Kalkutta.

Names of Note.—**Sir Charles Napier** (the conqueror of Sindh), 1782-1853.

(XIII.) SIR HENRY (AFTERWARDS VISCOUNT) HARDINGE GOVERNOR-GENERAL (A.D. 1844-48).

Governors of Madras.		*Governors of Bombay.*	
MARQUIS OF TWEEDDALE	1842-47	SIR GEO. ARTHUR .	1842-46
HENRY DICKENSON (Pro.)	1847-48	LESTOCK ROB. REID (Pro.)	1846-47
		SIR GEO. R. CLERK .	1847

Appointment.—Made in 1844 at the suggestion of Sir Robert Peel, and he arrived in Kalkutta on 23rd July of that year. At the time of Lord Hardinge's appointment he was about 60 years of age, and at the head of the War Office in England. He had previously seen much military service under the Duke of Wellington.

Resignation.—In 1847, but he did not leave India till 15th March, 1848. Sir Henry Hardinge was raised to the dignity of a Viscount after the first Sikh war.

Character.—Lord Hardinge was distinguished for his statesmanlike views and aptitude for business, and his humane spirit was shewn by his having persuaded twenty-three petty princes of India to pledge themselves to the extinction of female infanticide, Sutti, and slavery. Pacific in his views, he had nevertheless to conduct one of the most sanguinary campaigns recorded in Indian history, and in this he displayed much prudence and energy.

Wars.—I. With the Sikhs in 1845. It has already been mentioned that in 1841 Shir Singh was proclaimed king through the instrumentality of Dyan, a favourite of the late ruler, Runjīt Singh. In 1843 he was shot by Ajit, the nephew of Uttur, the Rāni's minister, and a boy, Dhullip Singh, only four years old, was proclaimed Māhārājā. A series of murders then took place at Lahore, where the government was utterly disorganized, and it ended in the Sikh army becoming the actual rulers of the state, and as late in the year 1845 they determined to invade the British territories, a proclamation was issued on 13th December by the Governor-General, confiscating all the Sikh possessions on the left bank of the Sutlej. On the 15th December the Sikh army under Tej Singh crossed the Sutlēj, and on the 18th met the British troops under Sir Hugh Gough, accompanied by Lord Hardinge, at Mūdki, where the English won the day, capturing seventeen guns. The loss of life was, however, very severe, Sir Robert Sale (the hero of Jellālabād) being among the slain. On 21st December the British army, numbering 24,000 men of all arms, attacked the Sikh entrenched camp at Ferozeshah (ten miles from Mūdki), occupied by 60,000 men with 108 heavy guns. The fight was renewed on the 22nd, and the British at length remained masters of the field, but at a dreadful sacrifice of life. On 28th January, 1846, the Sikhs were again defeated at Aliwāl by Sir Harry Smith. This was followed on 10th February by the battle at Sobraon, a formidable Sikh camp well fortified, which was carried by Sir Hugh Gough, and 67 cannon and 200 camel-mounted swivel guns captured. The same night the British army crossed the Sutlēj and encamped at Kussūr, thirty-two miles from Lahore, whither Gūlāb Singh was sent by the Sikh council to make terms with the conquerors. These were:—(*a*) The surrender of the territory lying between the Sutlēj and Beas rivers; (*b*) The payment of £1,500,000 as expenses of the war; (*c*) The disbandment of the Sikh army, and its re-organization on Runjīt Singh's system; and (*d*) No force to be raised without the consent of the British Government, and the internal organization of the Lahore Government to be settled by the Governor-General." This treaty was ratified on 8th March, 1846. Dhullip Singh joined the Governor-General's camp, and was allowed to remain as ruler, while Gūlāb Singh, for his neutrality, was made the independent sovereign of Kashmir and other neighbouring tracts of country, but to pay tribute to the British Government under whose protection he remained. This terminated the first campaign against the Sikhs. They had lost four general actions and 220 cannon, and the war was by far the most important in which the English had yet been engaged in India.

II. In 1844 disturbances took place in the small Maratta states of Kolapūr, and Sāwunt Warri in the Bombay Presidency. In 1827 a British force had been sent against the Rājā of the former state, who seemed desirous of becoming a second Siwuji. On his death in 1844 a Brahmin named Dāji was made Regent, but his conduct soon provoked a rebellion among the hill chiefs, and English troops were despatched to bring the latter to reason. The fort of Sāmungarh was captured after a delay of some weeks, and on 1st December the Punalla Fort was stormed and taken, but the insurgents fled into the Sāwunt Warri district, where Phōnd Sāwunt and Anā Sahēb were devastating the country. Colonel Outram was sent in 1844 to put down the insurrection, and his measures in six weeks quashed the disturbances. The rebels were dispersed, and two officers were appointed as political agents at Kolapūr and Sāwunt Warri, who completed the settlement of these disaffected districts.

Memorable Events.—On the completion of the first Sikh war, in 1846, Lord Hardinge set about reducing the national expenditure, which the state of the treasury urgently required. The numerical strength of the army was reduced, and the yearly expenditure was diminished to the extent of a million sterling. At the same time public works were not neglected. The construction of the great Ganges canal, begun by Lord Auckland, but suspended by Lord Ellenborough, was resumed during the administration of Lord Hardinge, and other canals were also cleared and opened out. One of these, the Western Jumna, was 445 miles long, and irrigated 1,015 square miles of land; its income in 1846-47 amounted to not less than £30,000. The Governor-General also completed the Grand Trunk Road from Kalkutta to Benares, on which no less than fifty-four bridges had been erected.

Lord Hardinge made arrangements for separating the Governorship of Bengal from the duties of the Governor-General, and Mr. Bird was appointed the first Deputy-Governor of that province. In 1845 the Danish settlements of Serampūr and Tranquebar were purchased by the British Government, the former selling for £125,000.

Sutti, which in 1830 had been abolished by Lord Bentinck throughout the British dominions in India, was, at Lord Hardinge's desire, partly put down within the territories of a large number of independent native princes.

In 1847 several stoppages occurred at Kalkutta among the banks and large business firms of that city, consequent, in a great measure, upon the numerous failures which had in that year taken place in England. These tended to create a general feeling of depression among all classes.

Madras.

The Governor of Madras (Marquis of Tweeddale), during his term of office, abolished transit duties, removed some obnoxious taxes, and expended much money in road-making in that Presidency.

Bombay.

In 1845 a fine causeway from Mahim to Bandora, in Bombay, was constructed by Lady Jamsetji Jijibhoy, wife of the Parsi Knight, at a cost of £17,000, and in the same year a "bund" (dam) was built over the Mūta-Mūla river at Pūna. The culture of silk, which had been tried in the Dekhun, completely failed in 1847. The foundation of a church (since called St. John's) at Kolāba (in Bombay) was laid in the same year; it was intended as a memorial of those British officers who fell in the disastrous Afghān campaigns of 1839-42. In 1844-45 the value of the imports from all countries into the three Indian Presidencies amounted to £10,754,000, and the exports from India to £16,590,000. In 1847-48 the Indian revenue was £18,748,000, and the public debt £43,085,263.

Names of Note.—**Sir Hugh** (afterwards **Viscount) Gough** (1779-1869.) **Sir Harry Smith. Major D'Arcy Todd** (1808-45), and **Major Broadfoot** (killed in 1845), military commanders. **Gūlāb Singh,** Māhārāja of Kashmir. **Sir Henry Elliott,** a distinguished Oriental scholar, (1808-53)

(XIV.) EARL (AFTERWARDS MARQUIS) DALHOUSIE, GOVERNOR-GENERAL (A.D. 1848-56).

Governors of Madras.		*Governors of Bombay.*	
SIR HENRY POTTINGER	1848-54	SIR GEO. R. CLERK .	1847-48
		LORD FALKLAND . .	1848-53
		LORD ELPHINSTONE .	1853

Appointment.—Made in 1847, and he landed at Kalkutta on 19th January, 1848. His father had previously held the post of Commander-in-chief of India, resigning it in 1832. Lord Dalhousie was Vice-President of the Board of Trade in 1843, and President in 1845, and when he accepted the Governor-Generalship of India, was only 36 years of age.

Resignation.—In 1856, and he left India in March of that year, after an able administration of eight years. His constitution had been greatly shattered by incessant toil in the service of his country, and he died on 19th December, 1860, in the 48th year of his age.

Character.—Lord Dalhousie was pre-eminently gifted with sound judgment and deep sagacity, and he displayed a vigour and devotion to business which was remarkable. He laboured incessantly to benefit the people of India with lasting and solid improvements. His policy of annexation, and what has been termed his "*lust of territorial aggrandizement,*" tended, it is said, to bring about the Sepoy revolt of 1857, but this, in the opinion of several eminent Indian statesmen, was not the case.

Wars.—I. With the Sikhs in 1848. Mūlraj, the Governor of Mūltān, having expressed a wish to resign his post, two young British officers, Messrs. Vans Agnew and Anderson, escorted by 1,400 Sikhs, were sent to Mūltān to receive the fortress from Mūlrāj, and instal Sirdar Khān Singh as Governor in his stead. On 19th April, 1848, they were received by Mūlrāj, who gave up the keys of the fort, but on their return unarmed they were assaulted, and afterwards cruelly murdered by the governor's soldiery. Messengers had previously, on the appearance of danger, been sent to the Resident at Lahore, and to Lieut. (afterwards Sir Herbert) Edwardes, at Bunnū, and the latter at once set out with all the troops he could muster to assist his countrymen. He prevented the spread of the insurrection, and, by the aid of the Sikh general, Van Cortlandt with 4,000 men, and with 5,000 men sent by the Khān of Bhāwulpūr, defeated the army of Mūlrāj at Kineiri on 18th June, and again on 1st July at Suddūsam near Mūltān. Shir Singh, son of Sirdar Chuttur Singh, now advanced in an apparently friendly spirit towards Mūltān with a body of Sikh troops, and on 18th August, General Whish was enabled to assume the command of a besieging force of nearly 28,000 men. Meanwhile, the troops under Chuttur Singh, in the Huzara district, had revolted early in August, and it was evident that another struggle with the entire Sikh army was close at hand. The siege of Mūltān proceeded but slowly, and when, on 14th September, Shir Singh and his troops went over to the enemy, it was raised, and the British forces retreated to Sūruj-kūnd, a fortified position some miles from Mūltān. Shir Singh in October joined his father,

Chuttur Sing, near Wuzirabād, but a British army for the Punjāb was now being rapidly collected at Saharun, and soon 38,000 men and a large park of artillery were ready, under the command of Lord Gough, who joined them on 21st November. On the 22nd, an attack was made by the British cavalry on a strongly fortified Sikh position at Ramnuggur, but it was repelled with great loss to the assailants. In December, the army before Mūltān under General Whish, was reinforced by a Bombay division, the besieging force now numbering 15,000 regular troops with 97 guns. On 3rd January, 1849, the city of Mūltān was stormed and taken, and on the 22nd the fort, together with Mūlrāj himself, was unconditionally surrendered. He was tried for the murder of the two British officers, found guilty, and imprisoned for life; the actual murderer was tried and executed. On the 3rd January, Attok was given up to the Sikhs after a spirited defence, and on the 13th was fought the sanguinary battle of Chillianwalla, in which the British lost 602 killed and 1,657 wounded. H. M.'s 24th Regiment of Foot alone had 11 officers killed and 10 wounded in this engagement. The Sikh army was afterwards joined by an Afghān division of 3,000 men, their united forces numbering upwards of 60,000 men with 60 guns, and these on 20th February encamped near the town of Gujerat, lying between the Chenāb and Jhilum rivers. The fall of Mūltān, on 22nd January, had enabled General Whish to join the Commander-in-chief, and on 21st February was fought the battle of Gujerat, where the Sikhs were utterly routed, with a loss to the British of only 97 killed and 706 wounded. The enemy were hotly pursued, the Afghāns driven out of India, the British prisoners recovered, and Chuttur Singh, with other chieftains and their troops, surrendered unconditionally. 158 guns and 16,000 stand of arms fell into the hands of the British during this campaign. The Māhārāja, Dhullip Singh, was deposed, and pensioned on £50,000 a-year, and by a proclamation of the Governor-General, dated 29th March, 1849, the kingdom of the Punjāb was annexed to the British territories. The country was at once placed under the management of a Board of Administration, of which Sir Henry Lawrence was appointed president, with two members, Messrs. Mansell and J. Lawrence (the latter afterwards Governor-General of India).

II. With the Burmese, in 1852, owing to the gross and unjustifiable ill-treatment of British subjects by the Burman authorities. In 1851, Commodore Lambert, of H.M.'s ship, "Fox," was despatched to investigate these cases, but the officers sent on a diplomatic mission to the Governor of Rangūn to adjust these differences were insulted, and Lord Dalhousie, finding that war was inevitable, prepared two expeditions, one at Kalkutta, and the other at Madras, and ordered round a steam flotilla of nineteen vessels from Bombay. The troops, European and native, to the number of 5,800 men, under the command of General Godwin, were conveyed without delay to Rangūn, where they landed on April 12th, and took the town on the 14th. On May 17th, Bassein, the western part of Burmah, was captured by General Godwin and Commodore Lambert, and Prome, which had previously been threatened by Captain Tarleton with a naval armament, was taken on October 9th. With the relief of Major Hill, who with 400 men had held out in the town of Pegu against 6,000 Burmese, all further military operations ceased. On December 20th, 1852, a proclamation was issued by the Governor-General, declaring that the Province of Pegu (33,400 square miles in area) had become a portion of the British territories in the East. This country, under the able administration of Sir Arthur Phayre, has since proved no burden on the finances of India, but has paid all its expenses.

Memorable Events.—Great improvements were carried out in the Punjāb (area, 97,548 square miles) after its annexation to British territory. The crimes of Thuggi and infanticide, both of which prevailed largely in that province, were put down. Roads were made, rivers bridged, groves of trees planted, and wells dug. The existing canals were cleared out and utilized, and an extensive work, called the Bāri-Doāb Canal, 466 miles in length, and irrigating an immense area, was constructed by Lord Dalhousie. The tea plant was introduced among the slopes of the Himalayas, about Kangra and the Murri hills. Nor was education neglected. At the time of the conquest, a large and consolidated system of education was found in force, and "female" schools were met with in the Manjha. The British authorities established central English schools in all the principal towns, and these were soon crowded with Sikh, Hindū, and Mussulman scholars. Though the land-tax was reduced twenty-five per cent. and several vexatious imposts abolished, the revenue of the Punjāb proper, the third year after annexation, reached 106 laks of rupees. The celebrated Koh-i-nūr diamond was presented to the Queen in January, 1850. It was found originally in the mines of Golkonda, and became the property of the Mogul emperor, Shah Jehān. Nādir Shah took it in 1739, and after his murder it passed into the possession of Ahmed Shah Abdāli Afghān. Runjīt Singh obtained it from Shah Sūjah, and after that it fell into the hands of the British.

Sattara.

In 1849, owing to the death of the Rājā of Sattara without heirs, that state was incorporated with British territory, liberal provision being made for the Rājā's family. The Rānis and the adopted son were permitted to retain property to the extent of 16 laks of rupees, and received also an annual pension of a lak of rupees.

Nāgpūr & Jhānsi.

In 1853, the Rājās of Nāgpūr and Jhānsi both died without heirs; the former had lived and died "a seller of justice, a miser, a drunkard, and a debauchee." His territory (in area about 76,432 square miles) was annexed by the Governor-General, and one-fourth of the revenue of the country was set apart for the support of the royal family and its retainers and dependants. In the same manner the small state of Jhānsi (2,500 square miles in extent) was annexed to the British dominions, on the grounds that its native rulers were only subjects of a sovereign, first of the Peishwā, and afterwards of the East India Company. In the same year, the Nabob of the Karnatik, Mahomed Ghouse, having died childless, the uncle of the deceased, Azim Jah, laid claim to the dignity and its prerogatives. His claim was disallowed by the Governor-General, as being only a collateral heir, and it was determined that the royal privileges and immunities of the post should cease. Azim Jah was allowed a suitable provision, and was recognised as the first native nobleman in the Madras Presidency; the dependants of the family were also provided for.

Karnatik.

It was in 1853 also that a treaty was made with the Nizam of the Dekhun for the transfer of certain districts including Berar, yielding an annual revenue of about 37 laks of rupees, intended for the payment of the Heidurabād contingent, and for effecting an equitable settlement of the interest and principal of the debt owing by the Nizam to the East-India Company. The allowances to the British contingent of 5000 infantry, 2000 cavalry, and four field batteries had been so repeatedly allowed to fall into arrears, that in 1843 the Nizam was directed to observe greater punctuality in these payments. In 1849, and again in 1851, he was told to make over certain districts to cover his obligation. These requests produced no result till 1853. Two years afterwards, a portion of these districts was restored to the Nizam, and subsequently (in 1861) all were given up, with the exception of Berar, the revenues of which were found sufficient to cover the expenses of the contingent.

Nizam.

The last of Lord Dalhousie's annexations was that of Oudh, with an area of 20,142 square miles. The terrible mismanagement of this fine Province by its native ruler had long been known to the British Government, and he had again and again been remonstrated with by successive Governors-General upon the inveterate abuses which everywhere prevailed in his kingdom. The king's army of 70,000 men preyed upon the people, and Rājpūt landholders, possessing some 246 forts scattered about the country, turned fertile land into a jungle and reduced whole districts to desolation. The journal and report of Generals Sleeman and Outram, both residents at the Court of Luknow, show the miserable state of the country, and that nothing less than the assumption of the Government by the British could effect any change for the better, and in these opinions the majority of the Governor-General's Council concurred. On 7th February, 1856, the Province was annexed to British territory, the king and his palace guards being allowed fifteen laks a year for their support, and the whole country went over to its new rulers without a single blow being struck in favour of the native dynasty. If all Lord Dalhousie's annexations be taken into account, it may safely be said that he added in eight years to British India upwards of 200,000 square miles of territory, an area larger than all France, and nearly double the extent of Great Britain and Ireland.

Oudh.

From 1848 to 1856 many beneficial reforms were introduced by Lord Dalhousie. A public works department was specially organized for carrying out the immense undertakings proposed by him for the improvement of the country. In matters of education a distinct department of Public Instruction was provided. At each Presidency a university was established, besides Government colleges of a higher character, and verna-

Administrative Reforms.

cular schools throughout all the districts. A system of grants-in-aid to all schools, without reference to caste or creed, was also inaugurated, and the cause of female education was upheld by the Governor-General as an object of national importance. In commerce the trade of Kalkutta was doubled, and that of Bombay increased to an enormous extent. Steamers were placed on the Indus where they had never before been seen. A low and uniform system of postage was introduced throughout the length and breadth of British India, whereby letters of a given weight might be sent to any part of the country for half an anna (about three farthings). Roads and canals were constructed with a lavish hand. Amongst the former was one stretching from the plains of Hindūsthān to the frontiers of Thibet; another connected Dakka with Pegu, while great military roads were made in the newly acquired territory of the Punjāb. The Ganges canal, a gigantic work, 800 miles in length including its branches, was finished during this administration, and opened on 8th April, 1854. The Eastern and Western Jumna and other extensive works of irrigation were also carried out. It was during Lord Dalhousie's rule that railways date their existence in India. In 1848 a guarantee of five per cent. was granted on two short and experimental lines in the neighbourhoods of Kalkutta and Bombay, but it was not before February, 1853, that the first fifteen miles of the Great Indian Peninsula Railway were opened between Bombay and Tanna. The electric telegraph was another benefit conferred on India by the Governor-General, and the first line constructed was that from Kalkutta to the sea at Kedgeri, which proved very useful during the Burmese war of 1852. By 1855 upwards of 3,000 miles of wire were at work, and this has since been extended to 12,000 miles. A remark made by Lord Dalhousie, "that the system of electric telegraphs in India may one day be linked with those which envelope Europe," has already been realised

In 1855 there occurred an outbreak among the Sonthals, a tribe inhabiting the hill ranges of Rājmahāl in the Bengal Presidency. Harassed by Bengali money-lenders they rose in rebellion, and descended into the plains sacking every European dwelling they came to, and spreading desolation in all directions. The hill-rangers sent against them were defeated, and it was not till the following cold season that the rebellion was extinguished, by the advance of regular troops against them. The district was afterwards made a non-regulation province, and placed in charge of a commissioner.

Sonthal Emeute.

The charter of 1833 expired in 1853, and the government of India was again entrusted to the East India Company under certain provisoes. The India Bill introduced in Parliament by Sir Charles Wood provided mainly—"(*a*) for a reduction of the Court of Directors from thirty to eighteen by ballot; (*b*) for the enlargement of the Legislative Council in India; (*c*) for entrusting the government of Bengal and Behar, previously under the Governor-General, to a separate Lieutenant-Governor, (Sir Frederick Halliday being the first incumbent of the new office); and (*d*) in withdrawing the patronage of the Court of Directors from the Civil Service, and throwing it open to unreserved competition."

East India Company's Charter.

The Supreme Government of India during Lord Dalhousie's rule consisted of the Governor-General and the following councillors, viz. the Commander-in-chief of the army, and three ordinary members of the Civil Service; the fifth, called the Legislative member, voted only in the making of laws and regulations. There were thus two separate bodies—the Legislative, and the Executive Government,—the first comprising the Governor-General and five councillors,

Government of India.

and the second, the Governor-General and four councillors.

Bāji Rao, Ex-Peishwā.

Bāji Rao, the ex-Peishwā, died at Bithūr, near Kaunpore, in January 1853, at the age of seventy-seven. He had drawn a pension of eight laks (£80,000) a year, since 1818, and had thus received in the aggregate, the enormous sum of £2,800,000. His adopted son, Dhūndū Punt, better known as "Nāna Saheb," petitioned the Indian Government for a continuation of this pension, which was refused, but a grant was made to him of the town and Jagir of Bithūr, rent-free for life.

Maisūr.

Since the introduction of British rule in this state from 1831, great results had been accomplished; the revenue had risen from forty-four to eighty-two laks, and marked improvement had taken place in every department of the state. In 1847, the Rājā requested Lord Hardinge that the government might be restored to him, but this was refused. A similar application to Lord Dalhousie, in 1856, met with the same fate.

Mutiny.

The same spirit of insubordination, which was shewn by some of the Bengal native regiments in Sindh during Lord Ellenborough's administration, was manifested in the Punjāb in 1849-50, and one of them, the 66th N.I., was disbanded by the commander-in-chief, Sir Charles Napier, and replaced by a Gūrkha corps.

Revenue.

The gross revenue of British India, which in 1849-50 was £27,758,000, had increased in 1855-56 to £29,613,573. The Indian debt, which in the former year amounted to £46,908,000, had increased in 1855-56 to £56,000,000.

Ecclesiastical.

In December 1849, Dr. Dealtry was consecrated Bishop of Madras in room of Dr. Spencer, who had resigned. In

1851, Dr. Harding was consecrated Bishop of Bombay in place of Dr. Carr, who resigned his see in that year.

Missions in India.

In 1852, it was ascertained by the Reverend Mr. Mullens, that there were in India and Ceylon 443 ordained missionaries (of whom 48 were natives) having the spiritual charge of a Christian community of 112,191 souls—47,504 boys were being educated in vernacular schools, 2,414 in boarding schools, and 14,562 in superior English schools. The entire Bible had been translated into ten languages, and the New Testament into five.

Educational.

The Doveton College, at Kalkutta, was established in 1855, from a sum of Rs. 2,30,000 left by a Captain Doveton to the Parental Academy, with which the college is connected.

Names of Note.—**Bāji Rao**, Ex-Peishwa (1776-1853), **Sir Walter Gilbert** (died in 1853), **Sir Joseph Thackwell, General Godwin, Colonel W. Havelock** (killed in the Sikh war in 1848), military commanders.

Mr. **James Thomason**, Lieut-Governor N.-W. Provinces (died in 1853).

(XV.) VISCOUNT (AFTERWARDS EARL) CANNING, GOVERNOR-GENERAL (A.D. 1856-62).

Governors of Madras.		*Governors of Bombay.*	
LORD HARRIS	1854-59	LORD ELPHINSTONE	1853-60
SIR CHARLES TREVELYAN	1859	SIR GEO. R. CLERK	1830-62
Recalled in	1860		
SIR HENRY WARD	1860		
SIR WILLIAM DENISON	1860		

Appointment.—Made in 1855, and Lord Canning arrived at Kalkutta on 29th February, 1856. He was the son of the distinguished British statesman, George

Canning, and was born in 1812. In 1841 he was Under Secretary of State for Foreign Affairs, and afterwards Postmaster-General.

Resignation.—On 12th March, 1862. He left India on the 18th of that month, but died in London on 17th June following. He was buried in Westminster Abbey.

Character.—Lord Canning was unquestionably not popular as a Governor-General. Though cold and reserved in temper, his manner was courteous and dignified, and he was at the same time just and impartial in his public duties. He held office in India at a most eventful period of its history, but the liberal and enlightened policy he displayed at the latter end of his administration contrasted favourably with that he had adopted at the commencement of his Indian career.

Wars.—I. With Persia, in 1856. It arose from the Persians having early in 1856 laid siege to and eventually captured Herat in Afghānisthān, in violation of a treaty concluded in 1853 between Great Britain and Persia, which provided for its non-attack by the latter. On 1st November war was declared against Persia by the Governor-General, and an expedition numbering 6,000 men, Europeans and natives, was fitted out at Bombay, under the command-in-chief of General Sir James Outram. On 26th November a fleet of about forty vessels, with the troops on board under General Stalker, proceeded to the Persian Gulf, capturing the island of Karrak and effecting a landing on the Persian coast at Hallila Bay, twelve miles from Bushire, which town was subsequently captured on 10th December. In January, 1857, Sir J. Outram joined the force, and on 8th February defeated the Persian army at Khūsh-āb. On 18th March an expedition of nearly 5,000 men was despatched to Mohamreh, a town near the confluence of the Euphrates and the Karūn, where it was reported a Persian army, 13,000 strong, had entrenched itself. On 26th March the troops landed at Mohamreh and advanced against the Persians, who retreated precipitately, leaving behind them their tents, ammunition, seventeen guns, and a large quantity of stores. In April news arrived of peace having been concluded at Paris between England and Persia on the 4th of the previous month. The chief terms of the treaty, which was ratified by the Shah on 14th April, were:—"(*a*) The Shah to withdraw his troops from Herat and Afghānisthān within three months after the ratification of the treaty, and to renounce all claim upon Herat whether for sovereignty or for tribute; (*b*) The British troops to evacuate Persia on the fulfilment of certain conditions; and (*c*) In any future quarrel between Persia and Afghānisthān, England to be appealed to as a friendly mediator." In May, 1857, the greater portion of the British army returned to India, leaving a small force under General Jacob at Bushire, which remained there till all the terms of the treaty had been complied with.

II. In the month of May, 1857, took place the **Indian Mutiny**, one of the most formidable military revolts on record. From the middle of 1856, a method of secret correspondence was carried on, consisting in "chupattis" (small cakes of unleavened bread) being passed on from village to village, beginning in the North-Western Provinces around Delhi, and extending from the Sutlej to Patna, but the English officials were unable at the time to understand its meaning. At the latter end of January 1857, a new cause of disturbance occurred. This was the refusal of the native troops at Dum-Dum (near Kalkutta) to use the cartridges prepared for the recently-introduced Enfield rifle, because they believed them to be greased with the fat of pigs and cows, and that their religious usages were, in consequence, about to be tampered with. On 26th February, the 19th Bengal N. I., who on this account became riotous at Berhampūr, a town in Lower Bengal, were disbanded in March, and exactly a month afterwards, similar disturbances occurred among the 36th Bengal N.I. at Ambāla, in the Punjāb, more than 1,000 miles from Kalkutta. On 29th March, the 34th Bengal N.I. having become mutinous at Barrakpūr, were, in the following May, disbanded and dismissed. On 24th of April the cartridge disturbance began at Mirūt, in the North-West Provinces, with the 3rd Bengal N. Cavalry, and on the 10th May, the great revolt may be said to have commenced at that station, by the joint mutiny of that regiment and the 11th and 20th regts. of Bengal N.I., who fired the bungalows in the native lines, and murdered and mutilated every European they met, without regard either to rank, age, or sex. The mutineers then marched to Delhi, the centre of Indian nationality, where, on 11th May, they were joined by the 38th, 54th, and 74th regts. of Bengal N.I., who at the time garrisoned that city, and then commenced a general and indiscriminate massacre of almost all the European inhabitants in the place. To prevent the magazine in the city, which contained immense stores of ammunition, from falling into the hands of the mutineers, Lieut. Willoughby, the officer in charge, blew it up, but the destruction was only of a partial character. Shah Alum, the aged king of Delhi, was then proclaimed by the rebels sovereign of Hindūsthān, and as it soon became evident that this city was the intended rallying point for all revolted corps from other parts of India, a siege-train was dispatched without delay from Ambala, and on 24th May, the Commander-in-chief, General Anson, left that station for Delhi, but dying of cholera at Kurnāl, on the 27th, Sir Henry Barnard succeeded him in the command. A siege army of three brigades was organized to retake the city, but a portion only reached the scene of operations in the month of May. Meanwhile the disaffection was spreading largely, as, during May, fifteen regular regiments of the Bengal native army (cavalry and infantry), as also the 7th

Oudh Infantry at Luknow, and the native sappers and miners at Mirūt, mutinied at different stations, while eight other regiments were disarmed by the authorities. In June the revolt had begun to assume formidable dimensions. On 8th of that month, Sir Henry Barnard arrived with the siege army before Delhi, and here the force took up its position, never to leave it, till the British became once more masters of the place. Hardly a day passed without an attack from the besieged, but re-inforcements came slowly in, and by the last week in June, the European portion of the army numbered about 3,000 men, the siege materiel consisting of 5 batteries mounting 15 guns and mortars, but these were small in calibre, and in consequence not very effective.

At Luknow, the position of the Chief Commissioner, Sir Henry Lawrence, became very critical during May. Disaffection had shown itself as early as the 3rd of that month, when the 7th Oudh infantry mutinied, and this was followed up by the revolt of four Bengal native regiments on the 30th May. During June, his position became still more critical, as on the 30th of that month, while engaging a rebel force at Chinhut, his Oudh artillery went over to the enemy, and he was forced to make a disastrous retreat, attended with considerable loss.

On 1st of July, the Europeans at Luknow were in a state of siege, and on the 4th, Sir Henry Lawrence died at the Residency from a wound received from the bursting of a shell, Brigadier Inglis succeeding him in his military command.

At Kaunpore (Kanhpūr), in the North-West Provinces, there were signs of an outbreak in the month of May, but no overt act of hostility occurred till the 5th June, when the 2nd Bengal N. C., and the 1st, 53rd, and 56th regts. B. I. mutinied, the few English troops under Sir Hugh Wheeler, with the European civilians, their families and native servants, retiring into the entrenchments previously thrown up in case of danger; these were provided with eight pieces of ordnance and a fair store of ammunition, but afforded a poor shelter for upwards of 900 persons.

It was then that Dhūndū Punt, better known as Nāna Saheb, an adopted son of the ex-Peishwā, Bāji Rao, appeared on the scene. He resided at Bithūr (six miles from Kaunpore), and was in the habit of exchanging hospitalities with the English garrison at this latter station, but he cherished a feeling of deep animosity against the East India Company, because the extravagantly large pension of eight laks of rupees (£80,000) was not continued to him after Bāji Rao's death. When the four native regiments mutinied at Kaunpore, he placed himself at their head, and proceeded to attack the entrenchments with six guns, two of them eighteen-pounders. Many of the women and children died from the excessive privations of the siege. On 24th June, Nāna Saheb proposed, on certain conditions, to provide for the conveyance by river to Allahabād of all the remaining occupants of the entrenchments, and to this General Wheeler consented. On the 27th the survivors of the 900 left the entrenchments, but they had not proceeded far down the river when they were fired upon from both banks, the men were killed excepting Lieutenants De La Fosse and Thomson, and one or two others who escaped, but such of the women and children as survived were brought on shore by the Nāna's orders, kept in close confinement for a fortnight, and then murdered in cold blood on 15th July, only two days before a victorious English column, under General Havelock, entered Kaunpore, but too late either to succour or to save. A beautiful and appropriate monument now covers the fatal well where 200 mutilated bodies of English women and children, the victims of that frightful massacre, lie together in one common grave, and a memorial church of handsome design stands at no great distance from it. They are not only fitting memorials to the dead, but lasting monuments of that horrible cruelty and treachery which seem to have distinguished the miscreant Nāna and his followers. Meanwhile the siege of Delhi was progressing with varied success. During June the rebels were found to be in great strength in that city, while the besieging force was small and much weakened by the perpetual attacks made upon it by the besieged. On 5th July, Sir Henry Barnard died, and was succeeded by General Reed, who held the command till the 17th, when he resigned it to General Archdale Wilson. By the middle of August the besieging force comprised 3,570 Europeans and 2,070 natives, with 28 horse-artillery guns and a small supply of siege artillery, but this increase was mainly owing to the arrival of Brigadier Nicholson on the 8th, with 1,100 Europeans and 1,400 Punjāb troops. Early in September the long-expected siege-train from Ferozepūr arrived, as well as additional reinforcements of both Europeans and natives, raising the British force to 13,000 men, and on the 14th September the city of Delhi was stormed, and by the 20th finally captured. This success was, however, greatly dimmed by the loss of the gallant Nicholson, who fell in the assault. One hundred and thirteen days had been spent by the besiegers before its walls, and the number killed and wounded during that period on the side of the British amounted to 3,807. The King of Delhi fled from the city, but was soon after taken prisoner, and three of his sons were shot down by Captain Hodson, who feared a rescue. The re-conquered city remained in the hands of the British, and was by degrees brought under the control of the authorities.

Mention has already been made of the death of Sir Henry Lawrence at Luknow on the 4th July, from which date till the latter end of September, fierce attacks were made at different times by the rebels on the Residency, but all were repelled, though with great loss to the besieged. It was but a few days after the capture of Delhi, that Generals Outram and Havelock, who had fought their way through Oudh, relieved the Luknow Residency; but the survivors of the relieving force were too few to escort safely the women and children from Luknow to Kaunpore, and they therefore remained themselves besieged till the middle of November, when a second relief took place under Sir Colin Campbell. On the 23rd of that month Luknow was evacuated by the British till the 21st March, 1858, when it was finally captured by Sir Colin Campbell, assisted by a Nipālese force under Jung Bahādūr. The army of Oudh was then broken up into separate columns, with the object of engaging large parties of rebels who were at the time scattered about in different parts of that province. It was during this campaign that Generals Neill (Madras Fusiliers), and Havelock, and Major Hodson, one of the Delhi heroes, lost their lives.

In Central India Sir Hugh Rose, at the head of a large field force, was busily engaged during 1858 in re-asserting British supremacy in that part of India. In January he captured the fort of Ratgarh; in February and March he relieved Saugor, and took a series of strongholds in Bundelkund; and on 1st April he defeated Tantia Topi, a rebel leader, outside Jhānsi, and the next day captured the town itself. Early in May he was in pursuit of the Rāni of Jhānsi and Tantia Topi, and on the 11th defeated them at Kūrreh, and between the 15th and 23rd was engaged with the enemy at Kalpi. This place was captured on the 23rd, the rebel chiefs retreating to Gwālior, which they took, after defeating the Mahā-rāja Sindia, the ruler of that territory. On 16th and 17th June, Sir Hugh engaged the rebels with success near Gwālior, where the Rāni of Jhānsi was killed, and on the 30th he occupied the capital, and re-seated Sindia on his throne. After this, the Central India field force was broken up, and detachments were sent to occupy the different towns and cantonments which had been re-captured. During the months of July, August, and September 1858, the work of re-establishing the Civil Government in all the Provinces re-taken from the rebels, went on hand in hand with the pursuit of the many insurgent bands which still infested several parts of the country. Wherever the enemy appeared, he was beaten, but it was the Province of Oudh which gave the greatest trouble, though even here, under Mr. (afterwards Sir Robert) Montgomery, the chief commissioner, British influence gradually regained its ascendancy. During August, the pursuit of Tantia Topi, the only rebel leader left of any note, was carried on for a time under General Roberts, with the Rājpūtāna field force, after which it was taken up at different times by Generals Parkes, Mayne, Smith, and Michel, the last-mentioned officer defeating Tantia severely at Sindwa on 19th October, and again on the 25th at Multhone. Tantia was eventually betrayed into the hands of Major Meade, then at Gūnah, by Rājā Mān Singh, of Porona (a district to the west of Jhānsi), on 7th April 1859, and afterwards tried and executed. The last general expedition against the rebels took place in February 1859, when they were driven into the hills near Nipāl. Here they were surrounded by Jung Bahādūr, when twenty officers and 2,500 men surrendered, and these were passed on to British territory, the Nāna and the Begum of Oudh remaining, it is supposed, in Nīpāl. With these two latter occurrences, the Indian Mutiny may be said to have ended. An act of indemnity was passed in 1860, making valid all acts done since 10th May 1857 by officers of Government, and others in connection with these disturbances. It was found that no less than seventy-two Bengal native regiments, twelve Madras, and three Bombay corps, had been broken up by mutiny.

III. In May 1859, a mutiny on a small scale took

place among the East India Company's European troops, and this, owing to the diminutive stature of the men engaged in it, was generally known as the "**Dumpy Mutiny.**" It began at Mirūt, and extended to Allahabād and Berhampūr, but no actual violence was committed, except by the 5th regiment of Europeans at the last-mentioned station, and this was unattended with bloodshed. The demands of the mutineers were, that they should be allowed either their discharge and a passage to England, or a new bounty for re-enlisting from the Company's army to that of the Crown, which latter they declared they had not engaged to serve. It ended in the greater number of the malcontents being discharged, and sent to England at an enormous expense to the Indian Government. This mutiny is supposed to have determined the home authorities in not retaining the local army as a separate force, but in amalgamating it with the royal army.

Memorable Events.—One of the most important events that occurred in connection with the great Indian Mutiny, was the dissolution of the East India Company as a governing power in India. There had been a great outcry against it soon after the mutiny began, and on 19th December 1857, the British Government announced to the Company an approaching change in its powers. On 12th February 1858, India Bill No. I. was brought in by Lord Palmerston, but it remained in abeyance, owing to the resignation of the Ministry eight days afterwards. On 26th March, India Bill No. II. was brought forward by Mr. Disraeli, but it never came to anything. On 17th June, Lord Stanley introduced India Bill No. III., which subsequently became Act 21 and 22 Vict. cap. 106, against which, as well as the two previous Bills, the East India Company offered the most strenuous opposition. The Bill passed the Commons on the 8th July, and the Lords on the 31st of the same month, and received the royal assent on 2nd August.

The principal features of this Bill were as follow:—"(*a*) the transfer of the governing powers, as also all rights, territories, and revenues, from the East India Company to the Crown; (*b*) the appointment of a salaried Secretary of State for India, with certain powers, to be aided by a council of fifteen members; seven to be chosen by the East India Company, and the remaining eight by the Crown; each to receive an annual salary of £1,200, with a retiring pension of £500 after ten years' service, but no member to sit in Parliament. (*c*) Council to be divided into committees by the Secretary of State for dispatch of business. (*d*) All property, credits, debts, and liabilities of the East India Company to be transferred to the Crown. (*e*) Of high Indian appointments, some to be made by the Crown, and others by the Council and Governor-General of India. (*f*) Existing establishments to be transferred to the Crown, and existing enactments and provisions to remain in force unless specially repealed. (*g*) The Court of Directors still to exist, but merely for the management of the Company's dividend, and a few minor matters." This Act came into force on 1st September, 1858, with Lord Stanley as the first Secretary of State for India, and from that day, the Government of the East India Company passed into a tradition.

On 1st January 1857, there were but 26,000 royal troops, and 12,000 company's Europeans in India, the Sepoy army on that date numbering 200,000 men. Up to April 1858, 42,000 royal troops, and 5,000 company's Europeans were sent to India, making a grand total of 85,000 British troops in India, but war and sickness had, up to that date, lessened this number to 50,000 effective men. In June 1860, Sir Colin Campbell (Lord Clyde), resigned the commander-in-chiefship of the Indian army, and was succeeded by Sir Hugh Rose (now Lord Strathnairn), who introduced many useful and salutary reforms. In 1861-62, took place the amalgamation of the Indian with the royal army; the staff-corps was formed about the same time, and Addiscombe College abolished.

Oudh.

Lord Canning issued his celebrated proclamation with reference to Oudh, in March 1858. Its leading provisions were, that "the proprietary right in the soil of that Province, under certain restrictions, was confiscated to the British Government, who would dispose of it as it thought proper." The result of this was the tendering of allegiance by two-thirds of the Talūkdars, and the settlement of their estates on them. In October 1859, the Governor-General met the Talūkdars of Oudh at a large Durbar at Luknow, where he referred to the rights and dignities which had been conferred on them. The military resources of this important province may be conceived, when it is mentioned, that from the year of the great mutiny, up to August 1859, no less than 684 cannon, 186,177 fire-arms, 565,321 swords, 50,311 spears, and 636,683 weapons of various kinds were given up to the British authorities. The number of forts destroyed, or ordered to be destroyed, was 1569.

N. W. Provinces.

In 1859, Lord Canning made a tour in the North-West Provinces, holding a great Durbar at Agra, in November, where he recognized the much valued right of adoption by the native princes of India. A terrible famine took place in these Provinces in 1860, principally in the districts of Muttra, Agra, Delhi, Mirūt, and Rohilkund. Large pecuniary subscriptions were raised, not only in India, but in Great Britain, to aid the sufferers. This famine affected thirteen millions of people, of whom 4 per cent. died; many thousands of starving creatures were supported by the Government, and an immense area of land was thrown out of cultivation. A famine on a smaller scale visited Travankore, in Southern India, in 1861, and in the same year, a violent flood took place in Bengal, destroying whole villages, roads, and bridges.

Owing to the murder of Captain Mecham, an English officer, while travelling in Kohat, in 1859, a small frontier war occurred in the Derajāt district of the Punjāb, where the offending tribes were defeated, and the chief delinquent delivered up to the British Government.

Punjāb.

In 1860, a British force was moved into the country of the Sikhim Rājā, in consequence of the kidnapping propensities of his subjects. The station of Darjiling in that territory had, in 1835, been annually rented as a sanitarium from the Rājā for 3,000 rupees, but, as in 1849, Doctors Campbell and Hooker (the former political agent to the Rājā), had been ill-treated and imprisoned in Sikkim, a military force was sent to effect their release, and the tract previously rented was annexed. In 1861, a treaty was concluded with the Rājā, the chief provision in which was the appointment of a Resident at his court. In 1860 also, military operations on a small scale were carried out against some savage tribes on the Pegu frontier, in Guzerat, and in the hill districts of Assam.

Sikkim.

In 1861, a treaty was entered into with the Nizam (of Heidurabād), by which a portion of the Raichore Doāb, and the Dharaseo district of Berar, were restored to him by the British Government, under whose control and management they had remained since 1853. A treaty was also concluded in 1862 with the King of Burmah, by which—(*a*) Englishmen were allowed to trade in Burmah, and pass through that country unmolested; (*b*) a British consular agent was permitted to reside at the capital; (*c*) 1 per cent. only to be levied by the king on goods conveyed on the Irawaddi from China to the Bay of Bengal.

Nizam.

Burmah.

Maisūr.

A large sum (£520,000) from the Indian revenues, usually known as the "**Maisūr grant,**" was, in 1861, by the order of the Indian Secretary of State (Sir Charles Wood), set apart for the maintenance of the numerous descendants of Heidur Ali and Tippū Sahēb, former rulers of Maisūr. This measure, passed at a period of heavy financial pressure, produced a great ferment in India.

Indigo Disturbances.

In 1859-60, a violent rupture took place between the Indigo planters and their cultivators in Bengal, mostly in the Kishnagur, Jessore, Furridpūr and Pubna districts. The latter complained of the great oppression exercised over them by the planters in the cultivation of indigo, and a commission was appointed to enquire into these disputes. Much difference of opinion was shown by the members, but as some remedy to this state of things, small cause courts were shortly afterwards established in sixteen of the Bengal districts.

Waste Lands.

In October 1861, Lord Canning issued an order permitting the sale of culturable waste lands in India, at the rate of five shillings an acre for uncleared, and ten shillings for cleared land, limiting the grant to each person to 3,000 acres, and also according permission to redeem the existing land revenue at a twenty years' purchase. This was, however, practically annulled by a subsequent resolution (9th June 1862), of Sir Charles Wood, directing such lands to be sold in plots or blocks by auction at an upset price, to be fixed by the local Government.

Legislative.

In 1859, a new Code of Civil Procedure (**Act VIII.**) in force in all Civil Courts in India, was passed, as also the Rent Law (**X.**), which provides a more efficient machinery for settling the claims of rent between landlord and tenant In 1860, the Disarming Act (**XXXI.**), was made the law, but as it treated Europeans and natives alike, it excited great anger among the former. A clause was subsequently inserted in the Act, rendering it of no effect except in Provinces where it might be specially enforced. In 1860 also, the celebrated Indian Penal Code (**XLV.**), was passed, but not brought into force till 1862. It was commenced in 1833, and is one of the most complete codes of criminal law in existence. In 1861, the Criminal Procedure Code (**XXV.**), was passed, but several of its provisions have to some extent been since amended. The Indian Council's Act was also passed, but not acted upon till 18th January, 1862, on which day the Council, at Kalkutta, consisting, with the President, of fourteen members, three of them natives, sat for the first time. The Bombay Council of eight members, met on the 22nd January, and the Madras Council of seven members on 4th February of the same year. An Act, throwing open the Indian Civil Service to competition, and another amalgamating the Courts of Law, and constituting High Courts at the Presidency towns, as well as a Currency Act (**XIX.**), providing for the issue of notes in exchange for current silver coin or bullion, were all passed in the same year.

Financial.

The first Budget ever published in India was issued by Lord Canning in 1859, and this showed a deficit of five millions sterling. At the latter end of the same year Mr. Wilson arrived in Kalkutta as Indian Finance Minister, and introduced the Income Tax for the first time in India. It met with strong opposition, and Sir Charles Trevelyan, Governor of Madras, even published a protest against its imposition in the newspapers of that presidency, for which he was recalled by the Secretary of State for India. Mr. Wilson died on 9th August, 1860, of acute dysentery. His successor, Mr. S. Laing, landed in India on 18th January, 1861, and after bringing out his Budget left that country in May, returning at the close of the year. The cost of the whole Indian army in 1856-57 was £12,750,000, in 1858-59 it was £24,750,000. The military police alone numbered in that year 353,783 men, but great reductions were made by Mr. Wilson in military expenditure during the years 1859 and 1860.

Indian Revenue in	1856-57	was	£29,702,854
"	1861-62	"	£43,830,000
Indian Debt in	1857	. . .	£59,461,969
"	1862	. . .	£107,514,159

Honorary Magistrates. Native Honorary Magistrates were first appointed in Bengal in 1861, and afterwards in the North-West Provinces, Oudh, the Punjāb, and other territories.

Star of India. In 1861 the order of the most exalted "Star of India" was created, Sir John Lawrence, Sir George Pollock, Lord Clyde, and several others distinguished in Indian history, receiving the honour of knighthood. Among the native recipients were the Māhārājas of Gwālior and Puttiāla, the Nizam of Heidurabād, the Rājā of Kashmir, and other Oriental princes.

Productions. The cultivation of the tea-plant seems to have been entered upon with much spirit at the latter end of Lord Canning's administration. Land was eagerly taken up in the Kangra district of the Punjāb, in Kumaon, and the Dehra Dūn of the North-West Provinces, while great energy was bestowed on coffee planting in the Madras Presidency.

Ecclesiastical. In 1861 the Bishop of Kalkutta (Dr. Cotton) established in India schools for the education of European children whose parents were unable to send them to England for that purpose. In the same year the Bishop of Madras (Dr. Dealtry) died; he had previously (1831) been archdeacon of Kalkutta. His place in the Madras see was filled up by Dr. F. Gell.

Names of Note.—**Sir Henry Lawrence** (1806-57), **Generals Lord Clyde** (1792-1863), **John Jacob** (1812-58), **Sir Henry Havelock** (1795-1857), **J. Neill** (1810-57), **J. Nicholson** (1821-57), **Sir Robert Inglis, Major Hodson** (died 1857), military commanders; **J. Wilson** (1805-60), Indian Finance Minister; **Sir Jamsetji Jijibhoy, Bart.** (died 1859); **Rāni of Jhānsi** (killed in 1858); **Tantia Topi,** a rebel leader (executed 1859).

(XVI.) EARL OF ELGIN AND KINCARDINE,

GOVERNOR-GENERAL (A.D. 1862-3).

Governor of Madras.		*Governor of Bombay.*	
SIR WILLIAM DENISON .	1860	SIR H. BARTLE E. FRERE	1862

Appointment.—In 1862, and he assumed the post of Viceroy at Kalkutta on 12th March of that year; Lord Elgin had previously been Governor-General of Canada, and had also been sent on two missions to China and Japan in 1857 and 1860, where he negotiated several important treaties.

Death.—Lord Elgin died at Dhurumsāla, a sanitarium in Upper India, on 20th November, 1863, from illness brought on by unwonted exertion in the Himalayan Hills. He was at the time of his death in his 53rd year.

Character.—From the short period (twenty months) Lord Elgin held the office of Governor-General, it is impossible to draw his character as an Indian ruler, but it is supposed, from his previous experience in offices of trust, that, had he lived to complete his period of service, his nomination to the Viceroyalty of British India would have justified the expectations formed of him.

Memorable Events.—Though there were no wars, but

merely a few frontier operations, carried on during Lord Elgin's administration, an important movement, known as the "Wahābi" conspiracy, was discovered in 1863. "Wahābism" may be considered as a revival of pure Mahomedanism, and having a religious rather than a political tendency, no great attention was paid to it by the Indian Government. It was, however, discovered that some agency existed in North-Eastern India for sending up recruits to Sittāna, a colony of Hindūsthāni fanatics on the right bank of the Indus, opposite Hazara, where hostilities were then going on, and that one Mahomed Shuffi, an influential government contractor, with several others, were materially aiding the conspiracy with both men and money. These recruits were brought from distant cities, such as Dakka and Patna, the latter generally considered as the head-quarters of Wahābism in India. Mahomed Shuffi and his accomplices were tried and found guilty of treason, but none of them suffered capital punishment.

Wahābi Conspiracy.

Lord Elgin, in February, 1863, left Kalkutta for a tour in the Upper Provinces. At Agra he held a large durbar, and afterwards went on to Simla, thence in the autumn he proceeded by the Rotung Pass to Dhurumsāla, where he died.

Tea.

It was in 1863 that tea speculations in India reached their height. In Assam the number of tea estates was 246, with an aggregate area of 122,700 acres, of which 20,144 were under cultivation, yielding 2,150,068 lbs., valued at 1*s.* 9*d.* per lb. In the North-West Provinces and the Punjāb the tea districts covered 38,566 acres, of which, in the former, 4,596 acres only were cultivated, while 9,518 acres were planted out in the latter.

There were, in 1862, in India and Ceylon about 1,190 churches, with 153,816 native Christians in connection with Protestant missions, and out of 659 ordained missionary clergymen, 140 were natives of India. The vernacular schools numbered 1,562, with 44,612 scholars, and the Anglo-vernacular 185, with 23,377 scholars. The Bible had also been translated into twelve different languages. The expenditure during the previous ten years was £285,000, and the local contributions were £45,325. It has been found that, while the educated natives of India have relinquished the idle fables of Hindūism, but few seem desirous of embracing Christianity. Many appear to hold a middle course, and have taken to **Brahmoism**, which is in itself a kind of Deism, with a strict observance of the moral law. Caste prejudices are believed to be gradually declining, and the educated natives have established among themselves numerous societies and associations for the discussion of questions of social science.

Protestant Missions.

From the death of Lord Elgin (November, 1863) to the assumption of the Viceroyalty by Sir John Lawrence (January, 1864), the temporary vacancy was held by Sir William Denison, Governor of Madras, who arrived in Kalkutta on 1st December, 1863. His attention was at once directed to the operations generally called the "Umbeyla Campaign," then being carried on by Sir Neville Chamberlain against the Hindūsthāni fanatics of Sittāna, a place already mentioned. It commenced on the 20th October, 1863, and it was soon found that there was a general combination of almost all the tribes, from the Indus to the Kabūl boundary, against the English, and that the Akhūnd of Swāt had been preaching a "jehad," or holy war, against the infidel. Owing to some temporary successes on the part of the hill tribes, and to considerable loss of life on the side of the English force, it was proposed to retire, but this was rejected by Sir W. Denison, and fresh troops

Umbeyla Campaign.

were pushed forward to the frontier. The British arms were then successful, the village of Umbeyla being destroyed by fire on the 16th December, and the stronghold of Mulka, the settlement of the fanatics, also fired on the 22nd of the same month. The object of the expedition having been accomplished, the British force was then withdrawn from the hills.

(XVII.) SIR JOHN L. LAWRENCE, BART. (AFTERWARDS BARON LAWRENCE OF THE PUNJĀB AND OF GRATELY), GOVERNOR-GENERAL (A.D. 1864-69).

Governors of Madras.		*Governors of Bombay.*	
SIR W. DENISON . .	1860-66	SIR H. BARTLE E. FRERE	1862-67
LORD NAPIER . . .	1866	SIR W. R. SEYMOUR V. FITZGERALD . .	1867

Appointment.—In 1863, and arrived in Kalkutta on 12th January, 1864. Sir John Lawrence is the son of Lieutenant-Colonel Lawrence, and was born at Richmond, in Yorkshire, on 4th March, 1811: he arrived in India in the East India Company's Civil Service in February 1830, and rose to be, in 1853, the Chief Commissioner of the Punjāb. In 1857 he was created a baronet with a pension of £2,000 a year, for his services during the Indian Mutiny, and in 1869 a peer, with the title of Lord Lawrence of the Punjāb and of Grately.

Resignation.—Sir John Lawrence resigned his office of Viceroy on 12th January, 1869, and was succeeded by the Earl of Mayo.

Character.—Lord Lawrence is an able Indian statesman, honest, conscientious, experienced, and an excellent administrator. Prompt, decisive, and energetic in action, and endowed with a thorough earnestness of purpose—qualities which he fully showed in the eventful period of the mutinies of 1857—Lord Lawrence must ever be considered one of the foremost characters of Anglo-Indian history.

Wars.—I. With Bhotan in 1864. A dispute with the people of that country existed as far back as 1837, by their having committed certain outrages on the inhabitants of a strip of level country at the foot of the Bhotan Hills, called the "Dūars," eighteen in number, for which the East India Company paid a yearly tribute, and again in 1861, when an English force had to be brought up to the frontier, owing to a threatened movement by the Bhotanese against Darjiling.

The Indian Government at length resolved to send a mission, under the Honourable Ashley Eden, with a suitable escort to the Deb Rājā at the Bhotan capital. It set out in November, 1863, and arrived, after many difficulties, at Punakha, the capital, on 15th March. Mr. Eden and his party were, however, here subjected to several gross indignities by the Bhotanese officials, and he himself compelled to sign a treaty ceding the Assam Dūars to Bhotan. The mission was then allowed to depart, and after a second series of difficulties it reached British territory about the beginning of April. After a futile attempt by the Indian Government to obtain the restitution of all British subjects then in captivity in Bhotan on the threat of annexing the Bengal Dūars, war was proclaimed in 1864, and a British force marched into the disputed territory, where, after capturing all the forts by the 19th of December, it was broken up. At the latter end of January, 1865, these forts were attacked by the Bhotanese, and the water supply being cut off from one of them, that of Dewangīri, the officer in command, Colonel Campbell, was compelled to evacuate it, with a loss of two guns, but the place was subsequently recaptured. The other forts resisted all the attacks made upon them. In 1866 a treaty was concluded with the Deb Rājā, by which the two guns lost at Dewangiri were restored, the British Government engaging to rent the Bengal Dūars for 25,000 rupees yearly, this sum to be doubled should the treaty be faithfully observed by the Bhotanese.

II. In 1868 an encounter took place with the Waghurs, a lawless tribe inhabiting a portion of Kattiawar, on the western coast of the Bombay Presidency. They were defeated, but with the loss of two British officers, Captains La Touche and Hibbert.

An expedition, generally known as the "Black Mountain Campaign," was also organized against some tribes on the North-West Frontier in September, 1868, in consequence of an attack made by them on a police station in the Agror Valley, a district situate on the left bank of the Indus, and not far from the seat of the Umbeyla war. The campaign was speedily terminated by the burning of several villages, and negotiations having been entered into with the heads of the hostile tribes, a peace was concluded on 10th October, 1868. (The Abyssinian war is not referred to in these outlines, as being unconnected with Indian history, except in so far as the supply of troops and stores from British India was concerned.)

Muskat.

In 1865 the Imām of Muskat was murdered, it is believed, by his son Selim, who was then raised to the throne, but his uncle, the Sultan of Zanzibar, who had hitherto paid tribute to his brother, refused to do so to the nephew. The Shah of Persia also prepared to seize Bundur Abbas, the sea-port rented by him to the Imām, but this the British Government refused to allow. About the latter end of 1868, Sultan Selim was driven from his throne by his brother-in-law, Azan-ibn-Gheis.

Afghānisthān.

Dost Mahomed, the ruler of Afghānisthān, died in 1863, after nominating his son, Shir Ali Khān, as his successor. The latter defeated his brothers, Afzūl Khān and Azim Khān, who had risen against him, the former being imprisoned while the latter obtained a refuge in the Punjāb district of Rawul Pindi. A son of Afzūl Khān, however, collected an army and drove Shir Ali from his throne, on which he placed his father, but the latter dying soon after, Azim Khān was made his successor by his nephew. Shir Ali in his turn now got together a large force, with which he recovered his sovereignty in July 1868, and this he has since maintained.[1]

Burmah.

In 1866 a rebellion broke out in the independent empire of Burmah, headed by two of the king's sons; the rebels were driven into British territory, where they submitted to the Chief Commissioner. In November, 1867, the King of Burmah agreed to reduce all frontier duties to a 5 per cent. rate, and abolish all royal monopolies except those on earth-oil, timber, and precious stones, but he subsequently withdrew his assent.

Oudh.

The Governor-General during his administration settled several important questions relative to tenure of land in Oudh. Lord Canning had previously conferred large rights on the Talūkdars, or ancient landholders in that province, expressly stipulating for the observance by them of all the existing rights of their cultivators; but as hereditary tenants were likely to be reduced to the position of tenants-at-will, Sir John Lawrence decided that—"1. No new rights were to be created by the government of India; 2. the privileges heretofore allowed as an indulgence to all cultivators, who had once been proprietors of lands, should be confirmed and placed on a legal footing; and 3, the cultivators should be entitled to consideration for improvements made by them in case the landlords should attempt to oust them,

---

[1] In 1869 Shir Ali was received with great state at Ambāla in Upper India by the present Viceroy, Lord Mayo.

or raise their rents." These principles were expressed in the Oudh Tenancy Bill (XIX. of 1868). Similar measures were taken to improve the rights of tenants in both the North-West Provinces and the Punjāb. This latter province was visited by the Governor-General in October, 1864, and a stately Durbar held at Lahore, which was numerously attended by the native chieftains of that and the surrounding districts.

N.W. Provinces and Punjāb.

In 1866 a terrible famine occurred in the Orissa district (in the Bengal Presidency), owing to a failure of the rains in 1865. From the report furnished by a commission appointed to inquire into the subject, it was found that timely measures were not taken by the officials of that district to provide against the impending calamity. At the latter end of 1867 this unfortunate province was inundated, and it is believed that little less than two millions of its people must have died from sickness and starvation.

Orissa.

In October, 1864, a very destructive cyclone visited Kalkutta and its neighbourhood; it extended over an area of 100 miles in diameter, and was followed by a storm-wave on the river Hūghli, between 20 and 30 feet in height, which submerged whole villages. At Kalkutta 155 ships were driven on shore, and many foundered. Out of a population of 6,000 souls on Saugor island, only 1,488 were left alive. On 1st Nov., 1867, another cyclone visited Kalkutta, causing a loss of life in all of 1,000 persons; 30,000 huts were levelled to the ground, and 200 brick houses destroyed.

Cyclones at Kalkutta.

Owing to the enormous wealth poured into the Bombay Presidency from Europe, consequent on the great rise in the price of raw cotton in 1863 and 1864, a spirit of wild speculation seized on all classes. It

Speculative Manias.

lasted but till July, 1865, when a reaction set in, producing the most disastrous failures. The Bank of Bombay became irretrievably ruined, resulting, it is supposed, from a neglect of reasonable precautions, and from a want of proper supervision on the part of the government directors. In May, 1868, a commission was appointed to inquire into its affairs. Madras remained unaffected by the speculative mania, but it was felt, though in a less degree, at Kalkutta, where several gigantic schemes were put forward but none carried out.

Administrative Reforms.

The administration of Sir John Lawrence was distinguished for the many reforms and improvements effected during his rule. In **Public Works** a system of irrigation was planned to benefit such districts as were liable to seasons of drought. He organized a separate branch of the Public Works Department to carry out this object, and had the Province of Rohilkund surveyed for irrigational purposes. New canals were cut in the Punjāb and North-West Provinces, existing ones re-modelled, and lines of navigable canals were projected in Bengal, in the Madras and Bombay Presidencies, in the Central Provinces, and in British Burmah. The E. I. Irrigation Company began its work in Orissa, in November, 1863, but was unable, from want of progress, to avert the great famine there in 1866; and in 1864, the Madras Irrigation Company commenced operations with a Government guarantee of 5 per cent. on its capital. In **Military Works**, large and commodious upper-storied barracks for European troops have been erected in several of the principal stations in India. Road-making by European soldiers in the regions of the Himalayas has also been introduced with marked benefit to the health of the troops so employed. Among **Civil Works** may be noticed several roads constructed in Rājpūtāna and Central

India, and during Sir John Lawrence's administration, 1,556 miles of railroad were opened, on which thirty millions of capital had been spent. On 1st May, 1867, the total number of miles of railway open in India was 3,637. The gross railway earnings in 1868 were £4,487,112, the net receipts £2,337,300, and the net annual payments £800,000. In **Telegraphic** communication, though the increase in lines had been but 505 miles, the length of wire had been increased from 11,661 miles in 1865, to 22,567 miles in 1869, while the tariff of prices had been very considerably reduced. Several lighthouses were erected on the east coast of the Bay of Bengal. A new and scientific system of forest management was introduced for the first time in 1864, and a college of engineering was founded in 1865 at Rūrki, on a plan designed by Sir Hugh Rose, its object being to qualify officers and students for the engineering profession. Sanitary commissions were appointed for eradicating abuses and proposing reforms, and, lastly, the police establishments, as also the subordinate judicial departments of the State, have both been re-organized, and the number of small cause courts greatly increased.

Legislative.

Among the most important enactments passed during Sir John Lawrence's tenure of office, may be mentioned, the Whipping Act (**VI.**) and a provision for Cooli Emigration (**XIII.**) in 1864. During 1865 an Indian Marriage Act (**V.**), referring to Christians only, and an Indian Succession Act (**X.**), but not applying to Hindūs, Mahomedans, or Būdhists, were passed, as also the High Court Criminal Procedure Act (**XIII.**) which abolished Grand Juries throughout British India. In 1866 the Native Converts' Marriage Act (**XXI.**) was passed, but it does not apply to either Mahomedans or Jews. In this year also a High Court was established at Agra in the North-west Provinces, and a Chief Court, possessing most of the powers of a High Court, at Lahore in the Punjāb. Among the enactments passed in 1868 the most important are the Oudh and Punjāb Tenancy Acts (**XIX.** and **XXVIII.**) as treating of Tenant-right.

Financial.

The revenue of British India, which on an average during the three years preceding the mutiny of 1857 was £31,980,000, had increased in 1863-4 to £44,613,000, and in 1868-9 to £51,657,658, the total Indian debt in the latter year being £108,866,189, with interest thereon of £5,044,171. In 1862-3 the Indian export trade rose in value from 43 to 63 millions sterling, but this increase was mainly due to the high prices of raw cotton then ruling. Still it is enormous when compared with that from 1840 to 1843, and from 1850 to 1853, the export trade in which periods was £13,610,000 and £19,503,000 respectively. Mr. Laing's first Budget, brought out in 1861-2, opened with a deficit of six millions, but that for 1862-3 showed an equalization of receipts and disbursements. Mr. Laing was succeeded as Indian Finance Minister by Sir Charles Trevelyan (a former Governor of Madras) in January, 1863, who was remarkable for his determined opposition to an income-tax. He resigned his office in 1866 to Mr. Massey, who in the following year introduced the license tax, against which a strong spirit of opposition was manifested at the time.

Productions.

The planting of cinchona-trees for the production of quinine has been carefully attended to since 1863, and in 1866 the plantations had greatly increased on the Nilgiri Hills. Facilities have also been afforded by the Indian Government for experiments in cotton cultivation, and cotton commissioners have been appointed in several districts to assist mercantile interests in this important staple. The cotton exports from Bombay which in 1857-8 were 24,000,000lbs. of the value of £4,036,875, had increased in 1865-6 to 512,750,000lbs. of the value of £25,534,416, and in 1868 to 522,777,428lbs. of the value of £15,975,569. In 1840 the district of Wynaad near the Nilgiri Hills was selected as a suitable spot for coffee cultivation; in 1866 the number of planters was 200, but the want of good roads is still a great obstacle in transporting the coffee to the sea-coast. In the article of Indian-grown tea, the quantity exported to England in 1856 was only 690,390lbs., whereas in 1868 it was 9,095,444lbs. of the value of £820,532. In 1869 the export was believed to be not under twelve millions of pounds, while the number of plantations in Assam, Darjiling, Silhet and Kachar was 374, with a cultivated area of 66,000 acres.

Educational.

Education made great strides in British India during the administration of Sir John Lawrence. The state expenditure on Education, which in 1856-57 was £195,494, had risen in 1867 to £763,230, but notwithstanding this large pecuniary grant, the great masses of the people remain still practically untouched. In Bombay the Jijibhoy family are supposed to have contributed in the aggregate not less than £200,000 to charitable and educational institutions in that Presidency. In female education the first great start was made in the Punjāb in 1862-63. In 1867 there were in that Province 296 government and 651 aided female schools: in the North-west Provinces 479 government and 68 aided; in Bengal 1 government and 257 aided; in the Central Provinces 130 government; in the Madras Presidency 75 aided, and in the Bombay Presidency 61 government and 12 aided schools. The entire number of educational institutions of all descriptions in British India, which in 1852-3 numbered but 413, had risen in 1865-6 to 19,206, and in 1868-9 to 23,300 with 757,667 pupils. The total expenditure in this latter year from all sources was £995,589, of which the Government of India contributed £590,452.

In connection with these educational statistics, it may not be considered out of place to treat of the different languages spoken throughout India and the countries adjoining it. These may be divided into two great branches—1. The Indo-Germanic, and 2. the Turanian.

Languages of India.

I. INDO-GERMANIC.

Indic Class.

1. Hindi (with numerous dialects).
2. Bengali.
3. Punjābi (with many dialects).
4. Sindhi.
5. Marathi.
6. Gujerathi.
7. Nipālese.
8. Uriya.
9. Assamese.
10. Kashmiri.
11. Doghra.

Iranic Class (*of which Zend is the parent*).

1. Persian.
2. Kurdish.
3. Ossitinian.
4. Pushtū.
5. Armenian.

II. TURANIAN.

Class I.

1. The Thaic (or Siamese) of which the Khamti is spoken in Burmah.
2. The Mōn, spoken in Pegu.
3. The Shan spoken in Tenasserim.

Class II.

1. Bhotia.
2. Lepcha, spoken in Sikkim.
3. Kiranti, Bramhu, Chepang, Pahri and numerous others, spoken in parts of Nipāl.

Class III.

The Lohitic or Burmese, with numerous dialects.

Class IV.

The Kol, with numerous dialects.

Class V.—Dravidian.

1. Telugu.
2. Tamil.
3. Kanarese.
4. Malayalim.
5. Tuluvu.
6. Kodugu (Kūrg).
7. Brahui (Bilūchisthān).
8. Singhalese (Ceylon).

The principal hill stations in Bengal and the North-west Provinces are—1. Simla (7,000 feet); 2. Dūgshai (6,000 feet); 3. Darjilīng (7,166 feet); 4. Landour (7,500 feet); 5. Kussowli (7,000 feet); 6. Mussūri (7,000 feet); 7. Nyni Tal (7,000 feet); 8.

Hill Sanitaria in India.

Subathū (4,000 feet); and 9. Murri (8,000 feet); all these are situated in the Sub-Himalayan range of mountains. In the Madras Presidency there are—1. The Nīlgiri Hills, having the stations of Utakamund (7,400 feet; Jackatalla (7,000 feet); Kotāgiri (6,570 feet); and Konūr (5,800 feet); 2. Ramundrūg (3,100 feet) in the ceded districts. In the Bombay Presidency there are the Māhāblēshur Hills (4,700 feet); 2. Mount Abū, near Disa (5,000 feet); 3. Purundhur in the Dekhun (4,300 feet); 4. Singhur in the Dekhun (4,200 feet); 5. Matheran, in the Konkun (2,000 feet).

Geological and Revenue Surveys.

It was about 1856 that a geological survey was established for examining the mineral resources of British India. Revenue surveys also with the object of assessing moderately and equitably all lands paying revenue to the Indian Government, were introduced about 1822, and have been attended with marked benefit to both the cultivator and the State. Up to 1868 nearly three-fourths of the peninsula of India had been surveyed trigonometrically.

Exhibitions.

An exhibition of arts, manufactures and produce on a large and pretentious scale was successfully carried out at Lahore in 1864; other Exhibitions, agricultural and industrial in character, have also been held at different times at Kalkutta, Benares, Luknow, Agra, Nāgpūr and in several places in the Madras Presidency. It is expected that these examples will be very generally followed in other parts of British India.

Ecclesiastical.

In October, 1866, Dr. Cotton, the Bishop of Kalkutta was drowned by falling into the river at Kūshtia in Assam, while attempting to get on board a steamer; he was much beloved for his earnest piety, untiring energy and great charity. He was succeeded by Dr. Milman, who was installed on 2nd April, 1867. Dr.

Gell, Bishop of Madras had visited the whole of his diocese, and had confirmed 6,600 persons (of whom 5,000 were natives). The number of baptized native Christians in his diocese was found to be 55,495, and the European and East Indian Missionaries, 53, besides 34 native clergymen. Dr. Harding the Bishop of Bombay resigned his see in 1868, and was succeeded by Dr. H. A. Douglas, who had previously filled the office of Archdeacon at Cape Town in South Africa.

Names of Note.—**Dr. Cotton,** Bishop of Kalkutta (d. 1866); **Sir Robert Montgomery,** Lieutenant Governor of the Punjāb; **Mr. S. Laing, Sir Charles Trevelyan,** Indian Finance Ministers; **Sir H. Bartle E. Frere,** Governor of Bombay; **Sir Hugh Rose** (now Lord Strathnairn), late Commander-in-Chief of the Indian Army; **Sir Herbert Edwardes** (1819-68); **Sir Neville Chamberlain, Sir Arthur Phayre,** Chief Commissioner of British Burmah.

APPENDIX.

THE DIVISIONS AND DISTRICTS COMPRISING THE BENGAL PRESIDENCY.

Divisions.	Districts.	Area.	Population.
		Sq. miles.	
Bhaugulpur.	1. Bhaugulpur	4121	1,082,650
	2. Monghyr	4200	925,040
	3. Purneah	5275	729,114
	4. Sonthāl Pergunnas	5375	522,000
Burdwān.	5. Bankura	4683	74,300
	6. Birbhūm	2330	827,624
	7. Burdwān	2692	1,088,813
	8. Hūghli	1457	1,370,120
	9. Howrah	550	520,000
	10. Midnapūr	5031	1,558,450
Chittagong.	11. Noakhalli	3000	544,998
	12. Chittagong	2717	800,000
	13. Tipperah	3600	1,000,000
	14. Chittagong Hill tracts	7000	250,000
Kuttak.	15. Balasūr	3065	494,056
	16. Kuttak	3370	1,293,884
	Tributary Mehals	16,608	750,000
	17. Pūri	2083	613,536
Dakka.	18. Bakurgunge	4000	866,632
	19. Dakka	3138	950,000
	20. Furridpūr	1500	624,176
	21. Mymensing	6586	947,240
	22. Sylhet	5500	1,504,289
	23. Kachar	5000	200,000
		102,881	19,675,802

Divisions.	Districts.	Area.	Population.
		Sq. miles.	
	Brought forward .	102,881	19,675,802
Nuddea.	24. Jessore	3651	957,152
	25. Nuddea	3296	551,229
	26. The 24 Pergunnas . .	2523	593,079
	27. City of Kalkutta . . .	7.8	1,000,000
Patna.	28. Gya	5439	1,367,392
	29. Champarun	3781	750,000
	30. Patna	2242	872,000
	31. Sarun	3000	1,200,000
	32. Shahābād	4403	1,600,000
	33. Tirhūt	9216	1,854,297
Rājshayi.	34. Rungpore	4500	1,259,362
	35. Bograh	2000	400,000
	36. Dinajpūr	3820	1,000,000
	37. Maldah	1484	305,563
	38. Mūrshedabād	2439	967,619
	39. Rājshayi	3035	710,290
	40. Pubna	2044	281,366
Assam.	1. Durrung	2912	178,163
	2. Nowgong	8712	247,500
	3. Sibsaugor	2821	226,000
	4. Kamrūp	3348	400,000
	5. Lukimpūr	5000	117,393
	6. Kossyah & Jynteah Hills	5000	118,925
	7. Nāga Hills	5000	250,000
Chota Nāgpore.	8. Hazaribaugh	7028	750,000
	9. Lohardugga	7000	750,294
	10. Maunhbūm	6396	528,340
	11. Singbhūm	3998	289,789
Kūch Behar.	12. Western Dūars	1427	30,000
	13. Darjiling	800	85,000
	14. Gowalpara	2672	230,000
	15. Garrow Hills	3390	80,000
	16. Kūch Behar	1287	80,000
		226,552	39,567,675

MADRAS PRESIDENCY.

Divisions.	Districts.	Area.	Population.
		Sq. miles.	
	1. City of Madras	27	450,000
	2. Ganjam	4457	1,136,926
	3. Vizagapatam	18,935	1,934,558
	4. Godaveri	7535	1,427,472
	5. Kistna	7227	1,296,652
	6. Nellūr	4546	1,168,664
	7. Kuddapa	9177	1,144,759
	8. Bellari	11,496	1,304,998
	9. Kurnāl	7470	766,204
	10. Madras	2183	804,283
	11. North Arkot	15,146	1,787,134
	12. South Arkot	4779	1,261,846
	13. Tanjūr	3735	1,731,619
	14. Trichinopoli	3565	1,006,826
	15. Madura	8790	1,946,389
	16. Tinnivelli	5146	1,521,108
	17. Koimbatūr	8470	1,408,829
	18. Salem	7604	1,619,233
	19. South Kanara	4206	839,688
	20. Malabar	6259	1,856,378
		140,753	26,413,626

BOMBAY PRESIDENCY INCLUDING SINDH.

Divisions.	Districts.	Area.	Population.
		Sq. miles.	
	1. Island of Bombay . . .	20	916,000
	2. Ahmedabād	4402	650,223
	3. Kaira	1375	580,631
	4. Punch Mahals	1563	400,000
		7360	2,446,854

Divisions.	Districts.	Area.	Population.
		Sq. miles.	
	Brought forward .	7360	2,546,854
	5. Broach	1351	290,984
	6. Surat	1482	492,684
	7. Tanna	5400	874,570
	8. Khāndēsh	12,078	778,112
	9. Pūna	5250	666,006
	10. Ahmednuggur	10,414	995,585
	11. Solapūr	8565	675,115
	12. Rutnagiri	4500	672,197
	13. Bēlgaon	13,106	1,033,373
	14. Dharwar	6070	754,385
	15. North Kanara	4300	483,336
	16. Sattara	9327	948,053
Sindh.	17. Kurrachi	19,240	340,000
	18. Heidurabād	10,974	630,300
	19. Shikarpūr	9042	650,304
	20. Frontier Upper Sindh .	2225	75,000
	21. Thur and Parkur . . .	13,000	127,035
		143,674	13,033,893

THE NORTH-WEST PROVINCES.

Divisions.	Districts.	Area.	Population.
		Sq. miles.	
Mirūt.	1. Mirūt	2361	1,199,593
	2. Alligarh	1859	925,538
	3. Seharunpūr	2512	866,483
	4. Muzuffurnuggur . . .	1647	682,212
	5. Būlundshuhur	1889	800,431
	6. Dehra Dūn	1020	102,831
		11,288	4,577,088

Divisions.	Districts.	Area.	Population.
		Sq. miles.	
	Brought forward .	11,288	4,577,088
Rohilkund.	7. Bareilly	2372	1,381,334
	8. Bijnūr	1882	690,975
	9. Moradabād	2761	1,095,306
	10. Budaon	1972	889,810
	11. Shahjihānpūr	2328	1,016,844
	12. Terai	438	91,802
Agra.	13. Agra	1873	1,028,544
	14. Muttra	1612	800,321
	15. Ferrukabād	1693	915,943
	16. Mynpūri	1666	700,220
	17. Etawah	1631	626,444
	18. Etah	1404	614,351
Allahabad.	19. Allahabād	2764	1,393,183
	20. Kaunpore	2366	1,188,862
	21. Futtehpūr	1580	680,786
	22. Banda	3030	724,372
	23. Humirpūr	2288	520,941
	24. Jounpūr	1552	1,015,427
Benares.	25. Benares	991	793,277
	26. Gorukpūr . . . . . } 27. Busti . . . . }	7500	3,439,513
	28. Azimgarh	2545	1,385,872
	29. Mirzapūr	5199	1,054,413
	30. Ghāzipūr	2225	1,342,234
Jhānsi.	31. Jhānsi	1608	357,442
	32. Jaloun	1542	405,604
	33. Lullutpūr	1947	248,146
Kumaon.	34. Kumaon	6000	369,223
	35. Gurwhal	5000	233,326
	36. Ajmir	2672	426,268
		83,369	30,007,871

THE PUNJĀB.

Divisions.	Districts.	Area.	Population.
		Sq. miles.	
Delhi.	1. Delhi	790	506,689
	2. Gurgaon	1939	682,486
	3. Kurnāl	1832	486,067
Hissar.	4. Hissar	3294	340,886
	5. Rohtūk	1340	551,000
	6. Sirsa	1270	151,683
Ambāla.	7. Ambāla	1832	1,003,974
	8. Ludiana	1377	527,722
	9. Simla, about	21	23,400
Jullundhur.	10. Jullundhur	1381	683,531
	11. Hushiapūr	2204	795,784
	12. Kangra	3207	692,977
Umritsur.	13. Umritsur	2024	883,319
	14. Sealkote	1350	711,472
	15. Gūrdaspūr	1675	800,000
Lahore.	16. Lahore	2826	543,495
	17. Firozpūr	2692	433,609
	18. Gujranwalla	3752	420,758
Rawul Pindi.	19. Rawul Pindi	5996	543,000
	20. Jhilum	5350	395,000
	21. Gujrat	1916	489,661
	22. Shahpūr	3500	301,769
Mūltān.	23. Mūltān	5634	411,386
	24. Jhung	5718	299,034
	25. Montgomery	4142	106,434
	26. Muzuffurghur	6122	248,802
Derajāt.	27. Dera Ismāil Khān	5745	434,180
	28. Dera Ghāzi Khān	6531	238,959
	29. Bunnū	4500	246,824
Peshawur.	30. Peshawur	2324	450,099
	31. Kohāt	2840	107,362
	32. Hazara	2424	310,000
		97,548	14,820,362

OUDH.

Divisions.	Districts.	Area.	Population.
		Sq. miles.	
Luk-now.	1. Luknow	1390	630,259
	2. Unao	1334	591,141
	3. Durriabād	1285	731,661
Khyra-bād.	4. Sitapūr	1828	743,235
	5. Hurdui	2099	909,984
	6. Mohomdi.	3046	527,390
Fyza-bād.	7. Baraitch	1721	570,778
	8. Fyzabād	1979	1,038,195
	9. Gonda	1900	750,000
Baiswa-rah.	10. Sūltanpūr	1526	433,016
	11. Pertabghur	1703	724,739
	12. Roy Bareilly	1331	676,249
		21,142	8,326,647

THE CENTRAL PROVINCES.

Divisions.	Districts.	Area.	Population.
		Sq. miles.	
Nāgpūr.	1. Nāgpūr	3682	634,121
	2. Bhundara	5601	748,161
	3. Chanda	10,000	537,295
	4. Wurdah	2392	343,485
Jubbulpūr.	5. Jubbulpūr	4856	620,201
	6. Saugor	3928	498,642
	7. Dumoh	2457	262,641
	8. Seoni	5365	455,462
	9. Mundla	5134	187,699
		43,415	4,287,707

Divisions.	Districts.	Area.	Population.
		Sq. miles.	
	Brought forward .	43,415	4,287,707
Nurbudda.	10. Hoshungabād	3997	427,418
	1. Feudatoryship . . .	215	13,015
	11. Baitūl	3600	244,854
	12. Nursingpūr	1916	336,796
	13. Chindwara	4255	327,875
	14. Nimar	3584	226,969
Chuttisgurh.	15. Raepūr	8453	952,754
	6. Feudatoryships . . .	6139	369,908
	16. Belaspūr	5873	699,468
	2. Feudatoryships . . .	1807	81,035
	17. Sumbulpūr	5632	452,348
	5. Feudatoryships . . .	10,496	360,000
	18. Upper Godaveri District .	2274	54,680
	1. Feudatoryship . . .	13,062	269,684
		114,718	9,104,511

BERAR.

	Districts.	Area.	Population.
		Sq. miles.	
	1. Umrawutti	5085	569,494
	2. Akola	3411	491,036
	3. Mehkur	3013	225,168
	4. Wūn	5875	300,349
		17,334	1,586,047

MAISŪR.

	Districts.	Area.	Population.
		Sq. miles.	
	1. Nundidrūg	9,095	1,535,742
	2. Ashtagram	7,345	1,306,550
	3. Nugur	10,563	1,058,443
		27,003	3,900,735

KŪRG.

	District.	Area.	Population.
		Sq. miles.	
	1. Kūrg	2116	115,827

BRITISH BURMAH.

Divisions.	Districts.	Area.	Population.
		Sq. miles.	
Pegu.	1. Rangūn . . . . 2. Bassein . . . . 3. Myanoung . . . . . . 4. Prome . . . . 5. Toungū	33,400	1,350,989
Tenasserim.	1. Amherst . . . . 2. Tavoy 3. Mergui . . 4. Shoayghin	28,000	443,695
Arrakan.	1. Akyāb . . . . 2. Ramri . . . . 3. Sandoway	18,630	428,042
		80,030	2,222,726

FRENCH AND PORTUGUESE INDIA.

FRENCH.	Sq. m.	Pop.	PORTUGUESE.	Sq. m.	Pop.
1. Chandernagore . 2. Karikāl . 3. Pondicherri . . 4. Yanaon . 5. Mahē . .	191½	229,000	1. Goa. . . .	1066	363,788
			2. Damāun . 3. Diu . .	238	44,808
				1304	408,596

TERRITORY UNDER NATIVE FEUDATORIES.

	Sq. miles.	Population.
Bengal (all India except Madras and Bombay)	515,533	38,702,206
Madras	51,802	5,213,671
Bombay	60,575	4,460,370
	627,910	48,376,247

The wealthiest and most important of these Feudatories are the following :—

	Sq. miles.	Population.	Ann. Income.
			£.
Nizam of Heiderabād	78,003	10,666,080	2,150,000
Māhārāja Sindhia	35,650	2,500,000	1,110,910
Gaikwar of Baroda	4399	1,710,404	600,000
Māhārāja of Jeipūr	15,250	1,900,000	500,000
Māhārāja of Travankore	6653	1,262,647	448,063
Māhārāja of Kashmir	60,000	2,000,000	400,000
Māhārāja of Jodhpūr	35,672	1,783,600	350,000
Māhārāja Holkar	8318	576,000	330,000
Māhārāja of Puttiāla	5412	1,586,000	300,000
Māhārāja of Udipūr	11,614	1,161,140	266,127
Māhārāja of Bhurtpūr	1974	743,710	263,692
Begum of Bhopal	6764	663,656	240,000
Māharao of Kotah	5000	450,000	250,000
Māhārāja of Ulwar	3300	1,000,000	200,000
Rāna of Jhallāwar	2500	226,000	150,000
Rao of Kutch	6500	409,522	150,000
Nawāb of Bhāwulpūr	2483	364,582	125,000
Rāja of Kochin	1131	399,060	108,000
Māhārāna of Dholpūr	1250	192,382	109,437
Nawāb of Tonk	2370	320,419	101,751
Nawāb of Rāmpūr	890	484,691	100,000
Rājā of Kolapūr	3184	546,156	100,000

RACES AND CREEDS IN INDIA.

Aboriginal Hill Tribes	12,000,000
Hindūs	145,000,000
Būdhists	4,000,000
Mahomedans	20,000,000
Parsis	200,000
Asiatics from beyond British India	500,000
Jews	10,000
Armenians	5000
Europeans, pure	149,812
Europeans, mixed	90,496
Native Christians (of all denominations)	1,100,000

DENSITY OF POPULATION OF ALL INDIA.

	Census year.	Per sq. mile.
British India	1864 to 1868	129
British India without Feudatory States	1864 to 1868	159
Madras	1867	214
Bombay and Sindh	Estimate	95
Lower Bengal Hūghli District	Estimate	900
N. W. Provinces, Benares District	1865	797
Punjāb	1868	184
Central Provinces	1866	183
British Burmah	1867	79
Maisūr	1867	145
Berar	1867	128
Kūrg	Estimate	48

QUESTIONS ON THE HISTORY OF INDIA.

1. When was the Mogul dynasty established in India? Mention, with dates, the names of some of the most distinguished of the Great Moguls.

2. What was the origin of the East India Company? When did it first establish itself in India? Describe its gradual extension.

3. What important measures in reference to the Government of India were introduced in the years 1773, 1784, and 1833 respectively?

4. On what occasions has the city of Delhi been taken and plundered?

5. Who were the following persons; mention when and where they flourished, and the most important facts connected with them:—Heider Ali, Siwuji, Akbar Khān, Runjit Singh, Sindiah, Holkar, Sir William Macnaghten, and Sir Eyre Coote?

6. What are the principal sources of the revenue of British India? How is the land-tax assessed? What was the Zumindari settlement, established by Lord Cornwallis in 1793?

7. Mention the dates and the occasions on which the following battles were fought, and their results: Mūdki, Plassi, Chillianwalla, Ghuzni, Buxar, Prome, and Ferozeshah.

8. Mention, with dates, the names of the most eminent Governors of India during the present century, and briefly sketch the most important events which occurred during the government of each.

---

9. Arranging the history of India under three religious systems – Hindū, Mahomedan, and Christian—when may

each be considered to have commenced and when to have sunk under partial subjection to its successor?

10. Was the distinction of caste among the Hindūs contemporary with the primitive faith, or was it of a later and political origin?

11. What was the nature of the pretensions of the Brahmin to superiority?

12. When do we find India first noticed by classical writers?

13. What is the date of Alexander's invasion of India?

14. Where did he enter India, and by whom was he encountered?

15. Where did Alexander finally halt in India?

16. Did any of the Seleucian princes of Persia invade India?

17. Did any Greek princes rule in India after these incursions? How many, for how long, and over what extent of territory?

18. Up to what date did Būdhism flourish in India?

19. In what countries is it now the prevailing religion?

20. What authorities have we for the Mahomedan history of India?

21. Who was Mahmūd of Ghuzni? At what date did he live?

22. How often did he make predatory incursions into India?

23. By whom was India invaded for the purpose of permanent subjugation?

24. What was the date of the battle which decided the struggle, and with what Hindū princes was it fought?

25. Who was the first Mahomedan king of Delhi?

26. Who was the second king, and what was his race and position?

27 What progress was made in the conquest of Hindūsthān under the first dynasty of the kings of Delhi?

28. What were the conquests of Ala-u-din?

29. For what is his successor, Firuz, celebrated in India?

30. What was the date of Teimūr's (Tamerlane's) invasion of India?

31. By what transaction was it signalized?

32. When and by what means did Baber establish the house of Teimūr on the throne of Delhi?

33. Who was Baber, and what means have we of knowing his character and adventures?

34. What was the character of Akbar?

35. What were his notions of religion?

36. Who was Akbar's chief minister, and what record has he left of his master's administration?

37. What was the character of Akbar's son Selim, afterwards known as Jehāngīr?

38. What English ambassador was received at his court, and what was the result of the mission?

39. What celebrated edifice was erected at Agra by Shah Jehān, and in whose honour?

40. Who were the four sons of Shah Jehān? Describe their characters, their contests, and the result?

41. What was the character of Aurungzib?

42. Who was Siwuji, and what political power did he found?

43. What was the state of the Mogul empire after the death of Bahādūr Shah, in 1711, to the accession of his grandson Mahomed Shah in 1718?

44. What two principal Subhēdars, or Viceroys, made themselves independent in the same reign?

45. Who are our best authorities for the history of the Christian or European period in India?

46. What is the earliest notice we possess of commercial intercourse with India?

47. What was the date of the first voyage to India viâ the Cape of Good Hope, and by whom was it effected?

48. Where did the Portuguese first land?

49. What European nation next entered the Indian seas, and under what circumstances?

50. Where were their principal establishments?

51. What is their present condition?

52. When was the first English association for trading to India formed, and by what monarch was a charter granted?

53. Under what circumstances did the Company obtain Bombay?

54. How came the Company possessed of the villages

now constituting Kalkutta and the twenty-four Purgunnas?

55. What European government first mixed itself up with the quarrels of native princes?

56. By whom was the fort of Kalkutta captured, and on what account?

57. By whom were the English stations in Bengal recovered?

58. When was the battle of Plassi fought?

59. Who succeeded Jaffier Ali in the Nawabship of Bengal?

60. What induced the English to make Kossim Ali Khān the Nawāb, and afterwards to depose him?

61. From whom and at what period did the English receive the Diwāni of Bengal, Behar, and Orissa, and what did that imply?

62. Who was the first Governor-General of British India?

63. What were the principal heads of the impeachment of Warren Hastings on his return to England? How long did his trial last, and how did it terminate?

64. What was the first important political transaction of Lord Wellesley's administration?

65. With what Maratta princes did hostilities ensue?

66. With what native state did hostilities break out soon after Lord Moira's arrival? on what grounds, and with what result?

67. Who were the Pindaris?

68. What were the Maratta States at this period?

69. What were the important results of the Pindari and Maratta wars?

70. By whom was the Marquis of Hastings succeeded?

71. What hostilities ushered in his government?

72. What accession of territory followed?

73. What were the principal domestic measures of Lord Bentinck's administration, and what was their tendency?

74. What induced Lord Auckland to take part in political events beyond the Indus?

75. Who was Shah Sūja?

76. How and when did Dost Mahomed become the supreme ruler in Kabūl?

77. What was the object of the negotiations with Dost Mahomed in 1838, and in what point did they fail?

78. How did the English connexion with Afghanisthān close?

79. What was the form of government in Sindh?

80. What is the character of its population?

81. What demands were made upon the Mīrs of Sindh by the Governor-General?

82. What military and political transactions ensued?

---

83. Name the principal works of authority for the Hindū portion of the History of India.

84. What vestiges remain of what may be considered as the aboriginal population of India?

85. To what class of the nations of antiquity are the Brahminical Hindūs supposed to belong, and what are the grounds for this classification?

86. In what part of India did the Brahminical Hindūs first settle?

87. To what degree of civilization had they attained some fourteen or fifteen centuries before Christ?

88. What are the primary distinctions of caste, and their several duties?

89. Was the classification contemporary with the earliest conditions of the Hindū community, or was it of later introduction?

90. What is the present state of the Hindū population with respect to caste?

91. What were the leading features of Būdhism, and when and by whom was it introduced?

92. When did it disappear from India, and why?

93. What is its present state?

94. To what works are we chiefly indebted for our knowledge of the history and doctrines of Būdhism?

95. What classical authors (Greek or Latin) have preserved any account of India prior to the Christian Era?

96. What is the date of Alexander's invasion of India?

97. How far did he penetrate, and by what route did he return?

98. How long did Greek princes exercise sovereignty in

India, and in what parts of it? Mention some of the most celebrated of these rulers.

99. Through which of the Seleucian kings of Persia was a friendly intercourse with India maintained, and by whom and to whom was Megasthenes sent ambassador?

100. What means have we of knowing anything of the political condition of India from the time of Alexander to that of the first Mahomedan invasion, and what does it appear to have been?

101. When and where did the Mahomedans make their first appearance in India?

102. Did they effect any permanent establishment?

103. Who was Mahmūd of Ghuzni?

104. How often did he make incursions into India?

105. What is the truth of his reported treatment of the idol of Somnath?

106. Under what prince and at what date did the Mahomedans first take a firm footing in India?

107. What was the name, nation, and original station of the first Mahomedan King of Delhi?

108. What were the several dynasties of the Mahomedan Kings of Delhi until the coming of the Moguls?

109. By whom were the Mahomedan arms carried first into the Dekhun?

110. Mention some of the tyrannical acts of Mahomed Toghlak.

111. In whose reign, and at what date, was India invaded by Teimūr (Tamerlane)?

112. What act of barbarity signalized his invasion?

113. How was Baber descended, and by what means did he become possessed of the sovereignty of Hindūsthān?

114. Humayūn was driven from India, and remained absent fifteen years; when and how did he chiefly spend this interval?

115. Who were the Kings of Delhi during that period?

116. What independent Mahomedan principalities flourished in the Dekhun at the time of Humayūn's restoration, and what was their origin?

117. What powerful Hindū principality in South India

was contemporaneous with them, and when was it subverted?

118. What were the most remarkable features of Akbar's character and policy?

119. Who was his financial minister, and what were his chief revenue arrangements?

120. Name the sons of Shah Jehān, with notices of their individual character and ultimate fate?

121. What was the great object of Aurungzib's military policy, and with what success was it attended?

122. Who was Siwuji?

123. What are the standard authorities for the history of Mahomedan India?

124. When did the Portuguese sail round the Cape of Good Hope and reach India?

125. Where did they establish themselves, and how long did they maintain a political ascendency?

126. What were the chief causes of their decline?

127. From whom and under what circumstances did the English obtain permission to form commercial factories in India?

128. How came the East India Company possessed of the lands on which the fort and town of Madras were erected?

129. How came they possessed of the lands subsequently forming the town of Kalkutta and adjacent districts?

130. Describe briefly the principal events that occurred in the Madras Presidency from about 1740 to 1760, in which the English first took part in native politics, and which in reality laid the foundation of their subsequent power.

131. By whom was Kalkutta captured, and on what account?

132. By what calamitous event was it signalized?

133. By whom was the ascendancy of the English restored, and extended in Bengal?

134. What were the grounds for the quarrel with Kossim Ali, and which party was more in fault?

135. By whom was the Diwāni of certain districts in

India conferred upon the Company's Government, and what did it imply?

136. What were the principal charges made against Warren Hastings, and what was the justice or injustice of each separate article?

137. What is meant by the perpetual settlement of Lord Cornwallis, and how has it operated?

138. What was the first military incident of Lord Wellesley's Government?

139. With what Maratta states was he engaged in war and what was the result?

140. What was the main object of Lord Wellesley's policy, and how did he seek to effect it?

141. What was the policy of Lord Cornwallis during his second administration, and by whom was it carried out? What were the objections to it?

142. What were the principal military events connected with Lord Minto's administration?

143. With what native state did Lord Hastings first find himself involved in hostilities, and with what result?

144. What was the origin and object of the Pindari war?

145. What was the conduct of the Peishwa and the Rājā of Nāgpūr, and what were the consequences?

146. What were the chief objects of the Government of Lord W. Bentinck?

147. What led to the war with the Afghāns?

148. Who were the Afghāns? Who was their first monarch, and what part did he take in the affairs of Hindūsthān?

149. How came Dost Mahomed to be at the head of the Government of Kabūl?

150. To what causes may be ascribed the disastrous and disgraceful failure of the military expedition against the Afghān ruler?

151. What was the constitution of the Government of Sindh?

152. What circumstances led to the annexation of Sindh to the British empire?

153. Name the principal authorities as the best guides

to a knowledge of the European portion of the history of India.

---

154. Into what periods may the history of India be most conveniently divided?

155. Are the Brahminical Hindūs to be regarded as the aboriginal inhabitants of India, and if not, who are?

156. To what family of nations do the Brahminical Hindūs belong? What are the grounds for this classification?

157. Have the Brahminical Hindūs of the North and South a common origin?

158. Name the chief races of Northern and Southern India, following the Brahminical religion, and point out the grounds of their difference or of their identity.

159. Specify the earliest authorities upon the religious institutions and traditions of the Hindūs, their names, their subjects, and which of them are wholly or in part translated into any European language.

160. What was the political condition of ancient India as indicated by these works, and what the degree of civilization then prevailing?

161. What are the four original castes, and what their duties?

162. In what respect does the condition of the Sūdra differ from that of the helot, the slave, or the serf?

163. Are there any classes still in a state of serfage in India, or attached to the soil, and to what extent?

164. What is the general state of the Hindū population with respect to caste?

165. Under which of the Seleucian monarchs did Baktria become independent?

166. By which of the Baktrian princes was that kingdom extended to India, and over what part, and to what date did their sovereignty extend?

167. By whom was the Greek dominion finally subverted, and about what period?

168. Name some of the most distinguished Greek and other princes who ruled in the North-West of India, and along the Indus, from the time of Alexander the Great, to the first part of the Christian era.

169. Who were the Andhrian kings mentioned by Pliny, and what notices have we of them in Hindū authorities?

170. When did Būdhism disappear from India, and where does it now prevail?

171. In what respect does the Jain religion mainly agree with, or differ from Būdhism?

172. When did it become the dominant system in Western India? Where are its votaries chiefly found, and in what condition?

173. What are the principal Rājpūt tribes, and what is their reputed religion?

174. For what are they chiefly noted?

175. Where was the city of Valhabhi (or Ballabhi) situated? when was it founded, and when destroyed?

176. Mahomedan writers speak of the city of Nahrwala (or Nahrwara) in Guzerat—What city is intended, and by what Rājpūt race was it ruled? When was it deserted?

177. The Arabian Nights' Entertainments and early European travellers spoke of a very extensive and opulent city in the south of India, under the name of Bisnāgar, or Bijnāgur (properly Bijāyanuggur)—Where was it situated, when founded, and when destroyed?

178. Are any of the descendants of the princes of Bijāyanuggur still in existence?

179. What was the site and origin of the Principality of Ghuzni?

180. By whom was it raised to independence?

181. For what was Mahmūd of Ghuzni celebrated?

182. How long did the Ghuzni dynasty of princes last, and what was latterly the position of their principality and its capital?

183. What is the fabled origin of the Princes of Gour?

184. By what stratagem did Shahab-ū-din, Ghori, obtain possession of Lahore?

185. In what direction did Shahab-ū-din (also named Mahomed Ghori) first carry his arms against the Hindū princes, and with what results?

186. What were the results of his second attack?

187. When and where was the battle fought which gave him permanent ascendancy in Hindūsthān?

188. Who was the Hindū Rājā that commanded against the Mahomedans, and what was his fate?

189. Who was the first Mahomedan king of Delhi?

190. Over what territories did the Mahomedan conquests extend under the two first kings of Delhi?

191. Is there any instance of the exercise of sovereignty at Delhi by a female?

192. Specify the different dynasties of the kings of Delhi, between the first conquest and that of the Moguls.

193. Who was Ala-ū-din, and by what military operations was his reign distinguished?

194. State some of the extravagant proceedings of Mahomed Toghlak.

195. Are there any grounds for connecting the appearance of the Gipsies in Europe with his reign?

196. What were the seven Mahomedan kingdoms in India between the death of Mahomed Toghlak and the invasion of India by Teimūr (Tamerlane)?

197. Who was Baber, and what were the circumstances of his early life?

198. Where was Akbar born, and under what circumstances?

199. Whilst finding protection from the Shah of Persia, it is said that Humayūn was compelled to adopt the profession of the Shia form of the Mahomedan religion—What are the great points of dispute between the Shia and Sūni Mahomedans, and by what nations are their doctrines respectively followed?

200. What is the story of Nūr Jehān, and what was her character?

201. Name the sons of Shah Jehān, describe their characters, and their fates.

202. What was the great object of Aurungzib's military policy?

203. What Mahomedan kingdoms did he overturn, and into what Sūbahs of the Dekhun were his conquests distributed?

204. Who was the founder of the Maratta kingdom?

205. Who was Aurungzib's successor, and what policy did he pursue towards the Rājpūts and Marattas?

206. What was the character of the religion of the Sikhs as taught by Nanuk Shah, and when and why did it assume a martial character?

207. What was the organization of the Sikhs before the time of Runjit Singh?

208. What change took place in the government of the Marattas under their Rājā Sāhū?

209. Name the two first Peishwas, and describe the success of their policy towards the Mogul Government.

210. Name the four successors of Bahādūr Shah of Delhi, their claims to the succession, and the fate of the last two?

211. Who was King of Delhi when that city was occupied by the English, and what had been his early relations with them?

212. What policy was observed towards him and his successors up to the deposition of the last king of Delhi?

213. When did the English first engage in trade with India?

214. What was the chief direction of their trade in the outset?

215. Where and when did they first obtain leave to establish factories on the continent of India?

216. When and where was the first factory on the Koromandel coast established?

217. When was it removed to Madras, and when was Fort St. George founded?

218. In whose reign, and through whose influence were the Company allowed to establish factories in Bengal? Where were these situate?

219. How came the East India Company possessed of Bombay?

220. How came the lands now constituting the site of Kalkutta, and the twenty-four Purgunnas, the property of the Company, and on what plea was Fort William constructed?

221. When was the battle of Plassi fought? What lea to it, and what were its results?

222. What were the principal judicial and financial arrangements made by Lord Cornwallis?

223. What are the principles regulating the revenue settlements in the North-West Provinces, as also at Madras and Bombay?

224. On what grounds was Vizier Ali deposed from the Nawābship of Oudh, and what was his subsequent conduct and fate?

225. What causes led to the war with Ava?

226. To what circumstances was the extreme loss of life, as also the inordinate expenditure of the Burmese war, attributable?

227. What political motives led to the war with the Afghāns?

228. What were the results of the war, and to what was the ultimate catastrophe to be ascribed?

229. Mention the principal territorial accessions that have been made to British India during the administration of Lords Ellenborough, Hardinge, and Dalhousie, with remarks on their justice or policy.

---

230. Name the earliest Hindū dynasties. To which dynasty did Rama belong? What were his exploits, and where recorded?

231. What was the occasion and result of the great war? Where was the decisive battle fought, and in what epic is it celebrated?

232. Describe the expedition of Alexander the Great to India.

233. In what year, and where, did Vikramāditya reign?

234. What were the early Hindū kingdoms established in the Dekhun?

235. How many expeditions did Mahmūd of Ghuzni undertake across the Indus? Give the date of the first and last, and mention his greatest exploit.

236. When, and by whom, was the first independent Mahomedan kingdom established in Delhi?

237. Name the five Mahomedan kingdoms which assumed independence in the Dekhun on the decay of the empire of Delhi towards the close of the 14th century.

238. When was the Hindū kingdom of Bijāyanugur

founded in the Dekhun? Name the battle in which it was extinguished?

239. Describe generally the career of the great Akbar. With what English monarch was he contemporary?

240. Name the chief events of Aurungzib's reign. Where, and at what age, did he die?

241. Describe the rise of the Maratta power, and the character of the Maratta policy.

242. When, under whom, and where, did the Portuguese arrive in India?

243. When was the East India Company formed, and who gave the first charter? When did the Company cease to govern India?

244. When and where did the wars between the English and French commence in India? Name the most illustrious commanders on both sides.

245. When and by whom was Kalkutta sacked, and by whom recovered?

246. Sketch Clive's career. What were the consequences of the battle of Plassi?

247. How long did Warren Hastings govern? What were the chief events of his reign?

248. Describe the rise of Heidur Ali, and the fall of his dynasty.

249. What were the most memorable events of the Viceroyalty of Lord Cornwallis?

250. Describe generally the events and character of Lord Wellesley's administration.

251. Under what Governor-General did the Maratta and Pindari war occur? What was the result of it?

252. What was the character, and what were the chief events of Lord William Bentinck's administration?

253. Describe the first and second Sikh wars.

254. What principalities did Lord Dalhousie annex, and what were the great improvements of the time?

---

255. What is known about the commerce between India and Europe, between the time of Alexander and Mahmūd of Ghuzni?

256. Write a short sketch of the reign of Shah Jehān.

257. Write a short account of the administration of the second Peishwa, Bāji Rao.

258. Give a sketch of the principal transactions between the Company and Tanjūr.

259. Write an account of the attempts of Shah Alūm to invade Bengal between 1758 and 1765. Give the terms of the treaty, and state how far they were carried out.

260. Write an account of Hastings' transactions with Cheyte Singh.

261. Give some account of Sir Eyre Coote and Lord Macartney.

262. Write a short account of Lord Cornwallis' two campaigns against Tippū. What were the conditions of peace?

263. Give an account of the Marquis of Wellesley's negotiations with the Nabob of Oudh.

264. Give a sketch of the condition of India south of the Nurbudda at the close of Lord Wellesley's government.

265. Write an account of the Pindāri war.

266. What were the principal measures of Lord Bentinck's administration?

267. What were the circumstances which led to the invasion of Afghānisthān?

268. When, and between whom, were fought the battles of Argaum, Dig, and Māhārājpūr? Give the principal conditions of the treaty of Bassein.

269. Write a short account of Yeshwunt Rao Holkar.

270. Give a sketch of the rise and history of Udipūr and Bhopal.

271. Compare Akbar's policy and method of administration with those of the British Government.

272. To what causes do you ascribe the failure of the French to establish an empire in India?

273. Give a sketch of Heidur's transactions with the Marattas.

274. Compare the political state of the different parts of India at the death of Akbar, the death of Heidur Ali, and the close of the first Sikh war.

275. Trace the gradual growth of our Indian empire between 1786 and 1806, as forced on by circumstances against the will of the Company.

276. Give the history of the removal of the restrictions on the press. Can you trace the influence of public opinion under the Mogul empire?

---

277. What reason is there for believing that, when the Hindūs first penetrated into Central and Southern India, they found the country occupied by tribes whose origin differed from their own?

278. What do you know of the languages and literature of India before the advent of the Mahomedans?

279. Sketch briefly the progress of the Mahomedan power in the provinces to the south of the Nurbudda?

280. Describe the state of the Mogul empire, and the operations of Aurungzib, in the interval between the death of Siwuji and the death of the emperor.

281. Mention the principal events that throw light on the decay of the Mogul empire, the growth of the Maratta power, and the rival pretensions of the French and English during the reigns of Ahmed Shah and Alumgir II.

282. Describe fully the state of India in A.D. 1761.

---

283. Give a brief sketch of the contest between Heidur Ali and the British.

284. Give a full account of the arrangements made by Lord Cornwallis for the permanent settlement of the public demand on account of land revenue in Bengal. What led to the adoption of those arrangements?

285. Describe the principal events that distinguished the governments of Lord Wellesley and Lord Hastings, and compare the state of British India at the dates of the retirements of those two Governors-General.

286. What do you know of the life and reign of Runjit Singh?

287. What alterations in the position of the East India Company took place during the government of Lord W. Bentinck? And what measures of administrative reform did he introduce?

288. State the consideration that led to the British expedition to Afghanisthān; the principal events that marked

the course of that expedition; and the most important effects produced by it.

289. What do you know of the recent state of the Sonthals, and their country?

290. Describe (geographically) some of the territories added to the British dominions in India after the cessation of the commercial privileges of the East India Company, and before the assumption of the direct rule in British India by the Crown.

291. In what wars was Lord Dalhousie engaged during his administration of British India? State the causes which gave rise to them, and their results.

292. In what year was the Punjāb annexed to British India, and what form of administrative government was provided for it?

293. Under what circumstances were the native states of Sattara, Nāgpūr, and Jhansi annexed to British India?

294. Give a brief account of the annexation of Oudh by Lord Dalhousie, and the state of that kingdom previous to its being made a province of British India.

295. What improvements were carried out by Lord Dalhousie during his administration?

296. What important event in connection with the East India Company took place in 1853? Show briefly the changes it brought about in the Company's government?

297. During whose administration was the first Anglican bishop appointed to British India, and what was his name?

298. Describe the constitution of the Legislative and Executive governments during Lord Dalhousie's rule, and of how many members did each consist?

299. Who succeeded Lord Dalhousie as Governor-General of India, and in what year?

300. Describe briefly the causes which led to the war with Persia in 1856. What was the result?

301. What great event occurred during Lord Canning's administration, and where did it first break out?

302. Describe briefly the position of the English garrison at Luknow, from the beginning of May, 1857, till the final

recapture of that city. When did this latter event take place?

303. What celebrated English officer died at Luknow in the early part of the mutiny?

304. What share did Dhōndū Punt (Nāna Sahēb) take in the Indian mutiny, and by what atrocious act will his name ever be held infamous?

305. When was the city of Delhi captured by the British army, and under whose command?

306. What natives of note in India were implicated in the great mutiny, and what afterwards befel them?

307. Describe briefly the course pursued by the Central India field force under Sir Hugh Rose during 1858, and its results?

308. What Englishmen (civil and military) greatly distinguished themselves during the Indian mutiny?

309. What event took place in 1859 among the East India Company's European troops in Bengal, and what was the result?

310. When and by whom was the India Bill, taking away the powers of the East India Company, introduced into Parliament; what were its chief provisions and when did it come into force?

311. What important legislative enactments were passed during Lord Canning's administration?

312. By whom was the income-tax first introduced into India, and when?

313. Who succeeded Lord Canning as Governor-General and how long did he hold the office?

314. What conspiracy took place in 1863 in North-Eastern India during his rule, and what was the result?

315. State what you know of the Umbeyla campaign of 1863. During whose administration did it take place?

316. When did Sir John Lawrence become Governor-General of British India, and what were his antecedents in the public service?

317. What wars took place during his administration?

318. What important questions concerning land in Oudh were settled by Sir John Lawrence during his tenure of office?

319. In what part of India did a terrible famine occur in 1865; how was it caused and what mortality is reported to have happened in consequence?

320. What administrative reforms were carried out during Sir John Lawrence's rule?

321. Mention some of the most important legislative enactments passed during his administration.

322. State in what respect education has advanced among the natives of British India from 1852 up to 1869, and what number of educational institutions of all kinds existed in the former and also in the latter year?

323. Where are the principal hill sanitaria to be found in British India? mention in what Presidency or Province each is situate.

A GLOSSARY OF USEFUL INDIAN WORDS.

Ana, the sixteenth part of a rupee, or about three halfpence.

Banglā (Bungalow), a word usually applied to the houses of Europeans in India.

Banian (properly Bunnia), a Hindū merchant.

Begum, a lady of rank, a queen or princess.

Bhātā (Batta), an extra allowance to public servants or troops when employed on special duty.

Brinjaris, the hereditary and professional carriers of India.

Caste, class, sect, from the Portuguese word *casta*, a race.

Chāwadi, native rest-house for travellers. Choultrie is an English corruption of this word.

Chout, a *fourth* of the revenues of a country exacted by the Marattas.

Compound, an enclosure, a corruption of the Malay word "Kampong."

Cowrie, the lowest coin in value in India; a shell.

Darbar (Durbar), a royal court; an audience or levee.

Daroga, a superintendent of police.

Diwān, a royal court; a minister, especially the chief financial minister.

Diwāni, the management of the revenue.

Diwāni Court, a court of civil justice.

Dūāb, a country lying between any two rivers.

Fakir, poor; a religious man who has taken a vow of poverty.

Firmān, an imperial grant, order, or charter.

Foujdar, a commander of military police; a criminal judge.

Ghāt (Ghaut), a landing-place; steps on a river side; a mountain leading up like a step to a table-land.

Gold Mohur, a coin worth about thirty-two shillings.

Huzūr, the royal presence; a respectful term applied to collectors, judges, or other high officials.

Jāgīr, a tenure by which the public revenues of an estate, &c. were granted to an individual as a reward for services done to a government.

Jāgīrdar, the holder of a Jāgīr.

Jezzia, the poll-tax imposed by Mahomedans on persons not of their own persuasion.

Kacheri, a court or office for public business.

Khān, a title of nobility answering to the English "Lord."

Khandi (Candy), a measure of weight and capacity. In Madras 500 lbs.; in Bombay = 560 lbs.

Khind, a narrow pass between mountains.

Kiladar, the commander of a fort.

Krore, ten millions of rupees; one million sterling.

Kūli (Cooly), a day labourer.

Lak (Lac), the number 100,000; £10,000.

Māhārāni, a queen, princess.

Mīr (Amir), commander; a title of princes and nobles, as the Mirs of Sindh.

Monsoon, a corruption of the Arabic word "*mausim*" a season; applied now to the periodical rains in India.

Mun (Maund), a weight varying in different parts of India. In Bombay it is 25 lbs.; in Bengal $87\frac{2}{3}$ lbs. since 1833.

Mūnshi, a writer, a secretary, a teacher of languages.

Mūnsiff, a civil judge of the lowest grade (now called "subordinate judge.")

Nāik, an officer in native armies corresponding to a corporal.

Nizām, an arranger; a title of the prince whose capital is Heiderabād in the Dekhun.

Nuwāb, literally means "deputies," and is the plural of "Nāib" a deputy. It is now a title of governors.

Pagoda, a corruption of the word "*but-kadah*" an idol temple; also a Madras coin worth from seven to eight shillings.

Pālegar (Polygar), a shareholder, a landed proprietor. A title of native chiefs in the Madras Presidency.

Peons, an Anglican corruption of the word "*piyādah*" footman.

Peshkash, tribute; an offering from an inferior to a superior.

Pēta, a native town or suburb.

Pice, corruption of the word "*paisa*," of which 64 go to the rupee.

Pīr, old; a Mahomedan saint.

Putta, a lease.

Rājā, a Hindū king, or prince

Rāni, the wife of a Rājā, a queen or princess.

Rupee, a coin valued at about two shillings.

Ryot, a corruption of the word "*raiyat*," a subject, a peasant.

Seer, a weight ranging from 12 oz. to 2 lbs.

Sepoy (Sipāhi), a native soldier.

Shah, a king; the title usually applied to the king of Persia.

Shastras, the sacred writings of the Hindūs.

Sirdar, a chief.

Sir-dēshmūkhi, the tenth of the produce exacted by the Marattas.

Sūbah, a Province and **Subēdar**, a governor of a Province.

Sunnud, a patent for office.

Tahsildar, a native collector of revenue.

Talūk, a district; a division of a province.

Umra, a Mahomedan noble.

Vakil, an envoy or representative; an attorney.

Vazir, a prime minister.

Zanānā, a harem.

Zila (Zillah), a province or tract constituting the jurisdiction of a circuit judge.

Zumindar, a landed proprietor.

INDEX.